## "He wasn't more than four or five feet away. . . ."

We spotted each other at almost the same instant. As startled as we both were, the small advantage was mine, for the German was right-handed and had to swing his "burp gun" around to his left before he could open fire.

For the first time in the war, I witnessed a disciplined and well-trained German soldier in action. This soldier's movements were automatic, and oh, he was fast. As he spun his body around to face me, I had the eerie feeling that I stared death in the face. The barrel of his Schmeisser moved at lightning speed, swinging in an arc toward my left side. I know my midsection must have contracted in anticipation of the bullets I knew were certain to spew from that horrible tunnel of death. I began to doubt that I'd have time to swing my Thompson the short distance to the left and pull the trigger. The advantage had been mine, but the superior training of this man from Rommel's Afrika Korps reduced the odds of my coming out of the engagement alive.

D0835147

# RECON SCOUT

## Fred H. Salter

BALLANTINE BOOKS • NEW YORK

Note: All names, characters and events depicted in this story are true. Conversational quotes are as close to being correct as my memory allowed, but are not necessarily the speaker's exact words. I have omitted a few of the characters' names to protect their privacy. Without having my personal war diary and the documented figures obtained from history books of World War II, my story wouldn't have been complete. I had no access to any War Department or military journals other than the report written to the U.S. Cavalry School by Lieutenant Colonel Harry W. Candler, former Commander of the 91st Cavalry Reconnaissance Squadron in Tunisia.

—The Author

A Ballantine Book
Published by The Ballantine Publishing Group
Copyright © 1994 by Fred H. Salter

All rights reserved under International and Pan-American Copyright Conventions. Published in the United States by The Ballantine Publishing Group, a division of Random House, Inc., New York, and simultaneously in Canada by Random House of Canada Limited, Toronto. Originally published by Scott Publishing, Inc., in 1994.

Ballantine is a registered trademark and the Ballantine colophon is a trademark of Random House, Inc.

www.ballantinebooks.com

ISBN 0-345-44693-3

Manufactured in the United States of America

First Ballantine Books Edition: December 2001

10 9 8 7 6 5 4 3 2 1

In humble
tribute to all the
men who served in the
Recon, especially to those men of
C Troop and their comrades in the 91st
Cavalry Recon Squadron. If this story helps
to rekindle memories of appreciation, and gives
recognition to the men still living and those
who died in combat while fighting in
Recon units during World War II, then
it has achieved its goal. Those men
contributed so much to
the final victory.

# Contents

# Acknowledgments

The author wishes to express his gratitude to the many faithful volunteers, without whose moral support, encouragement and assistance *Recon Scout* might never have been written. These include, but are not limited to, Pauline Salter, "The Authors of the Flathead," Graham S. Mitchell, Marlene Blessing, Dick Borgmann, Bob Bonham, Cecelia Salter, my three sons Fred, Mike and Cody Salter, and the men of the 91st Cavalry Recon Squadron.

# Tribute

Have you ever wondered what thoughts went through a young soldier's mind as he looked into the eyes of his enemy and squeezed the trigger of his rifle or submachine gun? To better understand the effect war has on a young man's mind, read this book.

There are many untold incidents and unanswered questions about World War II. The author has brought a few of them to the attention of the reader.

Who pays on the battlefield for the mistakes a general makes? What happens when almost half of a troop of men and their leader refuse to attack a hill? Why does a man repeatedly volunteer for night patrol duty when the odds against his survival are so great?

The horrors encountered in all wars have greatly affected the lives of so many of our youth. It is no wonder that thousands of them became either introverts, recluses to society, or wanderers like the author.

It's a good thing the army had young men in its ranks who were dreamers, men who should have been born 100 years earlier. Many of us grew up worshiping trappers, frontiersmen and cavalry scouts like John Colter, Bill Sublette and Kit Carson. We idolized the Native American warrior: Cochise, Geronimo and Crazy Horse. These men fought to save a land that rightfully belonged to them. Many of us young boys enlisted in the service, then volunteered for patrol duty and became scouts, not just because we were patriotic, but to satisfy a hunger for adventure.

Like the mountain men of the early West, we belonged to a different breed. Loners by nature, we seemed compelled to venture into the unknown. We sought a challenge that would fulfill the needs of our reckless youth. Many died seeking it, but would have it no other way.

# Preface

Nearly every battle and tactical aspect of World War II has long since been recorded in the pages of history. This story is mainly about a young man's feelings. It tells how the acts of violence he performed in combat come back to haunt him. His adventure is typical of those experienced by thousands of boys who joined the service and became part of the "eyes and ears" of an advancing army.

The episodes described could just as easily have taken place in France, Belgium or Germany, and been performed by men in any of the army's other Cavalry Recon units. The characters from C Troop of the 91st Cavalry Recon Squadron are real. Many of those comrades now lie in lonely graves in North Africa, Sicily or Italy.

To say that we were not afraid to fight or die would be like expecting a man to smile as he stood on a trapdoor with a noose around his neck. When we left the States in 1942, the end of the war seemed an eternity away. Because the life of a Recon soldier didn't hold much hope for the future, we lived for today.

This is a personal account of how I saw the conflict. Even though I had my war diary to fall back on, like smoke from the battlefield, the passing years have faded many of the details. A warrior is like a writer—he has to suffer and experience hardships before he can express his feelings. Each soldier has his own individual tale to relate. He may see the same battle from an entirely different perspective than the man carrying the rifle next to him. An insignificant incident to one man may become an episode of major proportion to his buddy. A soldier took another human's life only because of the difference in their political beliefs and the color of a uniform. There was nothing personal.

Many veterans will agree that the horrors and fears expressed in the story are authentic. At the time, I might have been unduly hard on a few of my superior officers. Fifty years later, I realize they were only human, like we men in the ranks. The men of C Troop followed many brave and competent officers into battle. They deserve a lot of credit for leading us in some of the fiercest fighting in World War II.

The admiration and love I have for the men I fought with can never be put into words. These comrades are the real heroes of my story. The deeds they performed greatly overshadow my humble actions. Because we passed beneath the shadow of death together, we became as brothers.

# CHAPTER I

# Boots and Saddles

The muffled sound of their boots on the cobblestones ahead told me it was a German patrol, not being overly cautious, because they were still behind their own lines. I dropped quietly to the gutter and lay prone with my Thompson submachine gun out in front of me. I knew that my buddy George, only a few yards behind me, followed my example. He had been in my squad for three campaigns. Night patrols weren't new to us, they were our way of life.

The night being pitch black, I felt secure in the knowledge that the German patrol would pass by without discovering us. As they came directly abreast of our position, I heard their squad leader whisper a few words in German. The squad halted, and they began talking in low tones, as if they were discussing their plans for infiltrating our lines. Even though my face and hands were blackened and my head was covered with a dark wool knit cap, my outstretched hands clutched the Thompson and eased the safety off.

At that moment, I noticed the glow of light on my wrist. I felt lit up like a Christmas tree. During the African campaign, I'd taken a beautiful luminous-dialed wristwatch from a Kraut soldier who had no further use for it. This watch was now exposed on my arm. I cherished the timepiece because it could be read so easily on my night patrols. Ordinarily I positioned it higher up on my wrist, concealed beneath the sleeve of my combat jacket. Now, that watch could be the death of me.

I was afraid to move a muscle, for fear the trash and dry leaves under my arm would give my position away. I had two

1

alternatives. I could swing my Thompson up fast and hope to get all the Krauts before they became aware we were in the gutter opposite them (this was doubtful), or lie still and hope none of them investigated the shiny fluorescent object in the ditch.

We were not on a combat mission, just a two-man recon patrol. Our main objective was to obtain information about the enemy's movements along the Rapido River in front of our sector of Cassino on the 5th Army front in Italy. We'd crossed the river below the ford leading into Cassino from the south, and worked our way to the outskirts of the town. The thick hard soles of my combat boots, I'd replaced with soft leather. They were as quiet on patrol as the moccasins I wore when roaming the woods as a boy. My clothing of dark wool material helped conceal my position if I brushed against branches or other objects.

I decided to take a chance and not move a muscle, even though some inner voice told me it would be better to die facing an enemy than be shot in the back while lying in a gutter. I hoped and prayed the Krauts wouldn't investigate. Never before on any of my missions had I regretted or questioned the reason I always volunteered to lead night patrols.

The German patrol continued to whisper. The minutes dragged slowly on. I felt like a condemned man waiting for the hangman to spring the trapdoor. As the tension mounted, a lifetime of memories crossed my mind. I've heard tell, that sometimes when a person is in a life-or-death situation, their whole life flashes before them. On other patrols, I'd experienced many close calls, but never had my past monopolized my thoughts as it did at this moment. Right now I couldn't afford to think of anything but survival. I wondered if this might not be an omen. Maybe the end was near.

As I awaited the outcome, my thoughts drifted away from the danger at hand. In that brief moment, when time seemed so precious, I relived my whole life.

My parents migrated to Pennsylvania from England and Wales after World War I, when my father received his discharge from the British Royal Air Force. My folks originally intended to continue on to Australia. Instead, my dad found work in America and decided to settle there.

The story of my childhood is full of episodes similar to those of Tom Sawyer and Huck Finn. Though these tales add a touch of humor to my life's memories, the years I spent roaming the woods and trapping the streams had a far greater influence on my army career. I learned to work alone and become self-reliant. Above all, I learned to understand and respect the forces of nature. Tending my trapline on moonless nights made me realize I had a friend in the darkness; that is the reason I later volunteered for night patrols.

On winter evenings, I'd often listen to the old-timers tell stories as they sat around a potbellied woodstove down at the village store. I'd be all ears as they painted a mental picture of cavalry and Indian scouts, the great Indian warriors, and of their own adventures in the Civil and Spanish-American wars. These tales, and those I'd read about, only added fuel to my boyhood fantasies, for I hoped to someday relive experiences such as theirs.

Never owning a breech-loading rifle or pistol until joining the horse cavalry, I became proficient in handling the muzzle-loading weapons and knives handed down to me by descendants of those early pioneers and adventurers. My youth played an important part in determining my destiny in the army.

That night at Cassino, when my life flashed before me, death seemed so close. Eventually the German patrol moved down the road toward the American front lines. They left George and me lying in the gutter, chilled to the bone from sweat. If we could have seen its color, it probably would have been tinted red. Once again, we learned how precious life really is.

My army career began much like it ended. It began with controversy.

Standing outside the army recruiter's office, I leaned against the building and signed my father's signature to the enlistment papers. Having the same name as Dad's, I figured I wasn't being completely dishonest. If only the army allowed a young boy to enlist without his parents' consent, I wouldn't have felt guilty. I thought to myself, "For what greater cause need a person bend the arm of the law, than for the opportunity of defending his country. If I'm guilty of a wrongdoing, then so be it."

After entering the building, I walked up to the recruiter's desk. Though nervous, I threw back my shoulders and tried to assume a military stance. When the sergeant asked me what branch of the army I preferred, without hesitating, I replied, "The U.S. Horse Cavalry."

Lowering his head, he looked out over the top of his glasses, and a faint smile crossed his face. He glanced down at my faded blue dungarees, then at my heavy flannel red-and-black checkered shirt. His eyes finally rested on the beat-up felt hat tilted back atop my head. He seemed intrigued with the pheasant feather sticking out of the hat. I'd pinned the right brim up alongside the hat, so as not to interfere with the ramrod of my muzzle-loading rifle when I seated a bullet. When he raised his eyebrows and slowly moved his head from side to side, I became defensive. I knew he must have known I'd just come down out of the hills, but he didn't say anything. I was thankful he never questioned the validity of my father's signature.

After I had received my physical, adaptability and I.Q. tests, an officer swore me into the service. The recruiter took me aside and, like a father telling his young boy about the birds and the bees, he said, "You know, son, you are qualified to join the Army Air Corps. Because we have an urgent need for pilots, I am going to assign you to that branch of the army."

Even after getting into the army under false pretenses and being in no position to bargain, I still didn't intend to be railroaded into the air corps. I spoke up and said, "Because I needed my parent's consent to enter the service, the recruiting posters say that I am entitled to join any branch of the army I choose. I want to be a cavalryman, not a pilot. If the army can't keep its word, then the first chance I get, I'm going to go over the hill."

The recruiter didn't get angry, but replied, "Young fellow, you are very foolish. I don't understand why you are passing up an opportunity to become an officer, just to pound leather on the back of some stinking bag of bones."

Taking another glance at my clothes, he pondered for a moment and said, "But then again, maybe I do understand."

After tearing up the air corps papers, on another form he wrote down that I be assigned to the Horse Cavalry Replacement Training Center at Fort Riley, Kansas.

The recruiting officer informed me that a buck private in the army received twenty-one dollars a month. "The paymaster will deduct six dollars and fifty cents from your pay each month for life insurance, and three dollars for laundry," he said. "With those kind of wages, you won't have to worry about opening a bank account. Your room, board, medical bills and all your clothes will be furnished."

Before long, I learned firsthand the meaning of the words to a popular song about payday in the army, "Twenty-One Dollars a Day, Once a Month."

Never having owned a wallet, let alone spending money to put in it, I made up my mind to be content with whatever the army paid me, for I didn't enlist in the army with the intention of getting rich.

The day of my enlistment, I joined a group of new recruits headed for Fort Meade, Maryland. After waiting at that camp for a couple of days, I traveled by train to Fort Riley, Kansas. While on the train, I met a boy from Reading, Pennsylvania. Paul Yenser remained one of my closest buddies until he lost his life in Italy.

At Fort Riley, I received cavalry boots, breeches, a jacket and a Sam Browne belt. The jacket came down almost to my knees. The wide-brimmed campaign hat, with its bright yellow band and tassels, signified that I belonged to the cavalry. Wearing the crossed-sabers insignia of the U.S. Cavalry brought me one step closer to fulfilling my boyhood fantasy of reliving the lives of Jeb Stuart and my other cavalry heroes.

Upon entering the barracks assigned to me, I almost bumped into a fifty-five-gallon oil drum mounted on top of a large sawhorse. Throughout my training, it remained a constant reminder that I had to become a good rider. A McClellan army saddle was cinched onto the barrel, and a bundle of hair from a horse's tail stuck out of the bunghole in the rear of the drum. The contraption reminded me of Washington Irving's tale of the headless horseman, with the horse wearing a suit of armor. On this make-believe cavalry mount, we recruits practiced the army's method of mounting and dismounting a horse. I often wondered if the carpenter who named the first sawhorses had at one time in his life been in the cavalry. After a couple of days riding our hollow-bellied steel horse, we started training on live mounts.

The horse stables were open at both ends, enabling the manure wagons to drive through the barn. Manure was pitched into the wagons from the stalls on each side of the long, narrow building. The men doing the work were called stable police, but the title didn't fit the task they performed. I soon learned that getting up at four-thirty each morning to work in the stables was a backbreaking job. A cavalryman didn't spend all his time in the saddle; there were countless other tasks to be performed. These jobs weren't advertised on the enlistment posters that enticed young men into the cavalry. Instead, they read "The Horse Is Man's Noblest Companion, Join the Cavalry and Have a Courageous Friend."

Before any of the cavalry mounts were assigned to us, they were broken at a cavalry remount station. We rode horses already trained to respond to cavalry commands.

I soon learned that these horses were far more spirited than the plow horses I rode back in Pennsylvania or on my friend's farm in New Hampshire. While riding on the Republican Flats and the surrounding plains of Kansas, I loved to hear Sergeant Tiller's Texas drawl when he gave one of the commands, trot, gallop, or column right, ho.

"Ho" was the signal to execute a command just given, like when the pioneer wagon masters yelled, "Westward ho, the wagons." The word "Ho" would barely be out of the sergeant's mouth, and those cavalry mounts would start to execute the command, even before we had a chance to neck rein or apply knee pressure to them. We soon learned that the horses were a lot smarter than us.

While in the saddle, if one of us disobeyed an order, the sergeant made the trooper trot with his feet out of the stirrups. The punishment wouldn't have been so bad if he hadn't ordered us to keep our knees away from the ribs of the horse. It's a wonder many a young cavalryman retained the ability to father children, especially when his privates became entangled in the slit of the McClellan saddle. This torturous punishment taught us not to disobey the sergeant. Before long, we mastered intricate cavalry maneuvers, like "thread the needle," and many other tactics used on the parade ground to impress the army brass.

Only three horse units trained at Fort Riley in the spring and early summer of '42; A and B Troop and the 8th Squadron. This last outfit was made up of all black troopers. Though segregated, these men were commanded by white officers. Some of the finest cavalry troops that ever fought on the Western plains were made up of black soldiers.

Joe Louis Barrow, the heavyweight boxing champion of the world, trained with the 8th Squadron. Joe rode out of the same stable that I did. When assigned to stable police, I talked to him a number of times in the tack room. Everyone liked Joe, and I considered him one of the finest men I had the pleasure of meeting at Fort Riley.

That summer, the War Department decided to make a cavalry training film. The army wanted to record the intensive training a cavalryman received. Some of the old die-hard cavalry officers still hoped to justify the use of horses in wartime, even though everyone knew their days were numbered. When it became known that the top brass chose Troop A to make the film, a lot of celebrities were allowed to enlist in it. Henry Morgenthau, the son of the secretary of the U.S. Treasury, joined the troop. DeCicco, the husband of beautiful young Gloria Vanderbilt, also became a member of the elite troop.

In contrast, the majority of the men I served with in B Troop were cowboys and ranch hands recruited off the

plains and out of the mountains from all over the West.
Quite a few rodeo performers were in our troop, the most fa-
mous being a cowboy named Turk Greenough, from Red
Lodge, Montana. Up until the time he enlisted in the service,
Turk worked the rodeo circuit all over the United States, in-
cluding Madison Square Garden. At Cheyenne Frontier
Days in Wyoming, he met Sally Rand, the famous queen of
the fan dancers. In the autumn of 1941, they got married.

Turk, the 37-year-old rodeo star, achieved the title of
champion bronco buster of the world six times. He soon became the idol of all the teenage boys in B Troop, with me his
greatest admirer. The reserved and quiet-mannered Turk
made me realize that a man didn't have to smoke or drink to
become successful in life. He abstained from both of these
vices. He was old enough to be my father, and I'd sit in awe and
listen to him spin yarns about his youth. He told us about life
growing up on his father Ben's ranch in Montana. Most interesting of all were his stories of riding the rodeo circuit. Turk
later made quite a few movies in Hollywood, using his expert-
ise with horses to star with celebrities such as John Wayne.
Throughout the remainder of my life, I was proud to say, "I
once rode with Turk Greenough in the Horse Cavalry, even
though I considered myself not qualified to curry his horse."

Frank Marshall, another well-known rodeo performer
stationed at Fort Riley, later served overseas with me.
Rodeo officials rated Frank the country's fourth money-
winner in the bull riding class. Even though A Troop
boasted its many celebrities, B Troop had its cowboys.

Just before the Fourth of July in 1942, Turk, along with
his beautiful wife Sally and their friends from the rodeo
circuit, sponsored a rodeo for the Army Relief Fund. They
held it at Junction City, Kansas, the town closest to Fort
Riley. Nationally advertised, the event drew performers
from all over the country. Turk's sisters Alice, the world
champion woman bronc rider, and Margie Greenough
came to participate. Along with Turk, they made up
Rodeo's Royal Family, "The Riding Greenoughs."

A few days after the rodeo, I witnessed an event that could

have been taken from a page in the book of *Life in the Peace-time Army.* The morning started out routinely with the bugler sounding reveille and our platoon sergeant yelling, "Off your ass and on your feet, this is reveille, it ain't retreat."

We ran from our barracks and lined up on the troop street for roll call. First Sergeant Hubbard, a career soldier and tough old Texan from Del Rio, began calling out troopers' names. Turk and another cowboy friend of his from Oklahoma were slow in lining up for formation. When the first sergeant saw Turk still buttoning his shirt while answering to his name, he proceeded to read him the riot act. Turk's buddy, feeling partly responsible for his friend's tardiness, entered the dispute and made Sergeant Hubbard boiling mad.

Prior to World War II, many first sergeants in the regular army were under the impression they had to be tough enough to whip any man in their command. Sergeant Hubbard, living up to this unwritten law, removed his shirt with its first sergeant's stripes and threw it on the grass. When I saw him flex his muscles and make them ripple like a rolling sea of buffalo grass, I thought to myself, "What a physique."

He motioned for Turk's buddy to step out of the ranks. "I'm going to show you men who's top dog in this outfit," he shouted. "No man in this troop is going to question my authority."

If the first sergeant thought the Oklahoma cowboy would eat crow, he was sadly mistaken. We all knew the rodeo performer had broke many a tough bronc and wrestled steers with a temperament just as ornery as the first sergeant's. Instead of waiting for Sergeant Hubbard to open the show and get in the first lick, the cowboy charged out of the ranks like they'd just opened the chute with him ridin' Turk's famous bronc "Midnight."

Captain Meadows, our troop commander, unlike Sergeant Hubbard, was a mild-mannered officer. Standing outside of the orderly room, he'd listened to the heated argument. When he saw his first sergeant take the bull by the horns, he knew what the outcome would be. Before Oklahoma had an opportunity to strike the first blow, the captain turned and

walked into the orderly room so he wouldn't be a witness to
the fracas. Though outranking the first sergeant, he always gave him a free rein when it came to disciplining the
men.

Oklahoma didn't realize it, but he caught the sergeant
off guard when he used a tactic we'd only recently learned.
During combat training, our instructor told us that in the
heat of battle, when defeat seems inevitable and your opponent is confident of victory, catch him off guard by doing the unexpected: attack. Our cowboy buddy swung the
first blow, but the sergeant, like a pro, warded it off and
countered with a right to the midsection.

The rough-and-tumble fight that followed was a sight
to behold. Sergeant Hubbard never expected his opponent
to fight by the Marquis of Queensberry Rules, but he also
didn't figure on tangling with a charging bull from the
ranks. Both men tried to gain a quick victory with their
fists, but to no avail. Time after time, each of them hit the
ground and mixed their own blood with the dust from the
troop street. When both men refused to stay down, they
resorted to different tactics.

These men weren't quitters, for all of their lives they'd survived conflicts with horses and cattle and brawled with some
of the toughest men in the West. Most of us troopers rooted
for the cowboy, even though we were certain that when the
fight ended, the sergeant would make us pay dearly for showing loyalty to our buddy. Because both men were in top physical condition, we knew it would be a long, knockdown fight.

Sergeant Hubbard, with clenched teeth showing from between bruised lips, spread his arms apart. A vampire about
to suck blood from the neck of an innocent victim couldn't
have looked more determined. With gravel flying from beneath the soles of his cavalry boots, he put his head down
and charged at Oklahoma. Caught off guard, Turk's buddy
tried to sidestep the wild rush of human flesh but couldn't
avoid it. Like a fist being driven into a punching bag, the
sergeant's head hit the cowboy in the belly. He encircled
Oklahoma's narrow waist with outstretched sinewy arms.

The force of the attack seemed to make Sergeant Hubbard's head disappear into the cavity between his massive shoulders. Oklahoma's midsection caved in as the force of the blow carried them both to the ground.

We thought for sure that our hero was a goner. Much to our surprise, the tough old cowboy used the momentum of the attack to his advantage. As his shoulders hit the gravel, he grabbed the back of the sergeant's web belt. In the same movement he drove his knees into the sergeant's groin and rolled backward. Sergeant Hubbard, forced to release his hold, somersaulted through the air and landed on his back. He bounced on the gravel like a slab of raw liver being thrown onto a butcher block.

Both men lay still for a moment, trying to recover from the brutal beating they'd taken. Too tired to swing their arms and fight with their fists, they crawled toward each other on their hands and knees. Evidence of the ferocious battle could be seen scattered about the troop street, for their undershirts were torn to shreds, leaving only battered flesh for groping hands to clutch. With neither man wanting to admit defeat, we couldn't help but admire their stamina and courage. Staring into each other's eyes, by mutual consent they realized they'd both met their match. Neither man uttered a word as they staggered to their feet and shook hands.

With his barrel chest heaving like a bull in heat and his nostrils emitting more steam into the early morning air than a lovesick stallion's, the first sergeant put on his shirt and resumed calling roll. When Captain Meadows came out of the orderly room, he never mentioned a word about the fight.

From that day on, Sergeant Hubbard was a changed man. He had a more humble attitude and never picked on Turk or the older cowboys again. Because I drew a lot more stable police than the others, I knew that he'd directed most of his wrath toward us youngsters who rooted for Oklahoma. Even though neither man defeated the other, we figured they both won. Like men raised on the Western frontier before their time, the two men fought to uphold the principles they believed in.

Most of the cowboys in our outfit found it extremely difficult to adapt to the cavalry's style of riding. In civilian life, while tending stock out on the range, their pants were literally glued to their saddles, for they rode Western style. The army taught us to post, which meant you had to rise from the saddle and return to it, in rhythm with the horse's gait. For a cowboy who'd spent a lifetime in the saddle, it was hard to learn a completely different method of riding. Many of the men never did post, and were continually in trouble with the drill sergeant.

Our training with horses continued, along with map reading, scouting and patrolling. Of all the schooling we received, the tactics we learned about scouting and patrolling interested me the most. I soon realized that the years I'd spent in the woods as a boy with Warren, the soft-spoken woodsman, were going to help me tremendously.

On the firing range, I became an expert with the rifle and the .30-caliber machine gun. The pistol they expected us to shoot proved to be a different story. As a boy, I'd learned to become a crack shot with my Civil War, .44-caliber cap-and-ball revolver. In the army, unlike any other branch of the service, a cavalryman had to qualify with the .45 semiautomatic pistol while riding at a gallop. With targets popping up from both sides as I raced through wooded terrain, I didn't score very high. I received a Marksmanship Medal, the lowest medal awarded. How I longed for my old .44 revolver with its extra loaded cylinder instead of the newfangled, short-barrel army pistol.

During our training, we carried the Model 1903 Springfield rifle. There were only a few of the new M1 Garand semiautomatic rifles at Fort Riley, and they were only used on the rifle range. What an improvement they were over the Kentucky muzzle-loading rifle I used back home. As a boy, when shooting squirrels, I made every shot count, for my cap-and-ball rifle had only one shot. This made firing the modern eight-shot breech-loading rifle a cinch.

Years later, I came across a postcard that I had sent home to my folks from Fort Riley. It was a photograph of Sally

Rand, Turk Greenough's wife, dressed in a cowgirl outfit and sitting astride her horse. On the back of the card, I wrote, "Next to the smell of chow, I like the smell of the stables best. We fired on the range yesterday. All week long, we've received instructions on how to handle a rifle. The drill sergeant gave me a kick in the pants as I lay in the prone position, while firing at a target five hundred yards away. He yelled, 'Salter, quit usin' Kentucky windage and start adjusting the sights on that rifle. You ain't shootin' squirrels back in the mountains now, you're in the army.' "

Even though I didn't take kindly to him forcing these new shooting methods on me, he taught me to shoot the correct way. The fellow marking the targets didn't have to hang up a large red flag called "Maggie's drawers" over my target, for I never once missed.

Every Friday afternoon, we assembled out on the parade ground for retreat ceremonies. Our horses and gear all had to be in top-notch shape. My cavalry mount knew a lot more about these cavalry maneuvers than I did, but he had one fault. He became upset if anyone touched his kidneys, the area behind the cantle on the McClellan saddle.

I don't know what got into me one afternoon on the parade ground. Maybe the hot Kansas sun penetrated my campaign hat and fried my brain, for I did a stupid trick. Hating the spit-and-polish ceremonies we had to endure, I longed for action of any kind to break up the monotony. When the bugler began to sound retreat, everyone remained at attention; everyone but me. Very slowly, I slid my right hand back across the top of the cantle and touched my horse's kidney.

The commotion that followed distracted the bugler so much that he hit a sour note and had to start playing retreat over again. Up on his hind legs my horse reared, just like those I'd seen in Western movies, the only difference being, my mount almost fell over backwards. While holding the reins in my left hand, I applied knee pressure to the horse's ribs to keep from sliding back over the cantle. If I hadn't grabbed the pommel with my right hand, I'd have polished the horse's rump with my breeches and landed in the pile of loose manure he'd nervously deposited on the parade ground.

Another maverick cavalryman drew uproarious laughter from the rest of the troopers when he yelled, "Ride 'em cowboy!"

My horse snorted so loud, he almost drowned out the officer on the reviewing stand who kept yelling "Attention! Attention!"

By the time I got my mount under control, the platoon sergeant had broken ranks and grabbed the bridle. Not trusting me to ride by myself, he led us back to the stables, saying, "You're in for it this time, Salter."

I never intended to steal the show and draw attention away from the officers intent on impressing each other, but that's what happened. When the senior officer yelled "Attention," and reprimanded the men for getting out of order, I thought for sure I'd end up in the stockade. After taking care of my horse and gear, the sergeant took me to the orderly room to await my fate.

When the retreat ceremonies were over, Captain Meadows and the first sergeant returned. When the captain questioned me about my misconduct, I played dumb and lied, saying, "All during the ceremonies, a darn bee kept buzzing around my horse's head. The only thing I can figure out is, the darn thing must have crawled up into my mount's nostrils, making him go berserk."

The captain said, "That's an unlikely story, Salter. You know, if the officers on the reviewing stand had their way, you'd be cooling your heels in the stockade right now."

I tried to seem as bewildered as I could, hoping the innocent look on my peach-fuzz covered face would influence his decision in my favor.

I believe my strategy worked, for he said, "Because I have no proof that you intentionally disrupted the ceremonies, I'll be lenient with you, and not because you deserve it. The first sergeant informs me that you do an excellent job on stable police, and enjoy getting up at four-thirty every morning." Shaking his head, he continued,

"From the looks of the record of your conduct, I can see why you've had lots of experience."

I saw a smile cross the first sergeant's face when the captain said, "Give him a week loading the manure wagons, Sergeant."

I tried not to show relief, but I considered myself lucky that the captain let me off so easy.

While stationed at Fort Riley, I witnessed my first cavalry funeral. I learned about the age-old custom of turning the deceased cavalry trooper's boots backwards in the stirrups, as his horse walks riderless in the funeral procession.

When I.Q. tests were given at Fort Riley, if a soldier had a high score, he could apply for officer's candidate school (OCS). Assuming command and being responsible for a group of men wasn't my ball of wax. Because I'd been a loner all my life, I had no desire to become an officer.

The commander of the cavalry training center asked for volunteers to join the OSS. This organization performed spy and undercover work in foreign countries, and became the forerunner of the CIA. Because I'd taken two years of French in school, the recruiter tried to convince me to sign up.

After giving it serious thought, I decided against it.

Unbeknown to any of us, the 1st American Ranger Battalion, under the leadership of Major William Darby, was in the process of being organized over in Scotland. Up until that time, the army had no specialized infantry units.

A group of officers at Fort Riley organized a volunteer training unit patterned after the famous British Commandos. Its purpose was to teach more advanced training in hand-to-hand combat, especially night fighting. We received nearly all of our specialized instructions while practicing night patrol tactics, for the classes were given after our workday ended. Because of the exhausting physical training, upon returning to camp everyone flopped on their bunks, completely worn out. The lessons I received in knife fighting saved my life one night while on patrol in North Africa.

Before entering the army, I bought a "Lone Ranger" guitar from Sears Roebuck and Company for five dollars.

While stationed at Fort Riley, I asked Mother to ship it to me. My friends and I spent many a Sunday afternoon playing and singing songs they'd learned out on the range and in the mountains of the West.

When given the opportunity to attend either horseshoeing or armorer school, I chose the latter. Now that I'd gotten a taste of handling modern weapons, I intended to learn all I could about them. There were more working parts to them than the old muzzle-loaders I'd been raised with. In armorer's school, I became familiar with the Thompson submachine gun, the weapon made famous by gangsters of the Prohibition era. I fell in love with the "Thompson," and the love affair lasted my entire army career.

Our rigorous cavalry training continued throughout the long hot summer. On many of our maneuvers, we were transported on large trailers that held a squad of eight men and their horses.

We trained extensively with the rifle, machine gun and pistol, and were taught the fundamentals of using a knife in hand-to-hand combat. In the cavalry's transition from horses to mechanized equipment, I imagine the top brass never thought of changing many of the horse cavalry's fighting tactics. If a cavalryman fought dismounted and used a fixed bayonet on his rifle, the army would probably classify him as an infantryman. For this reason, we never received training in the use of a bayonet.

Unlike the cavalrymen who fought in the Indian wars, we were issued Springfield rifles instead of carbines. We kept the Model 1903 weapon in a scabbard on the near side of the horse. Our blanket roll, we tied behind the high cantle of the McClellan saddle.

Though we weren't issued knives at Fort Riley, I carried a dagger all the time I served overseas. A knife always intrigued me, for I felt that someday I might need one to survive.

The most thrilling days of my life in the cavalry were the mock battles staged out on the open plains. Two troops of cavalry would face each other on hills that were sometimes a mile apart.

One afternoon, while waiting for the battle to commence, I sat astride my mount and let my thoughts wander back through time. In a few years, the cavalry charges we were making would be faded history. I thanked God for the opportunity he'd given me to be a part of the vanishing horse cavalry. We all knew that before long, the last trooper would ride off into the sunset.

I looked out across the wide expanse of prairie grass, wondering how long it would be before a plow disturbed the fertile soil hugging its roots. For the moment at least, here in the West a man could still hug his dreams.

The smell of sweating horses was drawn up into my parched nostrils. Glancing to my right, I saw the troop guidon colors waving in the warm breeze. While waiting for the bugler to sound "charge," so we could move forward against the opposing cavalry, I looked at the tense and excited faces around me. I saw tanned fingers grip sweaty reins so tight that the white knuckles behind them reminded me of tiny snowcapped mountains. I wondered if my comrades' hearts were pounding like mine, for the throbbing in my ears felt like the beat of distant war drums.

Before the first note of the bugle had time to echo back across the valley, I knew that "these were times to remember."

Oh, what a thrill to feel the wind in your face, as it lifts the brim of your campaign hat and ripples the endless sea of buffalo grass brushing high up on the flanks of your horse. It is like branding a never to be forgotten picture on the mind of a young cavalryman.

Though other experiences may get lost in the shuffle of a cluttered mind, these memories would never be erased. As our mounts raced toward the bottom of the slope, I saw the distant wall of horseflesh loom ever larger before me. The blood surged through my veins so rapidly, I thought for sure my heart would explode under the pressure.

Above the yells of my excited comrades, I heard a distant voice from out of the past. Keeping rhythm with the pounding of my horse's hooves, Tennyson's immortal words began to sound in my ear.

> *Theirs not to make reply,*
> *Theirs not to reason why,*
> *Theirs but to do and die:*
> *Into the valley of Death*
> *Rode the six hundred.*

As our opposing forces met, I tried to relive those days of old. I formed a mental picture of steel clashing against steel. Though it was only a figment of my imagination, I felt a saber slash the sleeve of my jacket. Not until my horse actually collided with one from the opposing forces, and a pistol discharged close to my ear, did I take charge of the situation and ride out of my fantasy world. When the firing ceased, and the mass of horseflesh untangled, I realized how much easier it is to dream than to face reality.

As we rode slowly back out of the valley, a hush settled over the men, for they knew their days in the horse cavalry were numbered. At that moment, I had a premonition that someday in the not-too-distant future, I would take part in a modern-day cavalry charge. When that day came, would I be one of those men riding back out of the valley of death? With these unanswered thoughts ringing in my ears, the same ghostlike whisper I'd heard earlier drifted down on the breeze from the surrounding hills:

> *Back from the mouth of hell,*
> *All that was left of them,*
> *Left of six hundred. . . .*
> *Honor the charge they made!*
> *Honor the Light Brigade,*
> *Noble six hundred.*

That day on the plains of Kansas, I rode with Custer at the Little Big Horn. I accompanied Jeb Stuart on one of his patrols leading Confederate cavalry behind the

Union lines, and I was one of the noble 600 who returned from the *Charge of the Light Brigade*. It's a wonderful feeling to be young and have such a vivid imagination. If o[...] horses were taken away tomorrow, and the horse cav[...] would be no more, these precious moments were w[...] lifetime of lesser memories. Never again would I [...] opportunity to relive the cavalry charges of a[...] years ago, or experience the thrill of how it felt [...] alryman of a lost era.

On Saturday nights, I usually went to Ju[...] Kansas, a small town outside the gates of Fort R[...] most military towns, Junction City had a tattoo [...] After completing my training in knife fighting, I had a [...] too put on my right arm: the design of a dagger penetra[...] ing a rose.

In time of war, the army wanted teenage boys to enlist, for they were adventurous, daring and sometimes reckless. All of these characteristics, when mixed with a strong feeling of patriotism, helped make a good fighting man. The discipline needed to mold these traits together was oftentimes hard to accomplish.

A couple of weeks after getting my first tattoo, I had a second design put on my left arm. It showed a picture of a dagger piercing a heart, with the words on a scroll, "Death Before Dishonor." Many of the fellows were accused of being drunk when they came back to camp with a tattoo, but I was stone sober when I received mine.

At the beginning of September 1942, most of Troop B left Fort Riley and were transferred to other cavalry units. With the rays of the western sun bouncing off spurs protruding from our boots, and yellow tassels flopping on the front of our campaign hats, we boarded a train for the East Coast and our new command. My hopes of being sent to the cavalry remount station at Front Royal, Virginia, faded. Most of us realized that our chances were also slim that we'd be sent to a regular horse cavalry outfit, for the army was fast becoming mechanized.

Our troop train took us to Bowling Green, Virginia,

where we loaded our gear on trucks and headed for Camp
A. P. Hill. We became part of an outfit that I remained
with throughout many campaigns. The 91st Cavalry
Reconnaissance Squadron, up until the 11th of September, had been assigned to the 1st Cavalry Division. Many
of the troopers still wore the yellow-and-black shoulder
patch in the shape of a shield with a horse's head on it, the
1st Cavalry insignia. After taking part in the Louisiana
maneuvers, and receiving desert warfare training at Indio,
California, the 91st traveled to the East Coast to make final preparations for combat.

We had no idea what theater of operations we'd serve
in, only that our commander was General George S.
Patton. The only American troops in combat at the time
were in the Pacific Theater of Operations. Being stationed
on the East Coast, it seemed only logical that our destination would be Europe. With the 91st recently completing
desert warfare training, we wondered if we might not be
sent somewhere in the vicinity of Rommel, the "Desert
Fox," still fighting the British in North Africa.

Those of us coming from Fort Riley turned in our
boots and breeches, and were issued woolen, olive drab
uniforms. Rumors traveling over the grapevine said that
we replacements were to receive a few weeks of intensive
cavalry reconnaissance training.

Because I'd fired the 81mm mortar a few times at Riley,
I was made first gunner in the mortar squad of the second
platoon in Troop C. Up until this point in my army career,
I'd lived in barracks, but at Camp A. P. Hill, everyone slept
in squad tents. September in Virginia proved to be a pleasant time of the year, with the weather warm enough for us
to take showers under a waterfall in a nearby creek.

Our troop had scout cars, jeeps and small weapons carriers with a 37mm gun mounted on the back. While receiving
recon training, I learned to drive a jeep, a far cry from the
horse I'd left behind at Fort Riley. We learned that a reconnaissance unit provided the eyes and ears for an army advancing into enemy territory, much like the job of Jeb

Stuart's Confederate cavalry unit in the Civil War. We were mechanized cavalry, but when in terrain too rough for vehicles, we trained to fight dismounted. Instead of a rifle, I carried a Thompson submachine gun and a bolo knife some doughboy had carried in World War I. On the firing range, I made expert with the Tommy gun.

With patrol work such an important part of our job, we received training in hand-to-hand fighting. The jujitsu, or judo training, wasn't as intensive as that taught at the commando school I'd attended, but I learned a few new tricks.

The large bolo knife was much heavier than the commando knives we used at Fort Riley, making me disappointed in the weapon. Its weight slowed down the maneuverability of the knife and the wide blade didn't have the penetrating capabilities of a dagger. Bolo knives were the only knives available to our squadron. Our country had only recently started to manufacture new equipment, and until the supply caught up with demand, many soldiers had to use outdated weapons. At Fort Riley, I'd qualified with the new M1 Garand rifle, but none were available for the 91st Recon.

Our squadron was equipped with the 1903-model Springfield rifle, the 1928-model Thompson submachine gun and the Model 1911 .45-caliber pistol. Each enlisted man carried one or the other of these sidearms, but the officers carried the old reliable six-shooter, .45-caliber revolver. Every squad had a .30-caliber air-cooled machine gun, a good dependable weapon.

A few of the fellows I'd trained with in the horse cavalry were in the second platoon of Troop C. It made things a lot easier to have a few old friends around like Paul Yenser, Jack Smith and Keith Royer. Keith had married his childhood sweetheart a couple of weeks before we joined the 91st. A few of my other friends were scattered among the other platoons in the troop.

I became a private first class shortly after joining the 91st. On my first weekend pass, I decided to buy a train ticket and visit my family in Pennsylvania. I took Jack

Smith, from Bellevue, Washington, home with me. Like me, Jack hadn't seen his folks since joining the army. We arrived in the village on a Saturday afternoon. After all the trouble I caused when I enlisted in the army, I felt reluctant about returning home, but soon realized my family held no animosity toward me.

That Saturday evening we attended the barn dance in the village. I played my fiddle with Jake and the old gang. After the Japanese attacked Pearl Harbor on December 7, 1941, I took the squirrel tail off the bottom end of my fiddle bow and replaced it with a small American flag. Everyone liked to see the flag waving as I played the hoedowns.

The following afternoon, Jack and I started back for camp. Walking through the village on our way to the train, Jerome Moore, a neighbor and former combat veteran from World War I, stopped us on the road. "Fred," he said, "you seem anxious to be headin' overseas, but do you realize what kind of an outfit you're in? Your job is to go out in front of the army as scouts. It's almost like a suicide outfit. Is it too late for you to transfer to some other unit?"

"Mr. Moore," I replied, "all of my training in the service had been for this type of a job. I believe the kind of life I led growing up here in the village prepared me for just such a task."

His sound words of advice fell on deaf ears, for I was too young and reckless to heed his warning. This is the main reason the army wanted youngsters like me. We never realized, or thought about the consequences of our sometimes foolish and carefree ways. We never thought of dying, or that we might be among the maimed and crippled returning from the war. Those things happened to the other fellow, not us.

When I arrived back at camp, I learned that Jack Jones, a friend of mine in his middle 30s, had sent home for his 16-year-old sweetheart to join him. Upon her arrival, the couple from the mountains of the South were wed in the village of Bowling Green, Virginia.

In the cool of the autumn evenings, Jack and I often

played and sang country music. He taught me the beautiful ballad called "Precious Jewel." Like many of the soldiers who married before leaving for overseas, he never saw his bride again after he left the country. A couple of years later, I lost a good buddy, for in June of 1944 in northern Italy, Jack lost his life in combat.

Our platoon sergeants were all cavalrymen from the regular peacetime army. The squadron commander, Lieutenant Colonel Harry W. Candler, graduated from West Point. In North Africa, he proved to the men of Troop C that he was one of the greatest fighting men to ever lead men into battle.

The 91st Cavalry Reconnaissance Squadron consisted of a headquarters troop and three recon troops mounted on scout cars, jeeps and weapons carriers. Another troop had thirteen light tanks, each with a 37mm cannon. This light tank troop, supposedly, would support the rest of the troops whenever needed. With about 1,000 men mounted in light vehicles, we were a fast-moving outfit. General Patton observed the 91st Recon operating with the 1st Cavalry Division at Fort Bliss, Texas. After working with them on the Louisiana maneuvers, he chose them to do his reconnaissance in the upcoming campaign.

Our troop was made up of a headquarters platoon and three combat platoons. Each platoon had two sections, with a section consisting of two squads of eight men apiece. Three of the squads in a platoon carried light machine guns, while the fourth had a mortar. Joe Montoro, from Gary, Indiana, the second platoon mortar squad leader, picked me as his first gunner.

The 81mm mortar had a three-inch-diameter barrel about three feet long. It fired shells weighing from six and a half to ten pounds. The mortar was the largest caliber gun in the squadron. The 37mm cannons and .50- and .30-caliber machine guns supplied the remainder of the troop's firepower.

According to the army field manuals, when the army advanced toward the enemy, recon units were positioned out in front, like fingers protruding from the palm of your hand. Usually, each finger contained no more than a platoon, and oftentimes only a squad of men. We were trained not to engage the enemy unless they attacked us.

Our main objective was to gather information, learn where the enemy planned to establish a line of defense, then locate their weak points. This strategy saved the main body of the advancing army from being drawn into a trap and annihilated. Far better to lose a few men in finding out where the enemy intended to make their stand than to lose the main fighting force. These main combat units, whether made up of infantry or tanks, were the ones that would determine the final outcome of the battle. Recon units were to an advancing army what scouts were to a company of infantry moving forward into battle.

In actual combat, we found that oftentimes the enemy drew us into a trap, then tried to close its jaws behind us. When this occurred, we needed to have enough firepower to survive until reinforcements arrived and, hopefully, came to our rescue. Sergeant Al Jerman from Pueblo, Colorado, our second platoon's radio operator, we considered to be one of the best in the squadron. When advancing into "No-Man's-Land," every few hundred yards Al contacted our rear command post and kept them informed of our progress and any changes in the enemy's movements.

The 91st Recon attained full combat strength after receiving its replacements. Even though we only had time to get a limited amount of training, I felt confident that we were ready for combat.

One autumn morning, we were loaded onto a troop train and sent to Fort Dix, New Jersey. After eating a turkey dinner fit for a king, we departed for New York, our point of embarkation. Upon our arrival, we marched to the troopships, our destination a mystery. I walked up the gangplank with my Thompson submachine gun slung over one shoulder, a barracks bag over the other, and carrying my battered old guitar.

The ship *Slaughterdyke* would be our home until we

touched down on solid ground again, which we hoped wouldn't be the bottom of the ocean. Still in the process of being outfitted, this Dutch vessel was having its first voyage as a troopship. Covered with canvas, a five-inch gun on the stern faced the New York City skyscrapers. A few antiaircraft guns mounted on deck pointed toward the autumn sky. Because none of the ship's crew were trained in the use of these weapons, our squadron's 37mm gunners operated the ack-ack guns. None of the friendly crew of the Dutch ship spoke English, but the language barrier never caused a problem.

Below deck, the berths were stacked four and five high like sardines. Soon after leaving New York harbor we ran into a terrible storm, during which nearly everyone got sick. Later, we learned that the autumn and winter of '42 and '43 were the worst in 50 years in the stormy Atlantic.

With no toilets in the hold of the ship, we made good use of our steel helmets. Some fellows emptied their loose bowels in them, too sick to even remove the helmet liner. They placed the helmet containing their smelly fecal matter under their chins, and filled it with the sour contents of their churned stomachs. Very few fellows made it up the ladder to the toilets on the deck above without spilling the contents of their helmet. I was lucky to have a top bunk, for most of the men lying in the lower bunks were continually being splattered with vomit from above.

Many men were unable to reach a toilet, or make it onto the deck in time to let the vomit be washed into the frothing seas to feed the fish. Soldiers who'd never set foot on a ship before, and even some of the veteran sailors, became deathly ill. Like everyone else, I came down with diarrhea. I spent half the voyage sitting on a toilet, with my head hanging over the toilet bowl next to me. With nothing left in my stomach, I barfed the dry heaves until I thought I'd vomited my insides out. By the time we found out that oranges helped to lessen our sickness, the ship's officers had put a guard over them.

A couple of days out of New York, we spotted the

periscope of a lone submarine. The stormy seas worked to our advantage, for the torpedo it fired missed its target. The destroyers escorting our convoy had their hands full trying to protect it from the submarine "wolf pack." In 1942, and even until the late spring of 1943, the Allies didn't have radar or sonar capable of detecting the German U-boats. Before the Allies finally perfected new technologies, like the Mark 4 radar equipment, German U-boats took a heavy toll on our troopships and all Allied shipping in the North Atlantic.

When the storm finally broke, though we were very weak, we enjoyed staying out on deck in the moonlight. Watching the flashing coded messages being signaled between our ships made us realize the seriousness of our situation. The convoy had to observe radio silence to escape detection by the dreaded U-boats.

I watched the bow of our ship part the fluorescent-filled waves. They slid by and tenderly caressed the steel hull, making a rhythmic splashing sound that almost lulled me to sleep. Like a tired old grandmother rocking her remaining years away, my body moved up and down with the motion of the ship. I took advantage of the peacefulness of the moment, and tried to peer into the future. I wondered what new adventures lay ahead, after the rolling seas calmed, and the waves washed up on the shores of our unknown destination.

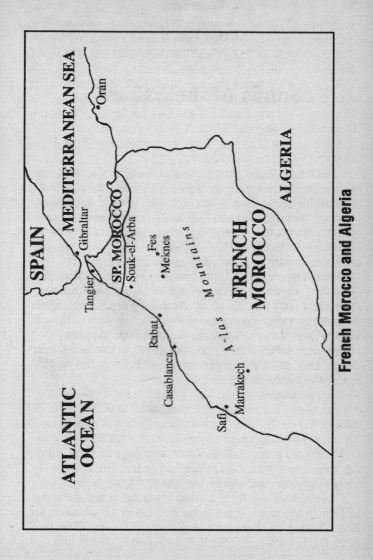

**Frensh Morocco and Algeria**

# CHAPTER II

# Sands of the Sahara

After what seemed like an eternity spent on the open sea, we men on the troopship *Slaughterdyke* received a clue as to our possible destination. Each of us was given a *Guide Book to Africa*. It explained the different customs of the Arabs and translated a few Arabic words into English. The booklet also contained a list of French words, their meanings, and some of the most popular phrases.

Because our convoy hadn't sailed through the Strait of Gibraltar, we knew we were still in the Atlantic Ocean, somewhere off the coast of Africa. When picturesque, snow-white buildings came into view, we were told we would disembark at Casablanca, in French Morocco. After an uneventful landing, we marched up the beach and headed inland. The invasion force that preceded us had silenced the opposition.

The Americans who landed along the northern coast of Africa, near Oran, met stiff resistance from the French forces loyal to the Vichy government. The troops invading the coastal area north of Casablanca, around Port Lyautey, also met strong opposition. After four days of fierce fighting, the French Admiral Darlan had ordered his men to lay down their arms and cooperate with the Americans.

General Patton's troops were scattered along the coast of French Morocco, from Agadir, south of Casablanca, to Port Lyautey to the north, a distance of over 300 miles. After the French capitulated, Patton's army dug in and occupied the entire country.

Although the 91st Recon hadn't taken part in the initial

landings, we were still nervous about stepping ashore on foreign soil.

When Christmas arrived and it came time for our first
holiday dinner overseas, we were each given a can of cold
hash and a cup of hot water. We grumbled as we waded
through ankle-deep mud and carried the meal to our pup
tents. Instead of hearing traditional Christmas music,
everyone lay back and listened to the rain and sleet fall on
their shelter halves. The cold mud oozing up through the
wet blankets was an added Christmas present from the
hand of fate. The cup of boiling water warmed our insides
and furnished enough heat to warm our hearts, so that we
could wish each other a Merry Christmas.

Our plight seemed a far cry from the scenes portrayed
by Humphrey Bogart and Ingrid Bergman in the movie
*Casablanca.* If those two actors had been served a meal under the same conditions as our first Christmas overseas, the
love scene in the cafe wouldn't have been quite so romantic.
Ever since we set foot on the shores of Africa, through no
fault of our kitchen crew, the quality of our meals wasn't
anything to write home about. We survived mostly on the
small cans of Type C rations, and were thankful to get them.
Most everyone realized that it took a tremendous amount of
food to feed an army the size of General Patton's.

When the men from the 91st Recon were ordered to un-
load supplies from the ships docking in Casablanca, our
morale received a boost, for it gave us a break from the daily
routine of training in the mud. No one complained about
working long hours on the docks. The large booms on a ship
lifted the slings and pallets from the hold of the vessel. Once
the pallets touched the dock, it became our job to transfer
the goods onto the waiting trucks or lorries.

In the early morning hours of December 31, we were
unloading a British freighter carrying food and ammunition. While removing cartons from one of the pallets, we
spotted a box of chocolate bars. The hard candy bars were
reserved for soldiers about to go into battle, for it gave
them a quick source of energy. Figuring the hunger in our

churning bellies was emergency enough to warrant a case of chocolate, four of us broke open a box.

With our pockets bulging with candy bars, we continued working. While waiting for the next pallet to be lowered from the ship, we decided to gorge ourselves with the mouthwatering delicacies. Before we had time to take the wrappers off the chocolate bars, the wail of an air raid siren broke the stillness of the winter night. We were experiencing our first air raid.

All lights along the waterfront were immediately extinguished. In their place, searchlights penetrated the sky, waving their beams like a hunter searching for a treed coon. Spellbound, we stood and watched the antiaircraft guns send their streaks of death into the heavens, but none of them found their target. Not until the German planes began dropping their bombs did we come to our senses. With no foxholes on the wharf, our immediate reaction was to dive under anything close at hand that would cover our bodies and protect us from flying shrapnel.

The first time a person is under fire, he's apt to do strange and stupid things. An innocent child would probably think that if the planes couldn't see him, he'd be safe. Our thinking wasn't much better. Aided by the beams of light reflecting off the clouds, we dove under the nearest shadow for protection. It happened to be a British lorry. All four of us felt a false sense of security, for now we couldn't see the planes, only hear the whistle and then the exploding bombs.

The air raid had interrupted our feast of stolen candy, but now that we figured we were safe, we lay back and munched on the tastiest food we'd eaten since landing in North Africa. That night on the docks of Casablanca, with our mouths full of tasty stolen chocolate, we experienced our first taste of war.

The "all-clear" finally sounded, and the lights on the ship illuminated the docks again. One of my buddies crawled out from beneath our bomb shelter, and yelled, "Hey you guys, come take a look at what we dove under for protection."

When we glanced up at the load of artillery ammunition

on the lorry, we were really shook up, but not half as much as we'd have been if one of those bombs had ignited the ammo. With that amount of explosives propelling us, four GIs, mixed with a case of chocolate bars, would be splattered all over the snowy-white houses of Casablanca. We joked about the stupid stunt we'd pulled, and said that our blood flowing over the candy would look like strawberry syrup running down the sides of a chocolate sundae. We learned a valuable lesson without having to pay the price.

In the latter half of January, Troop C was called upon to furnish a few scout cars for a top secret mission. The skeleton crew of each vehicle consisted of a driver and a machine gunner. Because my records showed I'd qualified as an expert machine gunner, our platoon sergeant assigned me to a scout car operated by Tom Thompson from Georgia. All the vehicles were driven into Casablanca and lined up in front of a large villa surrounded by a tall iron fence. Military guards were positioned all around the elaborate place.

Tom said, "Fred, with so many soldiers guarding it, there has to be someone doggone important inside that villa."

We didn't have long to wait to find out why we were summoned to Casablanca. Three black limousines drove out through the gate and lined up on the road in front of the villa. Scout cars were positioned in front of the column and between the limousines. Tom positioned his vehicle directly behind the last black car.

The sergeant in charge informed us that our destination was Marrakech. "The beautiful city lies in a fertile green oasis 90 miles from the Atlantic coast and about 150 miles south of Casablanca," he said. "Our orders are to provide protection for the convoy of dignitaries, and to halt the column every hour to permit its occupants to stretch their legs and empty their bladders."

Our curiosity became aroused as to the identity of the important people in the limousines. No one seemed anxious to provide us with information as to whom we were escorting along the snow-covered Atlas Mountains that bordered the Sahara Desert.

Tom said, "We'll find out who these VIPs are after the first hour is up. I don't care how much blue blood they have in their veins, they won't be able to hold their water all the way to Marrakech."

Orders were passed down along the column, "Load the machine guns and move out, but stay alert for any suspicious activity, especially until we reach the outskirts of Casablanca."

The long awaited first hour of our mysterious journey came to an end. By the time the convoy halted, we could hardly stand the suspense. The machine gun, mounted on a track running around the top of the chest-high sides of the scout car, could be moved to face in any direction. Because Tom's vehicle brought up the rear of the column, I'd positioned my machine gun on the back of the car. This let me cover our rear against a surprise attack. With nothing but desert visible in all directions when we stopped for the break, I saw no reason to be concerned where I located the gun. I moved it up to the front of the vehicle, to the right of Tom. With only the very top of my head showing above the scout car, I could observe everything going on around the limousines. Even though a steel protective cover shielded the windshield, Tom could still see out of a narrow slit in the cover.

Neither of us recognized any of the passengers who stepped out of the first limousine in the column. When the men occupying the middle car got out, none of their faces looked familiar. Finally, the right side door of the car directly in front of us swung open. The first thing I saw protruding through the door was the top of a gray felt hat with a black band above the brim. Its wearer, a short, stocky man in a dark pinstripe suit, had a watch fob chain draped across his chest. The dignitary looked vaguely familiar. I knew I'd seen his picture in the newspaper, but at the moment couldn't place him. Not until he put a partially chewed cigar in his mouth and walked to the rear of the limousine did I recognize him. I was looking at one of the most famous men in the world, and watching history in the making.

I ducked my head below the top of the scout car, removed my helmet, then peeked around the receiver of the machine gun. The dignitary walked to within a few feet of our scout car's bumper, then stopped. He faced in our direction, not realizing that Tom and I could see him clearly. With his back to the limousine, so its occupants couldn't watch him, he unbuttoned his trousers. After sitting in one position for over an hour, he couldn't defy the call of nature. His mind, like his bladder, must also have been under tremendous pressure, for he seemed oblivious to his surroundings.

Tom and I, with mouths wide open and eyes as big as saucers, unconsciously raised our heads above the top of the scout car and stared in awe. We watched the pressure slowly decrease the length of the stream, until it finally stopped altogether. As if hypnotized, I looked at the intermittent, trough-like impressions in the sand. They stopped between his highly polished shoes. The shallow marks reminded me of Morse code dots and dashes, ending with one large, moist dot. Vulgarity had nothing to do with my and Tom's curiosity, for we never intended to reveal the extent God had endowed the renowned man's reproductive organ. A smile crossed my face when I thought of how alike all men respond to the call of nature, even the man we were watching, Sir Winston Churchill, the most famous man in the British Empire.

After buttoning his pants, he happened to glance up and see Tom and me staring down at him from the top of the scout car. He didn't seem embarrassed, for he gave us one of his famous smiles.

"Hello Yanks," he said. "It's a pleasant day for a drive, isn't it? How are you lads doing?"

Both of us returned his greeting with a wave of the hand, thankful that he didn't get upset about having an audience while relieving himself. I nervously said, "We're fine, Sir, and are really enjoying the scenery."

Tom spoke up and said, "It sure is pretty down here along the Atlas Mountains, Sir Winston."

Nodding his head in agreement, the prime minister replied, "Marrakech is one of my favorite places to spend a holiday."

With a short wave of the hand, he turned and walked slowly back to the limousine. The convoy proceeded on to Marrakech without any further interruptions.

Unbeknown to any of us men in the scout cars, on January 14, 1943, a conference was held in Casablanca that lasted ten days. President Franklin D. Roosevelt, Sir Winston Churchill and General Charles de Gaulle of France were the main participants of the meeting. These three leaders of the free world made strategic plans for the offensive action to be taken against the Axis powers, after the anticipated defeat of Rommel's forces in North Africa.

Winston Churchill had often visited Marrakech before the war. He used the beautiful setting as a background for many paintings, and also as a retreat from the pressures created by his job as prime minister of Great Britain. He wanted to share his hideaway with Franklin D. Roosevelt before the President returned to the United States. Roosevelt was a passenger in one of the limousines in front of Churchill's car, but because of his infantile paralysis (polio), he'd been unable to get out of his vehicle.

In the years following the war, Tom and I often said that this incident turned out to be one of the most interesting experiences of our time in the service. Many folks can boast that at one time or another they had the honor of being in the presence of the prime minister of Great Britain. How many people can say that he stood before them with his gray felt hat atop his head, and a cigar protruding from his mouth, while they watched him empty his bladder and moisten the sands on the edge of the Sahara Desert. Of all the portraits made of Sir Winston, to have one of him in such a pose would be the most famous painting of them all.

Most people would be embarrassed, mortified and angry to be caught in a similar situation. The prime minister handled it with the same grace, understanding and tact that made him one of the greatest leaders the world has ever known. That day in the shadow of the Atlas Mountains, I learned why the British people chose to follow him, even though he offered them only "blood, toil, tears, and sweat." He gave them the strength and courage to fight against insurmountable odds, when he spoke these historic words: "We shall fight on the beaches, we shall fight on the fields and in the streets, we shall fight in the hills; we shall never surrender." Without him leading them, would England have survived?

When the convoy arrived in Marrakech, the black limousines entered a villa guarded by the men from our squadron. The scout cars and their occupants proceeded on to the French Foreign Legion barracks. The Foreign Legion troops were assembled on their parade ground for the great occasion. It wasn't every day that two world leaders visited their area. Watching the Legion decked out in their colorful uniforms and mounted on beautiful Arabian horses was a thrilling sight to behold. I'd never before witnessed such a wonderful display of horsemanship. Behind the famous horsemen and their mounts were the snow-covered Atlas Mountains. With their peaks brushing the low clouds drifting in a clear blue sky, they put the finishing touches to a panoramic scene. It was like looking into a magical crystal ball and witnessing an event of an era out of the past.

After cleaning our weapons and vehicles, we billeted with the Legion troops. This would be the only time I slept in a bed until I returned to the States. As colorful as we found the French Foreign Legion, much to our discomfort, we wound up with bedbugs. The insects only crawl out of their hiding places at night, so we didn't realize the straw mattresses were full of them. The following morning we were covered with welts from the bloodsucking insects. This was the first time I'd been bitten by bedbugs having a different nationality than mine. The second night of our stay with the Foreign Legion, we took our blankets and slept on the ground out in the courtyard.

The day after we arrived on the outskirts of Marrakech, a few of us took a walk into the town. A friendly Arab let us ride his camel, then tried to sell it to us. That afternoon we climbed over the walls of the Casbah into the forbidden

Arab section of the city. There we witnessed a custom we
thought had long since vanished from the annals of history.
Slave girls were being unloaded from a camel caravan that
had traveled over the mountains from the Sahara Desert. We
watched the girls being auctioned off to the highest bidder.
Veils covered many of their faces, but from our hiding place
we could see they were very young and beautiful. The
women coming in from the desert nomad tribes usually had
more freedom than those living in the towns and weren't
compelled to wear veils.

That evening, after returning to the French Foreign
Legion compound, we made preparations to hit the sack,
for we'd had a busy day. After crawling under my woolen
army blanket and canvas shelter half, I lay gazing up at the
stars that crept toward the mountains to the east.

As my eyelids began to droop, the stillness of the night
was broken by the distant sound of someone singing an
old cowboy tune. I knew the fellow had to be heading for
our bivouac area, for no Arab could imitate a drunken
Western drawl like that. A few minutes later, in through
the courtyard entrance staggered one of my old buddies
from the horse cavalry. He came abreast of me, singing
and feeling no pain. When he turned his head, the moonlight lit up his face, revealing a smile from ear to ear.

"What are you so all fired happy about?" one of the fellows asked.

"You'd be schmilin' too, if you'd a bin with me," he
said. "I schneeked into the cat howshh in Marrykech."

By now everyone in the courtyard was awake, eager to
hear the inebriated cowboy's story of success. Tom, lying
curled up in his blanket next to me, raised up on his elbow
and asked, "You know the whorehouse is supposed to be
off-limits to us, don't you? Did you protect yourself from
the venereal disease they say those prostitutes have?"

The old cavalryman dropped his chin to his chest and
thought for a minute before saying, "I don't think I did,
but if I didn't, I'll fix 'at right now. Don't ya go a worryin'
none, I'll dissinfeck myself good and proper."

He ended up disinfecting himself, but I don't know how effective or proper his method proved to be.

After fumbling around in his pocket, he finally found his prophylactic kit, then tossed the unused tube over his shoulder. We watched him stagger toward a scout car and then lean against it for support. We didn't know what our old buddy was planning to do. Because we'd all had a busy day and wanted to get some rest, none of us got out of our blankets. He proceeded to drag a five-gallon can of gas out of one of the vehicles. The can had a large hole in the top, about four inches in diameter, where a pouring spout could be fastened. Our intoxicated friend unscrewed the cap covering the hole. Glancing in our direction, he said, "Thish otta do the jhob."

It never dawned on us what his intentions were, not until he dropped his pants and stepped out of them. By the time he lurched forward and straddled the can, it was too late to stop him. In his drunken stupor, he lowered his private parts into the large opening, causing the full can of gasoline to overflow.

The shock of the volatile mixture coming in contact with the most delicate part of a man's skin somehow penetrated his alcohol-drenched body and registered in his befuddled brain. I don't think his actions completely sobered him, but as the searing red-hot flame of pain pierced the sensitive skin of his privates, he leaped to his feet. A horrible shriek, almost like the cry of a grown hog being castrated, broke the stillness of the desert night. Before anyone could grab him, he ran screaming out through the courtyard into the darkness beyond.

Upon hearing the bloodcurdling yell, the French Foreign Legion troops came running out of their barracks. Clad only in their underwear, they were a strange sight, a stark contrast to the men we'd seen earlier in the day in their spit-and-polish uniforms. They were certain we were under attack, for each of them carried a rifle.

All the men who'd watched the proceedings that led up to our friend's dash into the desert threw back their blankets and raced barefooted after him. With a group of men in white long johns racing after a lone figure naked from the waist down, we must have looked a sorry sight. When we caught up with our buddy, he lay facedown, moaning. Squirming around in the cool desert sand, he tried to relieve the pain in the shriveled up object that he'd subjected to such harsh treatment. Four of us carried him back to the courtyard. We poured water over his red and blistered privates, then put him to bed.

A few days passed before he could walk, and it took much longer before he was capable of a repeat performance of that night he spent in the house of ill repute in Marrakech. Tom asked him why he didn't write a book entitled *A Surefire Cure for the Prevention of Sexually Contracted Diseases.*

After we found out that he'd done no permanent damage to his manhood, we kidded him. I said, "The only reason you stopped running out into the desert that night was because you ran out of gas."

Fortunately, our amorous buddy never wound up with a venereal disease. From that time on, we noticed he kept his love life separate from his love for liquor.

Trying to understand the strange customs of the Arabs became a learning experience. I imagine that some of our habits in the Western world were just as strange to them. Nearly every Arab family owned a burro. These little animals were usually loaded down with so much brush or other heavy objects, sometimes you wondered why their knees didn't buckle. They lived up to the name given them centuries ago, "beasts of burden."

The Arab women always walked behind the men. Balancing a large object on the head while walking was probably responsible for the good posture. In preparation for their balancing feat, they first twisted a piece of cloth into a loose rope and placed it on top of the head in the form of a circle. This rolled cloth made a flat surface for the jug, or other bundle they were carrying, to rest upon. It still took a great deal of practice to balance the load and travel over uneven ground.

The Arab husband walking ahead of his wife carried nothing but a staff. If he had to go to the toilet, he squatted down in the gutter. As his loose-fitting robe folded up around him, it gave him all the privacy he needed. Without putting his staff down or using his hands, he relieved his bowels. When finished, he stood up and proceeded on his way. His wife walked around whatever he'd deposited in the gutter and followed him. The desert sun soon dried up the feces, leaving hardly any visible evidence.

To a person raised in a city of the Western world, this Arab custom probably seems crude and unsanitary. A man who's lived in the mountains, or the sparsely populated regions of our own country, will have a better understanding of the Arab. With no toilet paper available or water to wash their hands before they sit down to eat, it wouldn't be very hygienic for them to soil their hands. The Arabs don't use their right hand when they go to the toilet, for that hand has to remain free from germs when putting food in their mouth. Though we may scoff at some of their customs, in their own peculiar way, the Arabs are cleaner than we in the Western world.

After landing in North Africa, we soon learned to bring anything of value into our pup tents at night, for the Arabs stole us blind. It didn't take long for our squadron commander to deem it necessary that guards be placed around our camp at all times. We never became very upset with the Arabs, for we figured that stealing was their method of dealing with the Americans who'd disrupted their way of life. We enjoyed bartering the candy that came packed in our cans of type-C food rations for their almonds and oranges.

Winston Churchill and President Roosevelt only remained in Marrakech a short while. The day they left, we escorted the President to the local airport where a plane awaited to fly him back to Washington. We regretted having to leave the oasis city with its fine examples of Moorish architecture surrounded by beautiful gardens. While guarding the President at the airport, we had difficulty controlling the large crowd of curious Arabs. They all wanted to get a glimpse of the famous American. As aides pushed his wheelchair up a ramp into the waiting plane, we kept our Thompson submachine guns pointed at the crowd and our backs to the President.

I believe we were the most maneuverable outfit in General Patton's command, for like the cavalry of old, the 91st Recon could move on a minute's notice. As soon as we completed our mission of escorting the President and the prime minister, General Patton ordered us north on an urgent assignment. We traveled as fast as possible to the border between French and Spanish Morocco. Army intelligence reported that Hitler's forces might possibly move down from Spain and invade the coast of North Africa. Spanish Morocco bordered the Strait of Gibraltar, which at the narrow point was only eight miles wide.

Our squadron set up roadblocks at Souk-el-Arba and managed to capture a few Axis spies trying to infiltrate into French Morocco. Luckily, the rumored German invasion never materialized.

In one of the towns along the Spanish Moroccan border, I visited a movie house operated by French Moroccans and frequented by Arabs. There were no chairs in the place. Everyone sat crossed-legged on the floor and watched a Laurel and Hardy movie and a couple of other silent films. The Arabs laughed at the antics of the Three Stooges, even though no sound accompanied the picture. We enjoyed the antics of the Arabs more than we did the movie. They were like little children seeing a cartoon for the first time. When the show ended, I walked out of the movie house wearing a bright red Moroccan fez that a friendly Arab had placed on my head.

The Arabian women were very timid and humble and worked hard. In exchange for a small trinket, a few pieces of candy, or a can of C rations, they washed our clothes. We obtained bars of strong, lye GI soap from our supply sergeant and gave them to the women. After rubbing soap on the clothes, they bunched them together and either pounded them with a rock or jumped up and down on them with their bare feet. They usually used a large flat rock beside a stream as their laundry area.

Very few cars traveled the roads. Those that did were small European models with a tall 20- or 30-gallon tank mounted on the back. The automobile carburetors were converted to operate on carbide gas because gasoline was next to impossible for civilians to obtain.

Many of the Moroccans made a living by stripping the bark from cork oak trees. The bark could be stripped every seven to ten years without harming the tree. Selling cork provided a good income for those inhabitants living in the barren land on the northern edge of the Sahara Desert.

General Patton kept the 91st Recon continually on the move. We traveled all over French Morocco, checking on illegal border crossings, or investigating rumors of spies infiltrating the country. We had a very interesting job, for it afforded us an opportunity to visit Fes, Meknes, and most of the other towns and villages. We found that many of the ancient Moorish customs were still observed in Rabat, one of the four capital cities of Morocco. Visiting the Moslem mosques, and watching the military guards parade around the sultan's palace, made picturesque diversions.

On one of the many patrols we made along the Sahara Desert, I had a comical but educational experience. We'd stopped for the night outside of a small village next to an oasis. Before we had a chance to wipe the sand out of our eyes and the dust off our faces, the captain called us together. A very conservative man, he went strictly by the army's book of regulations. He oftentimes held himself aloof from the men in the ranks.

"It seems that every time we camp on the outskirts of an oasis or village," he said, "some of you men sneak into town at night and patronize the local cathouse. We are losing more men to venereal disease than we can get replacements for, and our troop strength is being depleted. Until today, every time we've bivouacked near a village, I've placed a walking guard around the local cathouse. That policy doesn't seem to have kept some of you men from climbing over the walls and entering the courtyard when the guard's back is turned. You all know that most of the prostitutes are infected with venereal disease, but that doesn't seem to put a damper on your sexual appetites."

Glancing around at my comrades, I could see that some of them were ill at ease, for they figured the captain was talking to them personally.

The captain spoke to us men much like a preacher reprimanding a teenage son who's been caught coming out of a burlesque show. He said, "Tonight I'm adopting a different policy; I am going to station a guard inside the whorehouse. The only men allowed to enter will be Arabs, Moroccans, and soldiers from the French Foreign Legion. I can understand the reason none of you men want to report to the medics. All of you know that if you contract a venereal disease, you'll automatically lose your noncommissioned officer stripes and be broken back to buck private.

"Is it right," he asked, "that the rest of us have to sleep with our first aid kits strapped to our bodies? We have to be afraid that one of our buddies will steal the sulfanilamide tablets, just so he can cure himself and not have to report for sick call. Those sulfa tablets are only supposed to be taken when you are wounded. That doesn't mean the type of wounds that some of you fellows are getting after you return from a night of physical combat with those whores."

When the captain finished reprimanding us, he looked out over the troops, giving us time for his words to sink in. Most of the men had their heads bowed and were busy shuffling the warm sand with the toes of their boots. As our leader's searching eyes moved back and forth, I knew he was looking for a candidate to enforce his new policy. I lowered my head, for I wanted nothing to do with the unpleasant task of policing my comrades.

The captain's eyes must have come to rest on me, for I heard him say, "Tonight, the guard inside the whorehouse will be Private Salter, and remember, Salter, no one touches those girls and that includes you. Report to the first sergeant for your instructions."

I asked myself, why did he have to pick on me? Was it because I still hadn't started to shave the peach-fuzz on my face? Maybe he chose me because I still looked like an innocent kid, who everyone said was a loner. I knew that just as sure as God made green apples, before the night ended, half the troop would be angry with me. None of them would take kindly to being deprived of one of the few pleasures these lonely patrols afforded us. Sheepishly, I picked up my Thompson submachine gun. After receiving my orders from the sergeant, and directions on how to find the whorehouse, I walked out of our bivouac area. All the villagers were aware that a troop of Americans was bivouacked next to the oasis. None of them spoke to me as I knocked on the large wooden door and waited to be admitted.

The madam of the establishment came to the door and greeted me. She seemed very young and beautiful to be running a business that could make a girl old before her time. The tattoo marks on her light tanned forehead were very pronounced when she smiled, and she displayed a beautiful set of teeth. I spoke only a few words of French, but understood enough of the language to let her know that I intended to keep the American soldiers away from her prostitutes. The front door opened into a large room, which I presumed to be the gathering place for the girls, and where they displayed what they had to offer. It was here that the client probably picked the young lady he hoped would satisfy his desires. As near as I could tell, the young women were a mixture of French, Berber and Arabian.

Most of the Arab girls we saw in the towns never ventured out in public unless they wore a veil, but these girls were of a different breed. Most of them were probably in their early teens. Without veils covering their faces, and the dark robes they usually wore discarded for more revealing clothes, these women were beautiful. Maybe I felt this way because I hadn't seen many girls without veils since I'd left the States.

After sitting down on a bench beside the front door, I became slightly nauseated from the smell in the whorehouse. I couldn't figure out where the strange aromatic odor came from. When my eyes became accustomed to the dimly lit room, I noticed a small column of smoke drifting toward the ceiling. The source of the smoke and fumes was a shelf fastened to the wall where three small clay monkeys about six inches tall were huddled together behind an oval dish. Incense burning in the container produced the sickening fragrance.

A long, narrow hallway branched off from the left side of the main room. On each side of this hall were small rooms. Loose-fitting curtains were draped across the openings leading to these cubicles. The brightly colored material afforded little privacy for the occupants of the room to perform their lovemaking.

When one of the girls walked out of her crib, I saw what I thought to be an ancient lamp made out of terra-cotta. It rested on top of a box used for a nightstand. The crude lamp burned some type of oil, and gave off a dim but pleasant glow. It made a very romantic setting for the events that took place there.

A large archway in the center of the far wall of the main room led to a courtyard enclosed by a masonry wall. The madam's quarters were in a medium-sized room to the right of the archway. Her lodgings contained more elaborate furnishings than those of her talented girls, and even included a bed with a metal frame.

I'd never ventured into a house of ill repute before, and had much to learn about the oldest profession in the world. As I glanced around at the girls, they all smiled at me with come-hither looks. My pulse quickened, and I began to get excited. An uncomfortable feeling came over me, but then I remembered the captain's final words, "No one touches those girls tonight, Salter, and that includes you."

When the first customer of the evening knocked on the solid wooden door, I turned the latch and admitted a French Foreign Legion officer. As the evening progressed, business started to increase. Quite a few of the local men came to sample the fruit from the madam's orchard of human flesh. The house provided the male population with the most popular entertainment in the oasis area.

About 10 P.M., when I opened the front door, I hated to refuse admission to one of my buddies from the 1st Platoon. "I'm sorry," I said, "but I can't let you in. You heard the captain's instructions. He'd nail me to the cross if I disobeyed his orders."

My friend walked away, cursing a blue streak. A short while later I heard a faint metallic sound in the courtyard. Walking out through the archway, I saw a grappling hook vibrating under pressure on top of the masonry wall. I recognized the hook as one made by a friend of mine, for it was wrapped with manila rope to muffle the sound when it hit against a solid object. A moment later the blond head of one of my friends in the 3rd Platoon rose up over the top of the wall. As he'd done many times before, he thought he could sneak in the whorehouse undetected. I hated to tell him to drop back down, but I'd no other choice. Without saying a word, he lowered himself to the ground, then shook the rope so the grappling hook would release from the wall. From the way my buddy yanked on the rope and sent the hook sailing back over the wall, I knew he'd become very upset.

When I returned to the main room, I looked up at the three clay monkeys sitting peacefully behind the incense burner. With expressionless faces, they still tended the smoldering fire. I stood for a moment and watched the smoke carry the fragrant odor throughout the room. The fumes did a good job of masking the telltale smells of a whorehouse.

The girls probably thought me stupid, for I talked out loud to the three silent monkeys. I asked them, "Why did the captain have to pick me for this blasted detail? Whatever his reason, by the time morning comes, I won't have a friend left in the troop. He's making a monkey out of me, and in my buddys' eyes, I'll stink worse than you three."

I remembered the legend of the three clay monkeys from when I was a child. My mother told me they know everything that goes on around them, and "see no evil, hear no evil, and speak no evil." That philosophy seemed like a good one to follow. The monkeys were probably smarter than most of us. By practicing those three things, they stayed out of trouble, especially when they saw and heard some of the things that went on in a whorehouse.

The next time a knock came at the door, an Arab and a soldier from the Foreign Legion appeared. The Arab pointed out a couple of the girls to the Legionnaire. I figured he must be a pimp, furnishing customers for the prostitutes. When I looked into the Arab's eyes, I almost vomited. He had the advanced stage of some type of venereal disease, for the whites of both eyes were horribly discolored. A heavy, white, pus-like fluid ran out of each eye and dripped down onto his cheeks. I turned away from him and glanced over at the tantalizing smiles on the girls' faces. Each of them was trying to entice the Legionnaire into her crib.

Under my breath, I muttered, "I'll bet the girls pay this pimp with their sexual pleasures behind those cubicle curtains."

Earlier in the evening, I'd been sorely tempted to lower my moral standards that the captain considered to be so high. I'd had a desire to taste the forbidden fruits of love the girls so willingly offered. Now, no amount of tempting could make me sample what on the surface seemed to be a rose from the garden, when underneath those swaying leaves of bright-colored cloth lurked a thorn on the vine. I had just received my first lesson in sex education.

Back in the States, when a soldier received his basic training, he saw movies that showed the different stages of syphilis and gonorrhea. What I'd witnessed was far more realistic and effective in keeping a young fellow on the straight and narrow path. The thought of sneaking into one of the cribs when business slacked off, I erased from my mind. I tried to forget about the sickening look of the Arab pimp's eyes. Though I hated the smell coming from the incense burner, it was easier to tolerate than looking into two eyes, boiling over like pus flowing out of a pair of carbuncles.

As the evening wore on, I became more at ease around the girls. Their charming personalities started to sway my biased way of evaluating prostitutes. I began to accept their lifestyle as a needed commodity for the lonely man. In my broken French and Arabic, I carried on a pleasant conversation with them. With the shield guarding my moral standards beginning to lower, I thought, these girls can't possibly be infected with a disease; they are too beautiful and friendly.

About two A.M., when business tapered off, I felt confident there would be no more interruptions from any of the men from our troop. All evening, I'd watched the money transactions between the customers and the girls, and knew what the best girl in the house charged for her services. Taking my wallet out of my shirt pocket, I approached the madam of the whorehouse. I handed her enough francs to pay for an evening of pleasure with her most beautiful girl. She gladly accepted the money. From the smile that appeared on her face, I knew she figured the fair-haired American had given in to his "holier than thou" attitude, and intended to pluck an apple from her tree.

A couple of the girls were bedded down in the cubicles with overnight guests. When the remaining girls saw me hand money to their madam, they immediately started to cozy up to me. I could tell they were more than willing to teach the shy Allied soldier some of the amorous tricks they'd learned from their love-starved customers off the Sahara Desert.

When I refused to give in to any of the girls' advances, the madam smiled and started to work her charm on me. She walked over and took me by the arm, certain that I wanted her more experienced favors above all the younger girls. When we reached the entrance to her room, she glanced over her shoulder, then rubbed her breasts against my arm. A young fellow can only stand so many amorous advances from the opposite sex before he loses either his virginity or his mind. My chest started to heave, like that of a buck rabbit thrown into a cage full of does. I saw the look of triumph appear on the madam's face when she winked at the other girls.

She pulled back the curtain, and like a lady matador waving a muleta or cape in front of a maddened bull, she swept her arm across her body and motioned me toward the bed. Just before the last of my willpower snapped, I raised my hand and stopped her advances. Shaking like a penguin stripped of its feathers, I told her that I did want a favor from her, but not her gorgeous body.

With her arm still encircling my waist and her bosom pushed tight against my chest, we walked back to the main room. I broke loose from her warm embrace and pointed to the three clay monkeys on the shelf. She made no move to stop me when I reached up and removed the incense burner. She just stood there dumbfounded. With their mouths wide open, the other girls were also struck dumb with astonishment. It finally dawned on them that I placed a greater value on three monkeys than I did on the sexual pleasures of one of the most beautiful women in North Africa.

Earlier in the evening, I had made up my mind that if I could keep my hormones under control, three monkeys would be the only physical remembrance I'd need of a night spent in an Arab whorehouse. Though the incense burner might not afford as much pleasure as the scented fruit offered by the girls, the companionship of the three monkeys would be a lot healthier.

At daybreak the captain sent word for me to report back to our bivouac area. I gladly relinquished my first and last assignment as a "Whorehouse Guard" on the edge of the Sahara Desert. Years later, my children would ask me, "What did you do in the war, Dad?"

Oftentimes I nearly blurted out, "I was a guard in a whorehouse."

How many returning servicemen can lay claim to having performed such an interesting task in the service of their country? You could even say that for a few hours, I helped to safeguard the physical well-being of a troop of American fighting men.

The 91st Recon Squadron's days in French Morocco drew to a close. The news of crucial military events taking place in Tunisia were very discouraging. We received word that General Rommel's war machine was once again on

## North Africa

the offensive. The American positions in Tunisia were in grave danger of being overrun.

Our commander, Colonel Candler, called the squadron together and said, "Because we are one of the most mobile units under General Patton's command in French Morocco, we are being force marched to Tunisia."

The 9th Infantry Division and volunteers from the 2nd Armored Division also prepared to leave for the front to join the army's II Corps. General Patton received orders from General Eisenhower to take command of the corps from General Fredendall.

Colonel Candler spoke to us before we left for Tunisia. None of us would ever forget his words of wisdom, for when we went into battle, he enforced this motto: "As you go into combat, always remember to have boldness of action and rapidity of movement."

Most of the troops stationed in French Morocco remained there until the Africa Campaign ended. General Patton personally requested that the 91st Recon accompany him.

When we first arrived in French Morocco, each soldier was issued a white, light canvas mattress cover. The sack-like cover could be filled with straw and used to make sleeping on the damp ground a little more comfortable. When the Arabs discovered our white mattress covers, they offered us almost anything they owned to obtain one. The covers could easily be made into white robes.

Traveling east through Algeria, en route to Tunisia, an event happened that strained the relationship between a few of the renegades of the Arab race and the easygoing American soldier, who was sometimes noted for playing mischievous pranks. Our convoy usually stopped once every hour for a five-minute break, to stretch our legs and maintenance-check our vehicles. Many of our rest stops were close to Arab villages, where we traded candy and cigarettes for eggs and wine. Nearly every time we bartered for wine, we found something other than wine in the dark-colored bottles. More than once, the Arabs had urinated in them. Nine times out of ten, we had to throw the contents away. Most of the eggs we received were either rotten or almost ready to hatch a young chick. We became so fed up with the Arabs' shenanigans that my jeep driver, George Johnson, and I decided it was high time to play a few tricks of our own.

A few miles west of Relizane, Algeria, we were about three minutes into our rest period when a group of Arabs walked by our jeep. In preparation for our planned maneuver against the Arabs, George unpacked his mattress cover and placed it over the back of his seat, in plain view. We saw the group hold a conference a few feet in front of our vehicle, then return to parley. The spokesman, a tall, exceptionally well-built fellow, had dark hair flowing from beneath a mantle that hung down around his shoulders. He held a bottle of wine in each hand. One of his partners carried a small basket of eggs. We knew these fellows were experienced in bartering, for in broken English the leader pointed to our mattress cover and said, "Trade for white cover."

George and I nonchalantly looked at each other. I shrugged my shoulders and raised the palms of my hands upward, showing the Arabs that it didn't matter to me if George made a trade. Being an obliging fellow, my buddy said, "Okay, we'll barter."

The vehicles ahead of us had already moved out and were a couple of hundred yards down the road when George started to remove the mattress cover draped over his seat. I reached out and took the basket of eggs and placed them on top of the ammunition boxes behind me. Reluctantly, the spokesman let me take his two bottles of wine, which I immediately placed on the floor between my legs. George wouldn't release his hold on the mattress cover until the wine and eggs were safely stored in our jeep. I noticed the cunning gleam in the leader's eyes when he gripped the white cover in both of his hands. The facial appearance on the rest of the group also changed. Where most Arabs wore a solemn mask, a cunning smile of victory appeared on their faces. They knew they could get a good price for the mattress cover in Algiers.

When George finally relinquished his hold on the mattress cover he said, "Let's get out of here."

In anticipation of making a fast getaway, he had previously pushed the clutch pedal clear to the floor. When he slid his foot sideways, the clutch engaged with a pop. At the same instant his right foot pressed the gas pedal so hard it's a wonder he didn't drive it into the engine compartment. I felt like I was back in the horse cavalry, for over 2,000 pounds of jeep reared up in the air. With gravel and dirt spewing from beneath the rear wheels, the little vehicle leaped away from the bewildered Arabs.

I turned my head and saw the Arab smiling from ear to ear, still clutching the prized possession to his chest. The jeep had sped about thirty feet from the Arab when his world exploded. The rope, tied around one end of the white canvas, uncoiled and extended to its maximum

length. The other end, we had securely tied around the machine gun mount pedestal bolted to the floor of the jeep.
Something had to give, and we were certain that the Arab's
determination to retain his trade goods would be no match
for the half-inch manila rope.

We had only planned on having a little fun with the
Arabs, but never expected to witness anything spectacular
and life-threatening. When the rope cracked like a whip, the
scene reminded me of a circus clown being shot out of a
cannon. We watched a bearded figure in a long, dirty robe
being lifted up into the air. His headdress came loose, and
the mantle that usually covered his head and hung down to
his shoulders became tangled around his neck, exposing his
coal-black hair. With his robe billowing out on both sides,
the wind velocity created by George's fast takeoff helped lift
him up in the air. No kite could have had a better takeoff. If
the poor fellow had been born with wings, he might have
been able to stay airborne, but like most everything that goes
up, sooner or later it has to come down. The Arab hit the
dirt and gravel road with a bone-crushing thud, but still he
wouldn't release his hold on the mattress cover. It continued
to drag on the ground like a toboggan beneath his body.

Above the roar of the jeep engine, I listened to his frantic
cries of anger mix with the dust swelling up from the roadbed,
"Allah" being the only word I could understand. The unfortunate fellow was probably asking the supreme being of the Islam religion for help, but his prayers went unanswered.

After watching a furrow being plowed in the soft
roadbed, I told George to slow down. Like all of us, when
the Arab died, his body would eventually turn to ashes or
dust. I didn't want to be responsible for speeding up the
process and see this man ground to dust before my very eyes.
Unable to retain his hold on the mattress cover any longer,
the Arab released it and rolled into the gutter. George
stopped the jeep and shifted into reverse with the intention
of helping the poor man. When the bundle of shredded
clothes came to life and stood up on the road shaking a fist
at us, we waved farewell and continued on our way.

After retrieving the mattress cover, all that remained tied to the rope were strips of dirty canvas, for it had taken the brunt of the punishment. If it hadn't been underneath his body, I'm certain the Arab would never have been able to father children.

Both George and I felt guilty for having pulled such a low-down trick, that is, until we took a swig of the wine. The fermented concoction was even worse than what we had traded a carton of cigarettes for the previous day. It tasted like a mixture of sheep manure and chicken bile. That evening, when we tried to fry up a couple of the eggs, the smell turned our stomachs so bad, we buried the eggs, basket and all. I placed a cross over the smelly mound, hoping one of the renegade Arabs would dig it up to steal a pair of shoes or the clothing from a corpse. Trying to add a bit of humor to our misfortune, George even removed his helmet and said a prayer when I lowered the remains into the ground.

It seemed a shame to lose a good mattress cover just to get even with a few outlaw Arabs. We didn't continue our crusade against the dishonest members of the race, for we knew the majority of the Moslems were fine people. Mohammed taught his followers not to kill, steal, or be guilty of adultery. Like the eggs we bartered for, there are good and bad in all nationalities.

One night, while camped outside of a village in eastern Algeria, I lay with my head on my helmet, listening to the Arabs chant their evening prayers. A devout believer of Islam prays to Allah five times a day. Before leaving Morocco, I'd found a book written in French that delved into the Arabs' customs, religion and the nomad way of life many of them practiced. That evening a French-Canadian boy in our platoon translated part of it for me. I learned that the Arabs were responsible for preserving many of the Roman and Greek works of literature and science.

When I found that Mohammed taught his followers about Abraham, Moses and Christ, and told them that all the prophets of God taught essentially the same things, my philosophy about religion began to change. I asked myself, "Who am I to criticize an Arab if he wants to believe in the Koran instead of the Bible?" From now on, as long as another man's faith teaches him the basic Ten Commandments, I will respect his beliefs.

It took an understanding of the Arab nomad and his religion to make me a more tolerant and better Christian.

On our forced march through Algeria, we never stopped to visit the cities of Oran, Algiers or Constantine. Four days after we left Morocco we arrived in Tebessa, an important road junction in northeastern Algeria located next to the Tunisian border.

As we drove southeast out of Tebessa and headed for the oasis town of Gafsa, German planes continually attacked our column. On this stretch of road, we received our baptism of fire from the Stuka Ju87 dive bombers. When the two machine guns in its wings and one in the rear cockpit strafed us, we were told to return fire with our rifles and other small arms.

The Stuka really put the fear of God into a man, even though it carried only a single 1,100-pound bomb beneath the fuselage. Like a hawk diving on its prey, when the Stuka went into a dive, the sound was terrifying. It made you want to crawl deeper into a foxhole that most of the time wasn't there. I very seldom shot at an approaching Stuka, but waited until it passed overhead, then raised up and fired. The psychological effect the plane had on a man when it came shrieking out of the sky was worse than the actual explosion of its bomb.

General Rommel's original plan was to destroy the American fighting force. On Valentine's Day he had broken through the American line of defense in Tunisia. After pushing his Afrika Korps through Kasserine Pass, he hoped to head north, capture Tebessa, and cut off the French XIX Corps and the British 1st Army.

The battle that ensued became a mass slaughter of American men and a gigantic trash heap of twisted equipment. For the first time in World War II, the unseasoned troops of the 1st Armored and the 1st, 34th, and later the 9th Infantry Divisions came face to face with the German war machine. Though the men fought courageously, their inferior armor and inexperienced commanders were no match for the battle-proven equipment and brilliant strategy of the "Desert Fox."

A number of factors foiled Rommel's plan of achieving a complete victory over the American troops. He received no cooperation from his bitter rival, General von Arnim, who commanded the German army in northern Tunisia. Von Arnim didn't want to see Rommel get control of any of his fighting units. Because of the conflict between the two generals, Rommel couldn't carry out his strategic battle plan. His fuel and ammunition supplies were also dangerously low. The delays he encountered gave the Allies time to move seasoned British troops and American reinforcements into the area. Lastly, the "Desert Fox" knew that General Montgomery, the hero of El Alamein, would be launching his attack on the German defense line at Mareth. This line extended westward from the Mediterranean Sea. Rommel had no other alternative but to call off the attack.

Shortly after these events took place, the 91st Recon, along with other American units, moved up to strengthen the U.S. II Corps and help plug the gaps in their line of defense. When General Patton replaced General Fredendall as commander of the corps in Tunisia, he quickly started to reshape his command into a fighting team that America could be proud of. Eager to show the world that the American soldier could distinguish himself in battle, Patton soundly defeated the Germans at El Guettar.

In the horse cavalry, we'd been trained that there are times when you can't go into battle astride a horse. Your mounts often had to be held by a few troopers, while the rest of the men fought dismounted. We did a great deal of this type of fighting throughout the war. Many times, we left our vehicles behind the lines to be attended by their drivers. Only when the Germans retreated and lost contact with our forces did we use our jeeps and scout cars and become mounted cavalry.

The main problem we had when fighting as infantry was that it left each platoon shorthanded. The mortar squads were affected the most because the first and second gunners were jeep drivers. The other three squads in the platoon operated machine guns.

When we experienced our first combat as infantrymen, the situation was so critical that our vehicles were left behind the front lines without drivers. Under cover of darkness, every man in Troop C moved forward to occupy a hill the Germans were determined to capture.

A foot soldier will never forget his feelings of fear and insecurity the first time he moves out into "No-Man's-Land." He wonders how he'll react under fire. Will he have the courage to advance when he meets the enemy, or will he turn and run like a coward? Experiencing an air raid, or being shelled from afar by artillery, is a completely different feeling.

Though surrounded by comrades, you walk alone with your thoughts. No amount of training can prepare you for the moment when you look into the determined face of your enemy, and it comes down to either his life or yours.

The stars were tiny ghostlike candles in the sky, casting their faint beams of light over the brush on the hillside. Eerie shadows gripped imaginary rifles that seemed ready to burst into flame with every step we took. The whites of your comrade's eyes stood out like those of a deer picked up in the beam of a poacher's light. Seeing them made you squint your own eyes almost shut, for fear an enemy waiting in ambush might sight his rifle between them. The tenseness of the moment made everyone overly cautious as we moved forward to meet the enemy for the first time.

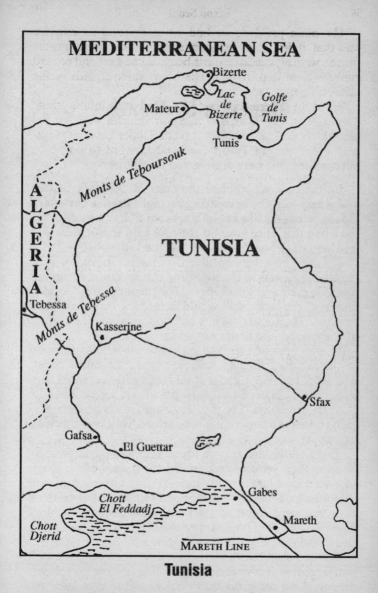

**Tunisia**

# CHAPTER III

# Baptism by Death

By the time we reached the crest of the dark, barren and windy hill, the drawstring of night drew a curtain of clouds across the display of stars that lit our way. Most of the earth that once covered the rocks on top of the ridge had long since been swept away to the valleys below.

Up until now, we considered ourselves lucky, for we'd beaten the Krauts to the top. How fast we could set up our machine guns and get prepared for the inevitable German attack to retake the hill would determine our chances of survival. The sooner we got our bodies below the surface of the ground, the better our odds.

If each man had a small pick and shovel, like the men in the infantry, digging foxholes would be much easier. The army training manual never dealt with a combat situation where cavalrymen dug fortifications a great distance from their mounts. The movies usually showed a cavalryman in battle either riding a horse or lying down behind his mount, using it as a shield.

Two or three men in each squad removed the large shovels from their vehicles and carried them up the hill; otherwise we'd have had a rough time digging our machine-gun emplacements. We had just finished setting up the machine guns and were about to start on our individual foxholes when the first shell landed atop the ridge. A German recon patrol had probably heard us digging.

Between shell bursts that sprayed the forward slope with hot, jagged, widow-making metal, I dug my first foxhole under fire. After using my heavy bolo knife to chip away the stones, I scooped the mixture out of the shallow hole with my canteen cup. To the front, facing the German lines, I built a breastwork. Oh, what I wouldn't give for a few large rocks to shield me from the ever-probing shrapnel.

Extra boxes of .45- and .30-caliber ammunition were hauled up to us by the kitchen crew. The ammo, left over from World War I, still had the dates 1917 and 1918 stamped on the boxes. Many of the shell casings were corroded a bluish-green. The ammo was distributed for use in our 1928 model Thompson submachine guns and our Model 1903 Springfield rifles. The .30-caliber air-cooled machine gun, our main defensive weapon, used the same ammunition as our rifles.

When I first arrived at Camp A. P. Hill, back in the States, I'd been appointed first gunner of the 2nd Platoon mortar squad. Corporal Joe Montoro was my squad leader. Over the past few months I'd become very close to the men in Joe's squad. I felt a sense of security in the knowledge that we could depend on each other when we entered combat. Because mortars weren't being used on this hill, the men of these squads were used as riflemen or machine gunners.

When the 3rd Platoon mortar squad leader got wounded and had to be evacuated to the field hospital, our captain ordered me to take over his squad. Being placed in charge of eight men that I'd never trained with gave me a feeling of loneliness. I hated the responsibility of having to command a group of men I hardly knew. I'd much rather have worked alone and not had to make decisions affecting the lives of others. Against my better judgment, I agreed to become a squad leader.

With no cover on the forward slope of the hill, the Germans were at a disadvantage. Each time they attacked, we drove them back, but not without suffering casualties ourselves. That first day on the hill, one of my men received a leg wound from small-arms fire and had to be evacuated. Though our numbers were depleted, we continued to keep the knifelike ridge from falling into German hands. Our captain was proud, for with the 9th Infantry battling on either side of us, we proved that the cavalry could also hold its ground.

In the early spring, the nights were cold in Tunisia. We were glad to be wearing our woolen, olive drab uniforms. Since joining the army, I'd corresponded with a girl from New Hampshire. She sent me a New Testament with a steel cover on the front. The small book was designed to be placed in your left shirt pocket, directly over your heart. I don't believe the piece of flat steel would stop a bullet fired at close range, but it did afford some protection from shrapnel. The word of God between its covers had a psychological effect on me. I thought of the warriors I'd read about in the Old Testament. I remembered the odds against David when he faced the giant Goliath, and of how Daniel faced death in the den of lions. I carried that New Testament in my pocket throughout the war.

When relieving our bowels up on the front lines, we had to be careful not to expose our underwear or our backsides, for they were both white. As yet, we hadn't been issued olive drab underclothes, and white made an excellent target for the German snipers. A man only needed one rectum.

The second night that we defended the hill where we received our first baptism of combat, Platoon Sergeant Smith received orders to send out a patrol. The captain told him to reconnoiter out in front of our lines and check on enemy troop movements. When he asked for volunteers, I raised my hand. There is an old army saying, "never volunteer for anything," but this wasn't a work detail, and I needed experience in patrol work.

All the members of the patrol were issued extra ammo and hand grenades. In the early days of the war, the only grenades available were the yellow practice grenades that we'd been issued back in the States. We never received green grenades until after the African campaign. I didn't hang the yellow pineapple-shaped grenades on my belt, but put them inside my jacket. A walking lemon tree would be an easy target for a Kraut rifleman.

On my first combat patrol I felt confident carrying the

Thompson submachine gun, but luckily, I never had to fire it. The days and nights I'd spent roaming the woods as a boy, creeping up on wild animals, and counting coup on my friends, like the Indians did against their enemies, provided good experience for patrol work. Volunteering for that first night mission set a precedent with me. From then on, I asked to be assigned to a patrol. After a while, the sergeant automatically picked me for night missions.

Unless the night was extremely dark, I figured I had a better chance of survival if I took my time, and waited for the moon to go behind a cloud before advancing into enemy territory. When approaching a clearing, I became extra cautious. I wouldn't move forward until I'd found a more concealed route around the opening, even though it meant taking longer. If at all possible, I tried to have an alternate escape route figured out in the back of my mind. When approaching an area where I suspected a German might be lurking in ambush, I tried to formulate a plan of escape if I were attacked.

To me, listening to the night sounds was like a blind person reading a book of braille, for I continually tried to detect and sort out the natural sounds from those possibly made by the enemy. Patrol work became a challenge. I knew that to survive, I had to take a scientific approach to my job and use every trick that I'd ever learned.

The dark wool clothing issued to the American combat troops in North Africa might be uncomfortable to wear during the day, but felt good on the cold desert nights. Wool doesn't make noise when it rubs up against a foreign object. For this reason, we replaced our steel helmets with wool knit caps. When traveling east across Morocco and Algeria, I picked up an abundant supply of cork. Before starting out on patrol, I smeared my face with a piece of burnt cork.

The army issued two pairs of high leather shoes to each soldier. Before we entered combat, I persuaded Supply Sergeant Roy Tyrpin, from Liberty, Kentucky, to have one pair of my boots soled with the soft leather used in the tongues of shoes. This pair of boots I saved for when we

were in combat. When I wore them, I could detect a
branch or any other object underfoot that would make a
noise when stepped upon. The soles were almost as soft as
my boyhood moccasins. As I'd ease my foot to the ground,
if I felt something foreign beneath the soft leather, I could
raise my foot and try another spot.

Not having a mortar squad to take care of, the majority
of the time we fought as infantry, I was readily available for
patrols. I couldn't explain my obsession for volunteering for
these missions. I believe I lived in a world of fantasy, never
wanting to own up to the fact that one small mistake out on
patrol could get me killed.

Soon after we completed the defense of our first hill, we
learned of E Troop's misfortune. This troop consisted of 13
light tanks, each mounted with a 37-millimeter cannon. A
number of their tanks were lost to the Afrika Korps' superior armor. Usually we were never in contact with any of the
other troops in our squadron. Each troop worked independ-
ently, and usually had a separate mission of its own. When
we heard of E Troop's loss and realized that many of our
comrades were killed in action, we were saddened.

Every hill we defended or attacked soon became just
another hill. Each one brought us closer to the day when
the Afrika Korps would be driven into the sea. Most of
the time, we men in the ranks didn't even know the name
of the hill we fought on, only that it had to be taken.

One hill in Tunisia that Troop C conquered left a lasting impression with us, more so than any other battle in
the African campaign. It became a major milestone for
our troop, for it molded us into a hardened combat team.
We gained the confidence that every unit needs to continue
defeating the enemy. The engagement would live in the
hearts and minds of those men who took part in it, for the
rest of their lives. I know that all the men who survived
and reached the top of the hill are proud to tell their children and grandchildren of the accomplishment. The story
of the battle is one of the shining hours of glory in
C Troop's hourglass of combat.

We had traveled all night on a forced march. Come morning, our captain told us we were moving into the front lines in support of the 9th Infantry Division. The Germans had breached the American II Corps' line of defense. Our job was to retake a hill and close the gap on the 9th Infantry's flank. We took all the machine guns off our jeeps and scout cars and prepared for our dismounted assault of the hill. The area was north of the Sahara Desert, in country broken by wadis and hills. The semiarid land contained patches of waist-high brush, surrounded by desert.

As dawn pierced the darkness over the Monts De Tebessa to the east, we moved against the German-held positions. We ran into no opposition until we reached a point just below the first bench. It was like running up against a hornets' nest, with small-arms fire filling the air with the sound of swarming bees.

A couple of sheepherder huts made out of stone, about ten or twelve feet square, nestled against the hillside on the far side of the sloping bench. They were defended by the stubborn German infantry.

This was the strongest offensive action we'd experienced so far in the African campaign. When German mortars and artillery laid down barrage after barrage on our positions, the attack came to a standstill.

A machine gun on the forward edge of the bench had to be silenced before we could attack the huts. I informed my squad to prepare to move to the left, that I intended to outflank the gun, for the brush leading up to the bench afforded a fair amount of cover. We had to move with caution, for if the Germans stuck to their standard tactics, they would have men on the flanks of the MG42 machine gun.

Gaining the protection of a large rock located to my left and a short distance up the hill became my first objective. I managed to reach the lower side of the boulder, but when I started to crawl around the right of it, I received the shock of my life. I almost bumped into a German soldier peering around the opposite end of the large mass of rock. He wasn't more than four or five feet away. His right knee rested on the ground and his back was toward me. When he heard my combat jacket brush against the rock, he turned his head and glanced back over his left shoulder. We spotted each other at almost the same instant. As startled as we both were, the small advantage was mine, for the German was right-handed and had to swing his "burp gun" around to his left before he could open fire.

For the first time in the war, I witnessed a disciplined and well-trained German soldier in action. This soldier's movements were automatic, and oh, he was fast. As he spun his body around to face me, I had the eerie feeling that I stared death in the face. The barrel of his Schmeisser moved at lightning speed, swinging in an arc toward my left side. I know my midsection must have contracted in anticipation of the bullets I knew were certain to spew from that horrible tunnel of death. I began to doubt that I'd have time to swing my Thompson the short distance to the left and pull the trigger. The advantage had been mine, but the superior training of this man from Rommel's Afrika Korps reduced the odds of my coming out of the engagement alive.

Chips of rock flew out in front of me as bullets from his "burp gun" ricocheted off the boulder to my left. Hoping to throw me into a state of confusion and gain the fraction-of-a-second advantage he needed to survive, he began to shoot, even before he'd gotten me into his line of fire.

In the heat of battle, the training I'd received instructing me to fire the Thompson in short bursts was forgotten. I did remember to keep downward pressure on the foregrip with my left hand to keep the barrel from climbing. As my finger froze on the trigger, the only thing I could think about was survival. I just knew I was going to die next to that rock, and that the pockmarked boulder would stand forever as a marker next to my grave.

Not until I'd emptied my thirty-round clip of ammunition did my Thompson quit bucking, but my finger wouldn't release from the trigger. It refused to respond to my command and seemed to be in a death grip. Could I be dead on my knees and not know it? Maybe the pain would come later, for I didn't see how my life could be spared. All firing had ceased and a calm settled over the area. Even the German machine gun remained silent, its operator waiting to learn the outcome of his comrade's engagement.

In a semi-trance, I glanced down at my body. I saw no blood, except for a few drops dripping from my face and hands from cuts caused by the flying chips of rock. I noticed where a couple of bullets had ripped through the left sleeve of my combat jacket. Only then did I raise my eyes and stare at the horrible sight before me. The courageous soldier was literally cut in half.

At that moment, I felt no remorse. Tense, excited and scared to death, "Yes!" Maybe I felt as I did because I'd been trained to kill. My mind and body were psyched up to such a high battle pitch, there was no room for compassion. That would come later.

I will never forget the astonished and determined look on that soldier's face, as he swung his "burp gun" into firing position. Years later, I would awaken from a troubled sleep, wringing wet with sweat. Out of the darkness, almost lifelike, that haunting face would appear, encircled in a "halo" of ghostlike light. The memories would be as vivid as they were the day we faced each other. I would close my tear-filled eyes and try to erase the horrible nightmare. It never left.

The years would fade away, but not the memories. Once again, I'd be back on that hill, reliving the first time I ever killed another human being. I could see the .45-caliber bullets from my submachine gun tear into human flesh. I'd tremble and think, "What if that German had seen me a fraction of a second sooner?"

Like me, he'd been taught to kill his enemies, but fate took his life instead of mine. By his actions and the strategy he used under pressure, I knew him to be a seasoned combat veteran. But for the grace of God, I would be resting next to that rock, or else under a white cross in some lonely cemetery in North Africa. Instead, that German soldier, who I now realize wasn't my real enemy in the war at all, took my place beneath the sod.

This was the first time I'd ever taken another man's life while looking into his face. As he stared into the muzzle of my submachine gun, he must have experienced the same feeling of impending doom that came over me. Why does the first time you take another man's life always come back to haunt you?

There is no honor in killing, and I wasn't proud of myself. Ever since joining the army, I'd been afraid of how I would react in combat when the chips were down. Every man knows fear, and there is no shame in being afraid. It has often been said, "The greatest challenge a soldier faces in combat is to be able to muster enough courage to overcome fear, before fear conquers him."

Not until after the tension and letdown of four more campaigns would I take the time to think about some of the dreadful things that happened in combat. Only then did my conscience begin to bother me to the point where it affected my mind. Oftentimes when I slipped into a deep depression, I wondered if I might not be going insane.

I believe the army wanted young men because they were dreamers, easily aroused to the glory and excitement of battle. That glory quickly disappeared, the longer a man remained in combat. Eventually, he began to realize that it would only be a matter of time before he wound up an invalid or else dead, like the soldier on the upper side of that boulder.

I landed on the shores of Africa a happy-go-lucky boy. When the campaign ended, I, like other young men in Tunisia, had been transformed into an entirely different human being, both in body and spirit.

Corporal Henry Trevino from San Antonio, Texas, a squad leader from the 3rd Platoon, witnessed my encounter with the German soldier. When he heard the exchange of small-arms fire, he moved his squad over behind my position to back me up.

He called out, "Did you get him, Fred?" I nodded my

head affirmatively, then replied, "I'm out of ammo, Henry, do you have any extra magazines?"

"No," he answered, "I only have one clip left. I think we better get down off this slope and forget about trying to take that machine gun. The rest of the troop has already retreated. We don't want to be left stranded up here."

With the machine gun still raking the brush around us, we crawled back down the slope to rejoin our comrades. The last of the stragglers were regrouping at the base of the hill. Every face held a depressed look. Driven off the slope in defeat, Troop C had failed to take the first major objective assigned to it.

We immediately began to dig defensive positions. The men in headquarters platoon brought us ammunition, for nearly everyone's ammo pouch was empty. That morning, a couple of the squads from the first platoon took .50-caliber machine guns from their scout cars and hauled them up the hill to support the attack. These men were totally exhausted. Because we didn't have artillery support, the captain hoped the heavier machine guns would boost our firepower. We never again used the fifties in dismounted action.

For the first time since entering combat, my spirits hit rock bottom, mostly because we'd lost a number of men that day. One of the fellows, a Mexican boy named Fimbrez, often played the guitar and sang with me around the campfires. After the machine guns were set up and our position made as secure as possible, we cleaned our weapons. The men didn't converse much that evening, especially after they learned that Colonel Candler had ordered our troop commander to move forward the following morning and renew the attack. None of us were as confident of achieving an easy victory as we'd been that morning. Sleep came in catnaps. We all took our turn at manning the machine guns and securing the perimeter.

When H-hour arrived, a tired body of dismounted cavalrymen crept silently up the hill. Once again we climbed the slope leading to the bench covered with tall grass and bushes. The Arabs had cleared the boulders off the bench and used them to build their huts, but the slopes were still strewn with large rocks. The previous day, the Krauts had made their stand on this bench.

Before the sun reached its zenith, our hopes soared. The enemy's line broke. The Germans made an orderly retreat across the bench and up the hill behind the sheepherder huts. Our victory was short-lived. We soon realized that they'd fallen back to the crest of the main hill to occupy a formidable second line of defense. To attack their new position, we had to move across the bench and advance up the long incline that was almost devoid of vegetation.

By midafternoon we'd crossed the bench and started up the main slope. A lad from Kentucky named Bert Gentry, myself and another man from my squad began moving up the long barren incline leading to the crest of the hill. Maneuvering from one large rock to another, we managed to reach a point just below the top. With luck, we might be able to silence the machine gun that swept the area with fire and breach their defenses. The moment we spread out to make our final push, the Krauts spotted us.

The machine gunner concentrated all of his fire on the three of us. With only a scattering of boulders providing cover, we were forced to retreat down the slope to the false safety of the tall grass and bushes on the bench. Crawling back down the slope, I squeezed my shoulder blades together. I tried to form an imaginary shield to ward off the bullets I expected to hit between them. It is a terrible feeling, to have someone shooting at your back. Facing an enemy isn't near as nerve-wracking as retreating from small-arms fire.

When I reached the bench, the high grass began falling all around me, some of it even landing on top of my back. The machine-gun bullets were slicing the grass and brush off, about a foot above the ground. It was as if a large scythe worked above our bodies, mowing down everything on the bench. It's a good thing the angle of the slope wasn't steep, or the gunner on top of the hill would have seen us crawling, and shot down into our backs.

Now we understood why the Germans baited us to move onto the bench below them. We were like sitting ducks. Eventually they'd have all the brush mowed down and annihilate us.

The gunner kept spraying the bushes around me until there was hardly any cover left. I had to find a low spot in the ground, or I'd never survive. The machine gunner was determined to put me out of action. A few seconds before he lowered his field of fire, I crawled into a small depression. The hollow, running parallel to the hill, couldn't have been more than six or eight inches deep. The gunner raked the area around me so intensely that I thought, "This is the end, the reaper operating that scythe-like weapon, shooting 900 rounds a minute, is going to harvest me for sure."

I felt something hit the "ditty bag" strapped on my back. Later, I discovered a bullet had cut through my backpack about an inch above my body. Sweat ran down along my backbone, and I knew it wasn't caused by the woolen clothing I wore. I had no alternative but to lie perfectly still. The machine gunner continued to rattle out a death chant just inches above my body. A couple of times I thought of moving out of the hollow, but knew I'd be committing suicide if I did.

Earlier in the afternoon, when the machine gunner had spotted me near the top of the hill, I almost messed in my pants. At the time, I thought maybe it was because he'd scared me half to death. As I lay in the depression on the bench, the urge to go to the toilet couldn't be ignored. My bloated stomach began to ache, and I felt feverish. I couldn't move, for if I so much as raised my head, it would be blown off. No way could I attempt to lower my pants and empty my bowels. I realized that I'd come down with a case of diarrhea.

When I pressed my body tight against the ground in response to another burst of machine-gun fire, my bowels let loose. With a swishing sound, like that of an artillery shell passing overhead, they emptied into my long-handled underwear. Once the pressure was relieved from my stomach, I felt a lot better. At least I was still alive, even though I smelled like the inside of a sunbaked latrine.

About half an hour elapsed before the Kraut manning the machine gun gave me up for dead. He concentrated his fire onto another target. Soon after the shadows lengthened and dusk settled over the mangled brush on the bench, I crawled down the hill to safety. By the time I reached the bottom, darkness covered the battlefield. Two days in a row, Troop C had failed to take its objective.

At the end of the second day's unsuccessful attack, we were completely exhausted. A haggard group of men, defeated both in body and spirit, limped back to the safety of the foxholes we'd left that morning. A sadness came over everyone when we saw how many foxholes remained empty.

My clothes were a mess. They smelled putrid, even after I threw my soiled underdrawers away. There didn't seem much to be grateful for, but I took a moment to lift my eyes to the heavens and say, "Thank you Lord, for my life."

When I asked Manley, our medic, for something to control my diarrhea, he told me to report to the aid station behind the lines. I ignored his instructions, for I couldn't leave my comrades. Many of them were in worse shape than I, and they still put duty ahead of their physical well-being.

When one of the fellows in headquarters platoon brought up a load of ammunition, I borrowed a portable, single-burner gas stove from him. On his next trip, he gave me a few small packs of powdered cream and tea. Putting the cream into a canteen cup of water, I scalded the mixture, then drank it. In an effort to plug up my semiwatery bowels, I also downed a potent mixture of tea.

All of us wondered what our next orders would be. We knew the top brass of Army II Corps depended on us to take this hill and close the gap in the front lines. We didn't have long to wait for our new instructions, for Colonel Candler personally came up to our defensive positions.

Our captain, only recently placed in command of the troop, seemed sincere about wanting to do right by his men.

He reminded me of a father trying to protect his family from harm. Because of his overly cautious attitude, he didn't impress me as being an aggressive officer on the battlefield.

The colonel approached him and said, "Captain, regroup your men. Make sure plenty of ammunition is brought up, then let the men get a few hours' rest. The last two days, you have waited until daybreak to attack. Tomorrow, H-hour will be at 0400 hours, and this time when you assault that hill, make sure you take it." Turning around to face those of us within earshot, he said, "The 9th Infantry Division is depending on you men to plug the breach in the line. The hill must be taken at all costs."

Our captain, a compassionate man, prided himself in looking out for the welfare of his men. He'd have made a wonderful friend in civilian life. In the eyes of the military, these characteristics didn't make him a good officer. Once again, the pep talk our squadron commander gave us before we left Morocco came to mind. Colonel Candler told us that a good officer must be capable of leading his men to victory. To accomplish this he must have boldness of action and rapidity of movement.

The number of men lost in the process of achieving a victory seemed to be of secondary importance to many commanders. Some of the armchair strategists and generals behind the front lines considered the gaining of an objective of more importance than the lives of the men who fought for it.

When we heard our captain's reply to the colonel's order that we take the hill at 0400 hours, everyone felt relieved. "Colonel," he said, "the men have gone without sleep for two days and nights. I'm sorry, but they need a day of rest before they are capable of attacking the hill again."

Shocked to hear a subordinate officer question his authority, in a stern voice the colonel replied, "I said, prepare to assault that hill at 0400 hours. That's an order."

The captain turned and looked out over his tired and beaten troop, who for two days and nights had given their all. He searched his conscience and decided that rather

than sacrifice the lives of the men who'd fought so gallantly for him, he would put his own military career on the
line. In a sympathetic voice choked with emotion, he
turned to the colonel and said, "I can't ask my men to do
more than they've already done. I am sorry."

My heart went out to our captain, for I knew he
thought only of us men. His decision wasn't the act of a
coward.

For almost a full minute, Colonel Candler remained
silent. We knew he was deep in thought. Now, he had a
tough decision to make. An officer under his command
had refused to carry out an order given on the battlefield.
Under the old military code, this act of insubordination in
combat was punishable by death. The colonel looked at us
men, some of whom couldn't even stand without leaning
on their rifles for support. Others lay exhausted on the
ground, unable to move. Having graduated from the U.S.
Military Academy at West Point, where duty, honor and
service to your country are valued more than life itself,
Colonel Candler's years of training forced him to make
the only decision possible.

Like a man with a heavy burden on his shoulders, he
walked a few paces up the hill in front of our foxholes.
With the heel of his high cavalry boot, he made a shallow
trench in the soft desert sand, about forty feet long and
parallel to our line of men. The stern cavalry officer reminded me of our army commander, General George Patton, and of General Rommel, "the Desert Fox." Their
military decisions also determined whether many of us
young soldiers would live or die.

Our colonel stood for a moment, bathed in moonlight
that cast a shadow across his deeply troubled face. He had
just made one of the most important decisions of his military career. We watched him retrace his steps back to the
center of the line in the sand. Crossing over to the uphill
side, he turned and faced us.

Standing straight and erect, that tall cavalry officer could
have been on dress parade reviewing troops back in the

States. Though he tried, he couldn't hide the look of pain on his face, not physical pain, but the suffering of a man fighting with his conscience. His voice was stern, but echoed of sadness when he said, "All those men who are going to take the hill at 0400 hours, cross over the line. Those who refuse to obey my command, remain where you are."

We looked to our captain for guidance in making the right decision, but he gave us no encouragement one way or the other. With head bowed and hands held waist-high, gripping each other, our fallen leader remained silent. Though it had nothing to do with the colonel's command, I glanced at the captain's twitching knuckles. Even in the moonlight, they were whiter than the desert sand. As each fist tightened, it intermittently turned red, then white, like the two were fighting each other. One of the captain's fists probably wanted to obey his superior officer, and the other wanted to protect the lives of his men.

None of our regular army platoon sergeants made any attempt to stand up. Lieutenant St. John, our 3rd Platoon officer, along with the two remaining buck sergeants, struggled to his feet. All of the squad leaders, the corporals, who were the lowest-ranking noncommissioned officers in the troop, stood up. One officer, two buck sergeants, and the corporals were the only commissioned or noncommissioned officers who made a move to cross over the line.

Lack of sleep and a bad case of diarrhea had weakened my physical condition to the point where I had a difficult time maneuvering. I smelled so rotten after having messed my pants that all the men in my squad avoided me. Like many of the young men around me, I knew I'd only one choice to make. I faced our colonel and walked toward him, leaving footprints in the sand that determined my fate. If I ever got out of this war alive, at least I could hold my head up and live with my decision.

Slowly, a group of privates, T/4s and T/5s, began to walk up the slope toward the line, that to cross over might mean the difference between life and death. Left standing or lying on the ground were our captain, one second lieutenant, and

the three platoon sergeants. Sprawled around them were
the remainder of the men who had crawled exhausted and
defeated down the hill only a short while ago.

Colonel Candler waited a couple of minutes, hoping
that more of the men would change their minds. When no
one else joined our ranks, he motioned for two of the privates on the uphill side of the line to step forward. Pointing down the slope toward the remainder of the troop, he
said, "Collect all of the guns and ammunition from those
men who failed to obey my orders. Divide their ammo and
grenades among the men who are going to follow me."

Our colonel looked at the captain and the men so physically tired and mentally exhausted, and said, "You are
now prisoners of war." He motioned for two privates to
come forward and told them, "Guards, march the prisoners back to the rear." Turning to us he said, "Extra ammunition will be brought up to you. In the meantime, make
sure your machine guns are manned in case the Krauts decide to counterattack. Lie down and try to get a little rest,
for at 0400 hours, you and I are going to take that hill."

My heart went out to those men who were made "prisoners of war," but I was especially sad for our captain. On
his shoulders rested the responsibility for the penalty they
all received, even though he'd made the decision in defense
of his officers and men. I never again saw any of the men
made prisoners by our commander.

As sorry as I felt for my buddies, I couldn't help but be
proud of our colonel. Right or wrong, I had made the decision to follow him. I wondered how, against such over-
whelming odds, we could ever hope to emerge victorious
from tomorrow's battle, or for that matter, even survive.

Sleep seemed far away that night as I lay in my foxhole
and looked up at the hill, standing like a sentinel beneath
the desert moon. I couldn't understand how a handful of
men, driven off that hill two days in a row, could possibly
reach the top on the third try. Like the old saying that it
is bad luck to light three cigarettes off a match, I felt that
the third day on the hill could spell disaster. We now had

only half of our original troop strength. As stubbornly as the Germans fought, it would take a miracle to defeat them. Trying to gain confidence, I realized that we were no different from other fighting men. Down through the ages, men have continually fought against superior odds. Sometimes they won, but most of the time they lost. A man can't go into battle with a defeatist attitude or he is licked before he starts. Our colonel had faith in us, and with him leading the way, maybe a miracle really would happen.

Unable to fall asleep, my thoughts drifted back to my school days, to a story that Mr. Zook, our history teacher, once told us. The historic tale left a lasting impression on my mind. Of all the nights in my life to remember the story, it seemed strange that night's events flushed it out of my book of memories.

The story took place back in the days when the powerful Persian armies were trying to conquer Greece. The Persian army outnumbered its opponent ten to one. With its back against a steep ravine having perpendicular sides, the small Greek force made a last desperate stand. They had to either surrender or fight to the death. Escape was impossible.

The general of the larger army seemed confident of an easy victory over his much weaker opponent. He sent a messenger to the commander of the Greek army, asking him to surrender or be annihilated.

The leader of the small courageous force listened to the ultimatum, then told the messenger, "I want you to remember every detail of the event you are about to witness, then return and tell your general the caliber of the fighting men he is facing."

The Greek commander called six of his soldiers forward and gave them orders to march toward the steep ravine. When the expected command of "Halt," never came, all six of the men marched over the cliff to their deaths. The leader of the fearless men turned to the messenger and said, "There is my answer to your general's surrender ultimatum."

When the battle resumed, the small, well-trained and disciplined force of soldiers came out victorious over the larger army of unruly and overconfident men.

Remembering the outcome of this story gave me renewed courage and a small ray of hope that everything might not be lost. After making the rounds to check on the men manning our squad's machine gun, I lay down in my foxhole. Before the moon dipped below the hill, I fell asleep.

We crawled out of our foxholes a few minutes before 0400 hours and formed a skirmish line behind Colonel Candler. The colonel lengthened the distance between each man, making it very hard to locate the men on my flanks. No second wave of men was behind us to move up and fill the gap when a man got hit.

I still had doubts that we could take the hill. With half of his original fighting force depleted, any other leader would have dug in and been satisfied to ward off a counterattack. No ordinary officer would have attempted to launch an attack under such conditions, but then again, our colonel was no ordinary man. The colonel staked his career on not failing, for not one man remained at the base of the hill in reserve.

Once again, a hidden voice whispered his motto in my ear, "boldness of action and rapidity of movement." By doing the unexpected, he lived his beliefs. I'm positive the Krauts never thought we'd attack; not after being defeated two days in a row. The German fortifications on top of the hill were provided with a good field of fire. On the other hand, the terrain we had to cross to reach them afforded very little cover during daylight hours. Because of these factors, the colonel decided to use a different strategy than our captain. He planned to approach the German defenses under cover of darkness. Hopefully he'd be able to catch them off guard in the early morning hours when their defenses would be the weakest. The success of the operation depended on the element of surprise.

The moon had long since disappeared from the sky, and storm clouds, heavy with moisture, drifted in from the west.

They covered the stars like a blanket and made the night blacker than the outside of a witch's cauldron. For once, the darkness of the desert night worked to our advantage. With a hint of rain, the cool breeze sliding down the hill away from the enemy helped soften the sound of our advance. Who knows, maybe the odds would swing in our favor.

Though we had difficulty keeping in contact with the men on either side of us, we moved silently forward. The colonel used a toy cricket to signal his commands instead of breaking the stillness with his harsh voice. One chirp meant stop, two meant go, and three chirps warned of impending danger. Each man knew that if he made one small noise, our advantage could be lost.

As we came up over the slope leading to the bench, I could just barely make out the faint outline of our colonel in front of us. Silhouetted against the darkened sky, he seemed to be the ghost of all the great warriors of the past who have led men into battles against odds such as ours. What must he be thinking at this moment, the man who placed so much confidence in the fighting ability of his men? Like us, did he feel alone, even though we trudged along together?

I wondered, what thoughts must have traveled through the minds of Pickett's troops in the Civil War at the Battle of Gettysburg? In one of the most daring attacks in history, 15,000 men advanced almost a mile through orchards and wheat fields, up the long slope toward the crest of Cemetery Ridge. Did those men have doubts about the outcome of the battle? Like our troop of dismounted cavalry, they marched against well-fortified troops waiting on top of a hill. Would the same fate befall us that Pickett and his brave men had suffered?

The only difference between Pickett's charge and ours was that, if our luck held, we might be able to take the enemy by surprise.

On the far side of the bench, the colonel stopped to re-align our ranks before starting up the final slope. How well I remembered the incline ahead. The day before, I'd barely gotten off it with my life. Almost barren of vegetation and with only a few boulders for cover, attacking it during day-light hours proved disastrous. If the Germans had any inkling we were approaching their positions, they would light up the hill with flares, and Troop C would be only a footnote in the history books.

We moved out and began the silent and final approach that would end in either victory or defeat. With each foot-step I prayed that the stones beneath our feet would re-main glued to the hillside and not tumble down the slope. The thin, moccasin-type leather on the soles of my boots felt every pebble beneath them, but the other men wore heavy-soled combat boots.

About halfway up the hill, one of the men stumbled. With all of us caught out in the open, we imagined the sound to be amplified ten times louder than it actually was. Immediately everyone stopped dead in their tracks. We waited. If the sound carried to the men on the crest of the hill, we could expect a flare to streak above us and light the sky brighter than Halley's comet.

The ground had been cooled by the approaching storm. The night air, made heavy when it came in contact with the cool hill, carried the air currents and sounds down to the valley. Without this help from nature, we'd have advanced no farther. The Germans would have discovered us. Once again we moved forward.

There could be no turning back now, for we could see the dim outline of the hilltop directly ahead. When we heard the colonel make a single chirp on his cricket, the long, thin line of men came to a halt. We waited for our leader to give the order to attack. The safety levers on the guns were eased off. Most of the men took a deep breath and slowly exhaled, trying to calm their tense nerves. The waiting was always harder on a man's nerves than the action.

The colonel wanted the Germans to believe we'd re-ceived reinforcements and were attacking their positions with a large force. Before starting out that morning, he'd briefed us on a demoralizing tactic he hoped would tip the scales in our favor. We never intended to use his ace in the hole unless we managed to get close enough to the enemy to launch our surprise assault. The Confederate "Rebels" often used the technique when attacking the Union "Blue Bellies" in the Civil War. A great majority of the men in our troop were Southern boys whose ancestors had fought in the Civil War. They were familiar with the tactic the colonel intended us to use. The time had come for those instructions to be executed.

When the colonel yelled, "Charge," the cool night air almost reversed its descent down the hill. The moment of truth had arrived.

On our last mock cavalry charge back at Fort Riley, I'd had a premonition of facing the enemy in battle, against odds similar to those faced by the men in Tennyson's poem, *The Charge of the Light Brigade*. When today's battle ended, would I be one of the men left of the 600 who entered "the valley of death"?

Inspired by the West Point cavalry officer, our paper-thin line of men let loose with "rebel yells" that almost drowned out the chatter of our Thompson submachine guns and rifles. The sound of the firing combined with the screaming must have sent chills down the spine of the bravest German warrior awakened by those yells.

The grandfather of one of the Southern boys in my squad had taught him one of the many versions of the rebel yell. My squad used an adaptation of that yell. It started with a combination of fox hunt "yips," followed by a shrieking "aye-EEEE-yaaaaa" that tapered off to end like the agonizing death chant of a ghost being strangled.

"Yip, yip, aye-EEEE-yaaaaa" became our battle cry. The rebel yells gave us courage and helped throw the German defenses off balance. I no longer smelled the stink from my diarrhea. My nostrils became filled with the acrid smell of burnt powder from the German mortar shells. The bombardment sprayed dirt and rock all around us. The dust floating through the air caused by shells exploding on the rain-starved soil churned together with the smoke and powder. The combination smarted our eyes and almost choked us as we dropped to the ground and inched our way forward. Some unknown force drove our tired bodies and gave us renewed strength, enabling us to advance into the face of the hailstorm of bullets.

If I'd had time to think about the situation we were in, it would have been very easy to cross over the line between loyalty and cowardice. In the darkness, I could have run back down the hill, but during the fighting, trying to stay alive occupied all of my thoughts. The word "courage" is often used in speeches to describe the quality of a man's actions in battle. In reality, the only word he knows at the time is "survival."

On your left, you look for the outline of your nearest buddy. When you can't find even a shadow to take his place, you feel alone at the mouth of the Devil's hideout. The flash of a comrade's Thompson machine gun penetrating the smoke, dirt and burnt powder on your right, means all is not lost.

The Germans continued to probe the darkness with their MG42 light machine guns, but still we moved on. A grenade tossed behind one of those muzzle flashes meant one less fire-breathing dragon to worry about. One by one, the eight-millimeter tubes of death were silenced. The German mortars stopped firing after they lowered their field of fire and learned they were dropping shells on their own troops.

The gray light of predawn approached much faster once the smoke from the firing began to slide down the sides of the hill, looking like slow-moving lava flowing from the depths of a volcano. How the miracle happened no one ever really knew, but the Germans were in full retreat. As tired and exhausted as we were, our colonel refused to let us rest on our laurels. He pushed relentlessly on and continued the attack. Victory was ours, but no one cheered. After three attempts, we occupied the hill.

Never have I been so proud of anyone, as I was of our colonel and my fellow comrades of Troop C. In the face of almost certain defeat, the men showed tremendous courage and loyalty to their leader. A feeling of pride came over me to think I belonged to a unit such as the 91st Recon.

No man that followed our colonel's charge to the top of the hill will ever forget that day. If our colonel had been killed, our squadron would have lost a great leader. It wasn't his duty to personally lead us into battle. I often wondered if he wasn't trying to prove to himself, even if he lost his life, that he could gain a victory in battle where others had failed.

Teddy Roosevelt led his "Rough Riders" in a dismounted cavalry charge up Kettle Hill during the Battle of San Juan in the Spanish-American War. Our squadron commander led us in a similar charge, just to show that with the right combination of leadership and men, the impossible can be accomplished.

Most of the men in our troop were not professional soldiers, but citizens from all walks of life who took up arms in defense of their country. They were willing to die for that country and for the colonel from West Point who led them to victory.

A soldier in World War I once said, "Few men live to know real fear."

Thousands of men in the armed forces lived through battles similar to the one we experienced in Tunisia. None of them are ashamed to say, "I was afraid."

In the army, when an order is given for a soldier to face in the opposite direction, the command is "about face." Keith Royer, from Newton, Kansas, received his training in the horse cavalry along with me. He gave the hill the only name we were ever to know it by, "About Face Hill." It seemed an appropriate name, for we retreated off the hill two days in a row.

When our squadron commander, Lieutenant Colonel Harry W. Candler, returned to the States after the African Campaign, the army assigned him to the Cavalry School at Fort Riley, Kansas. Up until that time in World War II, the 91st Reconnaissance Squadron was the only recon squadron fighting in the European Theater of Operations. Our colonel helped train other units, soon to be sent overseas.

He made an official report of his combat experiences in the *U.S. Cavalry Journal.* Concerning About Face Hill, he wrote, "Troop C, having been dismounted and in constant contact with the enemy throughout the period, was withdrawn to squadron support. Its performance had been magnificent. The entire troop, driven back from its position by a German counterattack late one evening, had moved forward before daylight and retaken not only its former position, but successfully attacked and occupied the one previously held by the Germans."

In the colonel's document, he never mentioned the major role he played in the attack. Without his leadership and encouragement, we couldn't have completed our mission. I don't believe our colonel received a medal or even recognition for his heroic deed. The only officer that could have recommended him for a medal, Lieutenant St. John, was killed in action shortly afterward. If ever a soldier deserved a medal, it was our colonel.

The men who lived through the charge very seldom talked about the battle or of the events leading up to the final victory. No soldier wanted it known that so many of his comrades, who had fought so well, were removed from the battlefield by their own commander. Those men left, not in disgrace or because they were cowards, but because they had reached the limit of their physical endurance.

After the battle, when we were relieved from the front lines, we marched to the valley below. For the last time, we gazed up at the hill that had drained the life's blood and broken the spirit of so many of our comrades. The survivors tucked their feelings away inside of a book of memories, thankful to be among the living who rode out of "the valley of death."

# CHAPTER IV

# A Poppy Lives Forever

After emerging victorious from the Battle of About Face Hill, we continued our push northward through Tunisia. My most unforgettable experience of the war occurred on this drive. The incident came back to haunt me, more so than anything else I've done in my entire life.

The Afrika Korps, now under the command of General von Arnim, continued to retreat. They left rearguard units behind. These men fought a delaying action, with the main purpose of slowing II Corps' advance. This enabled the German army to establish a new line of defense.

Recon units were usually out in front of the advancing American army, acting as scouts. We only moved forward during daylight hours, for it was very easy to be lured into a trap.

One night, after locating a good defensive position, our captain ordered us to dig in our machine guns and get a much needed rest. He didn't seem worried about a counterattack, because the terrain up ahead wasn't suited for the Germans to make a stand. There were no large hills on either of our flanks.

This particular evening, my squad wasn't called on to set up a machine gun on our perimeter. After digging my foxhole, I lay down and covered myself with a shelter half to keep the morning dew off. In a very few minutes, I fell asleep.

About twelve o'clock, Lieutenant St. John, our 3rd Platoon officer, woke me up. He said, "Corporal, I've noticed that you volunteer for every night patrol that comes along. You must like the challenge."

Of all the officers I'd met in the army, this lieutenant
was the only one I ever confided in, or felt at ease talking
to. "Lieutenant, I have a lot to learn about patrols, and I
need all the practice I can get," I replied. "I grew up in the
woods, and used to fantasize about becoming a scout like
Kit Carson and the other frontiersmen, but now I realize
how little I really know. It could be a long war, and with
no one to teach me all the skills and tricks of survival, I
have to learn through experience."

"We aren't expecting any trouble," he said, "but to be on
the safe side, I'd like you to have a look around the area."

The only officer in our troop to accompany us up About
Face Hill the day we conquered it, made his order seem like
a request. I had more respect for this man than any other officer in our troop. He'd shown his true colors in combat.

"How about making a swing out in front of our lines," he
said. "Move out on the left flank, cross our front, then return into the 3rd Platoon's defensive positions on the right
flank. Before leaving, make sure you alert the machine gunners that you'll be coming back through the lines in the early
morning hours. Keep your eyes peeled for Kraut patrols,
and take particular notice of any enemy activity. Make sure
you return before sunup, for we intend to move out soon afterward." As he walked away, he turned his head and said,
"Don't forget the password. Good luck."

Ordinarily, two men would be sent on patrol to cover
each other's leapfrog movements. If one man happened to
get wounded or killed, hopefully the other could make it
back with any vital information. The lieutenant didn't expect me to run into any trouble, for we hadn't seen any
signs of the enemy all afternoon.

I picked up a couple of extra grenades, replaced my helmet with a dark wool knit cap, then rubbed burnt cork on
my face and hands. After checking my Thompson, I
moved silently out through our lines.

It was an exceptionally good night for running a patrol.
The clouds looked like floating icebergs under an arctic
sky. They afforded plenty of cover as they moved along in

front of the moon, but still traveled fast enough to let light filter through for good observation. Before I'd gone 50 yards, I checked my bearings with my night compass, just to be on the safe side. Though I might have a little difficulty finding a familiar constellation between the clouds, I didn't plan on using the compass. If they were visible, I could usually take my bearings from either the Big Dipper, Little Bear, North Star or the Dog Stars.

Taking my time, I moved a couple of hundred yards further out in front of our left flank, before making a 90-degree turn to my right. I worked my way in front of our sleeping troop, thinking how nice they had it, lying down in their foxholes. Even though I could have shortened the time it took to run the patrol, I didn't hurry. After every few steps, I stopped to listen and observe, for I couldn't rely on the enemy to be as peaceful as this beautiful spring night. When I realized the first light of day would soon appear, I moved on.

Off to my left, I spotted a couple of stone huts on top of a knoll. The crudely built cabins were spaced about 60 feet apart. They had no window openings, and their entrances faced to the north. It was typical of the Arabs to use this type of shelter during bad weather, especially in the winter. I'm making pretty good time, I thought. As long as I get back to our lines by daylight, I'll be okay. When the moon goes behind the next cloud, I'll move up on that hill where I can observe everything out in front of me.

After walking up the slope, I carefully inspected both shacks. Neither had anything draped in front of the door openings. After finding them vacant, I figured the goat- or sheepherders who used them had taken their flocks back in the mountains. I squatted down on my haunches in front of the doorway of the hut closest to our right flank and watched the area to the north. For the first time since starting the patrol, I relaxed my guard. I listened to the night sounds, and smelled the fragrance of the spring grass growing in patches around the shack. The moon, playing a game of hide-and-seek, peeked from behind a cloud and brightened up the whole area. Because it shed its silvery light from behind the hut, I felt secure, for I remained hidden in the shadows.

After studying my surroundings for about fifteen minutes, I decided it was time to move on. Before I had a chance to stand up, out of the corner of my eye I saw a movement off to my left, in the brush below me. Because he stood out in the open, exposed in the moonlight, I could tell it was a man dressed in a dark uniform. The intruder studied the two huts for a couple of minutes, then nonchalantly walked up the incline toward the hut on my left. If I made an attempt to stand up or descend the slope, he would surely spot me. Still resting on my haunches, I duck waddled backward into the deeper shadows of the doorway.

My heart skipped a beat when I saw the moonlight reflect on metal headgear. Taking a closer look, I recognized the slightly box-shaped and flared edges of a helmet. It could only belong to a German soldier. He walked up the slope as if he hadn't a care in the world. With his Schmeisser burp gun slung across his back and his hands swinging freely at his sides, I knew he never expected to encounter any Americans this far north. Except for Troop C, all the Allied forces were miles to the south.

Before he reached the hut, I heard the soldier call out in a low voice, "Karl."

By his actions, I surmised that he and a buddy named Karl were either stragglers or had been left behind as rear guards when their outfit retreated. The two men probably became separated, and this man was searching for his partner before he moved on to the north.

With only the peak of my wool knit cap protruding past the edge of the door opening, I watched the soldier poke his head into the hut on my left. Again he called out "Karl."

When no answer came, he began walking toward the hut where I was concealed. He probably wanted to see if his comrade had fallen asleep inside it.

The first thing that entered my mind was, I'm not on a combat mission, maybe I can slip away without being detected. Why hadn't I made a move when he stuck his head into the other hut? Should I make a break for it now? I could run around the corner of this building and across the clearing. Maybe I could stay out of his line of fire by keeping the building between us. Could I reach the brush at the bottom of the knoll before he discovered me? At the moment, my life depended on too many uncertainties.

A man doesn't get many chances when he makes a mistake on a patrol. I realized too late that I'd made a grave error when I approached these two huts in the clearing. The only means of escape lay across an open area. I wondered if the Good Lord would give me a second chance to get out of my predicament. If he did, I swore I'd never put myself in a situation like this again.

The sky had already started turning the gray that comes just before dawn, and the moon, though fading, was still playing tag between the clouds. With daylight fast approaching, I knew I couldn't conceal my movements. I'd never make it across the clearing without being discovered. The German would unsling his burp gun and shoot me as I ran down the hill.

I thought: I'll have to take him with my Thompson, but I still have to cross that opening after I kill him. What if Karl is nearby and discovers me? No, I can't take the chance of making that much noise.

If the soldier had his burp gun unslung and ready for action, I'd have no alternative but to open up with my Thompson and deal with Karl later. I eased back inside the hut, and quietly placed my gun on the floor. I didn't lean it against the wall, for fear it would slide on the stones and clatter onto the dirt floor.

I stood flat against the wall, with my left side about six inches from the opening. My heart pounded so loud, I thought it might drown out the sound of his approaching footsteps. The few tense seconds that I waited seemed like hours. In the short period of time left, I had to ready myself psychologically for what I was about to do. I needed all the confidence I could muster. Closing my eyes for a split second, I tried to get them accustomed to the darkness inside the hut. Hopefully, my commando training had prepared me for just such a situation, but I was scared to death. When I took a deep breath, the dank smell coming up from the dirt floor filled my nostrils.

I didn't hear his footsteps coming through the grass. The shadow I saw move across the floor of the hut told me he'd arrived. With my head turned to the left, I watched the light coming through the doorway fade away. He must have placed both hands against the outside of the opening, because the only parts of his body that protruded through the opening were his head and massive shoulders. They leaned a few inches into the room, filling up most of the opening. Because he'd been out in the moonlight, I knew his eyes weren't accustomed to the dark interior of the hut, but there was no time to waste.

My left arm remained extended at my side, with the palm of my hand pressed against the cold stone. I held my right arm slightly bent, and a few inches from the wall, poised for action.

The moment he began to utter his comrade's name, I pivoted on my left foot and made my move. "God, give me the strength."

Before "Karl" left his lips, to echo into eternity, a loud grunt-like sound filled the room. He didn't scream, but slowly pushed himself backward and dropped to his knees directly outside the doorway. I stood facing him as moonlight filtered over his shoulders and cast death's shadow on the ground.

For a moment, I thought he would fall on his face, but he remained bent over. I looked down at his stomach and saw the slit in the front of his bloodstained trousers. The wound extended from the lower part of his abdomen up to the metal buckle on the leather belt around his waist. This buckle stopped the upward thrust of the dagger. The light wasn't bright enough for me to see the words Gott Mit Uns, or the emblem with the German swastika on the belt buckle, but I knew they were there.

Like a can of huge worms being emptied, his intestines slid slowly out of the incision. He placed both hands, which were soon filled to overflowing, under the wound. In desperation, he tried to push his mangled intestines back into his stomach, hoping to make himself whole again. Along with his life's blood, they slipped out between his fingers, the contents of the severed intestines dripping onto the ground.

In training, whenever possible, we'd been taught to go for a man's stomach. There were no bones there to stop the knife's penetration, like in a man's chest or the other parts of his body.

I looked into his uplifted face, a face that showed no anger, just shock and disbelief. I saw eyes that held no tears, but eyes pleading for my help. In a state of shock, I seemed frozen in place. My eyes were glued to the dying soldier's face. Maybe God wanted it this way, to make sure that I remembered the scene for the rest of my life, as punishment for what I'd done.

When the military instructors show a soldier how to kill his enemy, they try to make the training as realistic as possible. One thing they can never teach is how to cope with the look in a dying man's eyes. This soldier looked up into my face, pleading and begging with those eyes for help; help that I knew I couldn't give.

Later in the war, maybe I would feel differently about a few of the fanatical and arrogant Nazis in the Waffen-SS, the military arm of the dreaded *Schutzstaffel*, or SS organization. Not all the German soldiers were made from the same mold. The look on this young boy's innocent face seemed different. When I looked into his eyes again, I realized that's what he was, just an overgrown boy.

In a whisper, I asked, "Dear God, what have I done?"

At that moment, I snapped out of my trance. Without wiping the blood from the blade, I shoved the dagger back into its sheath. Reentering the hut, I picked up my Thompson submachine gun from the floor. When I stepped between the doorway and the soldier I'd eviscerated, I saw him bow his head. He wavered, while staring in disbelief at his intestines. They left his body, taking his life with them.

I turned my head away, for I couldn't stand to see the tears falling on his blood-drenched hands, knowing that in a few minutes he would be gone.

I threw caution to the wind. I forgot about how important it is to wait for cloud cover before moving, or to not make a noise. I had to get away from the horrible scene. Without looking to right or left, I ran around the corner of the hut, across the clearing and down the hill to the safety of the brush below. Sick to my stomach, I was too scared to dwell on my physical and mental condition. I had only one concern, to get away before "Karl!" heard the commotion and opened up with his burp gun at my cringing back.

What a coward I'd turned out to be. Why hadn't I slit the young soldier's throat, or shot him? I should have put him out of his misery. Instead, I'd left him to suffer and die a horrible death, all alone. I didn't even know his name. Why didn't I ask his forgiveness, or at least say "I'm sorry"? No man should have to die alone, whether he's your best friend or your worst enemy. He should have someone to hold his hand, and comfort him in those final moments.

I was destined to carry to my grave the memory of that young soldier's pleading eyes, begging for my help. The full impact of what I'd done hit me before I reached the safety of our defensive perimeter. I sat down in the brush and shook uncontrollably, then I vomited. I couldn't return to the lieutenant and tell him or anyone else how I'd been afraid to fire my Thompson and make a noise, just to save my own selfish hide.

The stars had already gone to sleep beneath a blanket of blue, before I entered the 3rd Platoon's outpost. When I made my report to Lieutenant St. John, I couldn't look him in the eye. I told him that I'd run across sign, showing where Krauts recently were in the vicinity, but that it looked like they pulled out.

As I turned to leave, he said, "Corporal, you better

make yourself a cup of coffee before we take off. You look a little peaked around the gills, probably from not getting enough sleep last night."

The only time in my life that I ever used a knife against another human being brought back memories of a story I once read about the Civil War, called *The Red Badge of Courage*. Like the soldier in that book, I too had been a coward. It would be over 40 years before I could talk about, or tell anyone, the horrible thing I'd done. The young soldier in the Civil War had only been doing his duty, and serving his country, just as I had. Though ashamed of my actions, I tried to force them out of my mind. I was part of a team, with a job to do. Somehow, I vowed to redeem my cowardly act. No other living soul knew about it, but I had to bear the shame and live with my conscience for the rest of my life.

That morning, our vehicles were brought up to our positions. Once again we became mounted cavalry for II Corps. The Stuka dive bombers were out in force, continually attacking our advancing column. As if in answer to my prayers, an incident occurred that gave me a much needed spiritual uplifting. A plane coming out of the blinding sun swooped low over our troop and released its single bomb. We leaped from our vehicles and actually dove headfirst into an Arab wheat field next to the road.

Spring, in northern Tunisia, arrived early in the year 1943. On that April morning, bountiful gifts of nature were visible throughout the countryside. The wheat, though tall enough to afford visual cover, was no protection from the wrath dealt out by the German planes. The bomb just released made a direct hit on Stanley Czech's weapons carrier. The vehicle, mounted with a 37-millimeter cannon, almost disintegrated. The pilot of the gull-winged J-87 Stuka must have felt elated when he turned his head and watched the black column of smoke rise up and pierce the blue Tunisian sky. Stanley Czech, from East Canton, Ohio, survived the attack, but later lost his life in Italy.

When I dove into the wheat field and hugged the

ground, I received the surprise of my life. My face pressed against a beautiful, bright red poppy, one of many that grew in the field. I lifted my head away from the gorgeous flower, then reached down and plucked it. To find beauty in the midst of a wartorn battlefield held me in a trance.

The plane swooped low over us again, spitting out its torrent of instant death. Though the machine-gun bullets cut the wheat down about four feet from me, I continued to clutch the dark-red poppy in my hand. Somehow, I couldn't release it. It reminded me of the blood shed by many of my comrades, in just the short period of time we'd been in combat. I asked myself, "Before this war ends, will my blood be staining the ground in some foreign land, like these red poppies scattered over this wheat field?" I came back to reality, and reached in my left shirt pocket for my steel-covered Bible. Gently, I pressed the poppy between its pages.

Years later, whenever I opened that small Testament, my thoughts drifted back to the day I blocked out the sound of exploding bombs and tried to ignore the whining bullets. I would relive those moments when I became spellbound by a small, innocent flower. That poppy wanted no part of war; it only asked for the opportunity to live out its life in peace. Like the once brilliant colors of that flower, I too grew old, and faded with the passing years. I spent almost a lifetime searching for a lasting peace. By the time I found it, I was as faded as the flower pressed between the pages of the pocket Bible.

Some greater power made me stop and pick a poppy that day. Maybe God meant me to grasp a token of beauty from amidst the horrors and destruction of war, and preserve it as a symbol. He might have put me on this earth as a witness, to tell the world that you can find beauty in everything he has made and that the good things in life never really die, but continue to live on in our memories.

After the Stukas dropped their bombs and emptied their machine guns, we continued reconnoitering to the north. We passed through the minefields left by the retreating forces. In front of our column loomed a large, isolated hill, strongly defended by the Germans. They were using it as an observation post from which to direct artillery fire on our advancing troops. Our II Corps commander gave the difficult task of taking the hill, called 609, to the 34th Infantry Division. The 34th sustained many casualties and took a tremendous beating from Rommel's Afrika Korps in southern Tunisia.

A short distance north of Hill 609 stood another hill only a couple of hundred feet lower, also strongly defended by the Germans. II Corps needed this high ground to establish an observation post from which to direct their own artillery fire. The hill, called Djebel Ichkeul, was defended by men from one of Hitler's crack combat units, the famous Hermann Goering Division.

Troops A, B and C of the 91st Recon Squadron were given the task of clearing Djebel Ichkeul of Germans. The north and east sides of the hill were bordered by a salt lake. A swamp covered the remaining approaches, helping to make a natural defensive barrier. The swamp varied in depth from ankle to waist deep. In late afternoon of the day before we were scheduled to attack the hill, our troop moved forward to a wooded area, a few hundred yards south of the swamp. Our camp was located far enough away from the hill to be out of rifle range.

The mortar platoons from the three troops received orders that later in the evening, under cover of darkness, they were to proceed to the southern edge of the swamp and dig in their guns. Corporal Charles Atherton, from Calhoun, Kentucky, was in charge of C Troop's 1st Platoon mortar squad. Corporal Joe Montoro, from Gary, Indiana, had the 2nd Platoon squad, and I led the 3rd's squad. All the men from our troop volunteered to carry mortar rounds to our guns after it got dark.

We had a few hours to wait before setting up the mortars. With a clear field of fire and a swamp in front of us, there wasn't much danger of the Germans making a surprise attack on our positions. After protecting our perimeter with machine-gun emplacements, we relaxed for the first time since entering combat.

When we finished cleaning our weapons, a few of us built a small campfire behind a knoll. I unstrapped my old battered guitar from the back of my jeep and tuned it. Everyone wanted to put tomorrow and the task assigned to us out of their thoughts. They knew that singing would ease the tension a lot more than sitting around worrying about the outcome of tomorrow's battle.

We sang "Back Home Again in Indiana" for Joe Montoro and the other men from the Hoosier state. For Al Jerman, Vic Molinski, Joe Martinez and the Colorado boys, we sang "Moonlight on the River Colorado." "The Yellow Rose of Texas" was always a favorite of the fellows from the Lone Star State. As the evening progressed, we sang "Utah Trail," "Night Time in Nevada," "Home in Wyoming" and "Montana Plains." We had a song for nearly every state represented in our troop. These old melodies brought back memories of home and our loved ones. Toward the end of the evening, when someone requested "My Buddy," the words were sung with deep emotion. Many of the voices that had once joined us in song were now silent. We wondered if the Germans, knowing they were going into battle tomorrow, might not be up on Djebel Ichkeul singing "Lili Marlene" and other songs about their homeland.

After we landed in North Africa, our 3rd Platoon officer, Lieutenant St. John, joined the 91st as a replacement officer. Unlike most officers, he quite often fraternized with the men in the ranks. As we sat around the fire, which by now was only a glowing heap of embers, he came and joined us in song. I'd recently written a poem called "The Zero Hour," and composed a melody for it. The lieutenant leaned over my shoulder so that he could read the words I'd scribbled on a folded piece of paper. He sang this song along with me.

## THE ZERO HOUR

*I'm just a lonely sentry,*
*Out next to "No-Man's-Land,"*

*Who early in the morning,*
*Will fight and make a stand.*

*The stars just seem to whisper,*
*Brave soldier boy, don't fear;*
*Have faith, and think of loved ones,*
*Be glad that they're not here.*

*I walk my post and wonder,*
*If the moon, o'er the hill*
*Will shine upon us soldiers,*
*When all the guns are still?*

*Though we may not all return,*
*If it's my final fight,*
*There'll still be boys to follow,*
*For God and might, makes right.*

*The cold gray dawn is breaking,*
*The "Zero Hour" is here,*
*Though "No-Man's-Land" looks empty,*
*Our enemy is near.*

Little did Lieutenant St. John realize that the following day he would lose his life in the assault on the 1,500-foot-high Djebel Ichkeul. Every time I read the poem "The Zero Hour," my thoughts drift back to that evening on the plains of North Africa. I can still hear our gallant lieutenant singing the ending to the song. The night wind carried the last words he ever sang, out past the campfire's glow, to trail away into the darkness. On the morrow, the warm breeze ascending the hill whispered the words of the last verse back to him as he moved forward into battle—

*I pray that I will come back,*
*But my heart holds no fear.*
*I'd die there for my country,*
*And freedom we hold dear.*

Later that night, we moved the mortars into position on the edge of the swamp. All the men from the troop helped dig a small depression to partially conceal the mortar and the rounds of ammunition. Working under the very shadow of Djebel Ichkeul, we realized we'd be exposed to machine-gun fire once we opened up our barrage in the predawn hours. Being so close to the hill made it necessary to take the bipod legs off the mortar and use just the base plate and barrel. I'd have to wear gloves to raise and lower the barrel and fire the gun without sights, for they were fastened to the discarded bipod. The mortar crews, along with a platoon of 37-millimeter antitank guns from headquarters troop, were given the job of softening up the Krauts' defensive positions on the hill. The top of the mortar barrel had to be lowered close to the ground and fired directly at the German positions like a rifle. Because of this, we all knew that when the German machine gunners opened up, we'd have very little protection. H-hour arrived just before daylight. To conceal the attack of our troops advancing through the swamp in the predawn light, we used phosphorus shells to lay down a smoke screen. The moment we began firing, the German guns on the hill zeroed in on our mortar's muzzle flashes. The steady hail of machine-gun bullets made it difficult to drop shells into the three-foot-long barrel. The incoming bullets that didn't plunk into the swamp or breastworks in front of us buzzed by our heads like a swarm of bees returning to their hive. One bullet bounced off the mortar barrel, ricocheting between me and my first gunner.

First gunner Arnold Eckert, from Bovey, Minnesota, had the job of dropping the shells into the muzzle of the barrel. When the shotgun shell in the bottom of each projectile came in contact with the firing pin at the base of the barrel, it exploded. This small explosion ignited the increments of powder attached to the projectile, which in turn propelled the shell. Because the barrel became very hot, I had to wear asbestos gloves while holding it.

Because of the acute angle of the barrel, Arnold had to literally shove the shells into it, or else they would hang up in the middle of the tube. Just as daybreak arrived, one of the shells traveled down the tube too slowly and failed to explode. This meant we had a live shell in the barrel. During the firing procedure, just before the number one gunner dropped the shell in the tube, the number two gunner pulled the safety pin. This pin was located in the point-detonating fuse on the tip of the projectile. With the pin pulled, the slightest pressure on this fuse could cause the shell to explode.

Many times in practice we tried to prepare for just such an emergency, but we'd never used a shell with the safety pin removed. What made matters worse, the enemy machine guns were trying their darnedest to knock us out of action. We were like fellows with dynamite in their hip pockets, standing in front of a red-hot potbelly stove, warming their backsides.

With my right knee resting on the ground in a kneeling position, I placed the top of the barrel on my raised left knee. Arnold unhooked the bottom of the barrel from the base plate. He lifted it up in the air until his end of the tube was about a foot higher than my end. Nothing happened. Even after he raised it another six inches, the projectile still wouldn't slide out. By now, we were almost frantic. If Arnold lowered his end of the barrel and the shell broke loose and hit the firing pin, the force of the explosion would be worse than being kicked by a dozen mules. Raising the barrel much higher meant that once the projectile freed itself, I would have a rough time trying to keep it from hitting the ground.

We looked at each other, and Arnold hollered, "What'll I do?"

"It's either the machine-gun bullets or the shell; lift it higher," I yelled.

He wasted no time in raising the barrel. The sudden upward thrust on his end of the tube did the trick, for when it reached a height of almost two feet, the shell broke loose. I continued to grip the front of the barrel with both hands, leaving a triangle-shaped opening between my thumbs and forefingers. The live mortar round slid down the barrel and almost tore my hands loose from the tube. The point-detonating fuse was touching the edges of my fingers. I quickly slid them back from the sensitive fuse and grasped the shell, which weighed almost eleven pounds. If the fuse had pressed any harder on my fingers, our whole mortar crew would have been wiped out. After this life-threatening incident, Arnold made sure he shoved the shells down the barrel a lot faster.

With the enemy only a few hundred yards in front of us, according to the army manuals, a mortar shouldn't have been used in this sort of situation. Determining the exact angle to elevate the barrel was a matter of guess-work, which made it extremely dangerous for the troops we were firing over. By visually spotting where each shell exploded, and with the aid of a walkie-talkie portable radio carried by one of the fellows in our troop, we managed to keep the shells above the heads of our comrades.

When we were almost out of ammunition, Arnold tapped me on the shoulder and pointed to the barrel. It had turned a bright red at the bottom, with a combination of blue and purple hues reaching almost to the top. If we didn't quit firing, the tube would ignite the increments of powder on the shells before they ever reached the firing pin, possibly killing us all. Because of our rapid rate of fire, we'd burnt up our mortar barrel.

The troop had already crossed the swamp and worked their way a couple of hundred feet up the incline. The drive to take the hill seemed to be progressing smoothly, which meant that our job of giving covering fire had been successful. There seemed no reason for all of my squad to stay down at the bottom of the hill and guard a burnt-out mortar barrel. I left one man behind, and the rest of us grabbed our rifles and followed the troop up the hill. I figured that the remaining mortars and 37-millimeter guns could furnish any support the troop needed.

The previous day, I'd picked up a 1903 Springfield rifle and left my Thompson submachine in the back of my jeep. The rifle, because of its longer range, was much more ef-

fective than the ten-inch barrel on my Thompson during
daylight hours. I now carried a belt of rifle ammo around
my waist, plus a bandoleer of ammunition draped over
each shoulder that crossed my chest.

As the troop advanced up the hill, some of the Germans on the lower slopes surrendered, for they realized
they were being surrounded. It would be only a matter of
time before all of them were either captured or killed. The
Krauts manning the observation posts on top of the hill
were determined to hold onto their positions as long as
possible, so they could keep directing artillery fire on the
Americans advancing from the south.

Sergeant Orel Ogg, a close friend of mine from Ada,
Oklahoma, and one of the best demolition men in the
squadron, was wounded in the initial attack. I had a
young cowboy in my squad from Texas, named Wardel,
who also got hit. When the battle ended, we all smiled
when we remembered Wardel's remarks to us after he'd
been wounded in a very private part of his anatomy. He
didn't seem the least bit worried about losing his life, only
whether he'd be able to father children.

With the army in dire need of more officers than the
West Point Military Academy or the R.O.T.C. programs
throughout the country could furnish, young men were
being trained in Officer Candidate Schools. After receiving
his basic training, a soldier having the qualifications to become an officer could enter the school. In 90 days he graduated as a second lieutenant. We called these officers
"90-day wonders." Most of them proved to be competent
officers, sometimes having more sense than their supposedly superior West Point comrades.

Though only a "shavetail" second lieutenant, not long
out of Officer Candidate School, my favorite officer,
Lieutenant St. John, was killed on Djebel Ichkeul. With
every one of our junior officers out of action, an officer
from another troop, and a close friend of the lieutenant's,
was assigned to C Troop on temporary duty.

When Lieutenant St. John lost his life, his fellow officer

became very embittered. It is heartbreaking to lose one of your best friends in combat and hard to still remain rational toward the men responsible for his death. Our replacement officer shouted an order to our advancing troop, "From this moment on, there will be no more prisoners taken."

Thankfully, the 30 prisoners C Troop had already captured were safely down the hill. A few minutes after the officer issued the inhumane order, one of the men from the 2nd Platoon started to march a couple of prisoners back behind the lines to be interrogated. The officer saw him and yelled, "I said no more prisoners will be taken."

His orders were carried out. The fighting became more intense as the day progressed, for I believe the battle-hardened men of the Hermann Goering Division realized what was happening to their comrades who surrendered. Even after the final truce was signed at the end of the African Campaign, many of these German soldiers hid in caves on Djebel Ichkeul and refused to surrender. Their captain said, "A German general would not sign such an order." Not until two days later when General Krouse, the German commander who signed the surrender order, confronted him, did he and his men reluctantly agree to lay down their arms. Many of the officers of the Waffen-SS were true Nazis.

As darkness approached, C Troop controlled the left, and B Troop the right section of the hill. This meant that II Corps could now place an artillery observer on Djebel Ichkeul. Troops B and C were ordered to move off the hill and let A Troop hold the ground already taken. A Troop had the job of cleaning out the remaining Germans. The squadron had a more urgent mission assigned to it. We were being attached to Combat Command A for an advance on the town of Ferryville.

A tired and ragged group of men trudged off Djebel Ichkeul. Some were limping from their wounds and others were being carried by their comrades. White bandages spotted the ranks of the silent band of men. Joe Priel, from Louisville, Kentucky, had been wounded and was unable to walk. Al Jerman and Tom Thompson carried him back across the waist-deep swamp on a makeshift stretcher. Tom and Al had taken a canvas shelter-half and wrapped it around each of their rifles, using the guns for sides of a stretcher.

Acts of heroism were performed among the men that no one ever knew about, except those involved. No one ever expected a medal for his actions; their only concern was to help fallen comrades.

Most of the men in the ranks never learned the name of the hill on the edge of the swamp until after the war. Fifteen-hundred-foot-high Djebel Ichkeul, a rocky ridge about one and a half miles wide and five miles long, would forever be stained with blood, shed by the brave men of the 91st Cavalry Recon.

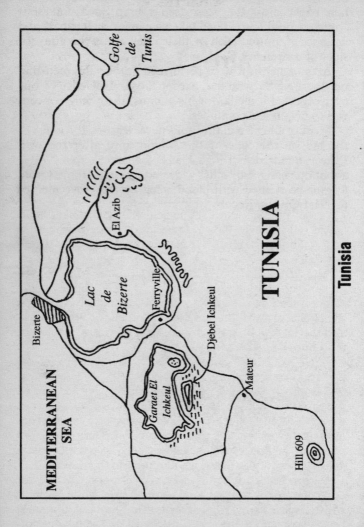

Tunisia

# CHAPTER V

# Afrika Is Ours

Thus far in the African Campaign, fighting as dismounted cavalry became a way of life for the 91st Recon. That policy changed in the latter phase of the campaign, when we were detached from the 9th Infantry Division and transferred to Combat Command A of the 1st Armored Division. With our 3rd Platoon lieutenant killed, and many of the enlisted men either casualties or made prisoners of war at About Face Hill, our platoon was drastically understrength.

The Afrika Korps had retreated from the Mareth Line in southern Tunisia and joined up with General von Arnim's forces to the north. Before successfully attacking the Djebel Ichkeul, the 91st Recon helped the 9th Infantry and the 1st Armored Divisions capture Mateur, a strategic road hub in northern Tunisia.

After the fall of Djebel Ichkeul, Troops B and C advanced as mounted recon in front of the 1st Armored. The two troops headed for Ferryville, a small town located on the southern shore of Lac de Bizerte. We were elated when we drove through the town. The civilians treated us like conquering heroes, waving, cheering and showering us with bouquets of flowers. For the townspeople's sake, we were glad we'd captured the town without having to destroy it.

We proceeded north out of Ferryville. Upon reaching the edge of town, I noticed a one-story, clean white building with a large red cross painted on its side. I thought, that must be the hospital for the area. Little did I realize how important a role the building would play in my life within the next

couple of hours. Our troop climbed the hill on the far side of
town, and I forgot all about the quaint little hospital.

The moment we reached the crest of the rise, a heavy
enemy artillery barrage scattered our column. Many of
the troop's vehicles raced back down the hill as incoming
shells passed overhead. I told my driver to pull off the
road, then motioned for the rest of my men to follow suit.
With my squad now dismounted, we looked for cover.

On top of the hill we saw an open pit, about 150 feet in
diameter and 20 or 30 feet deep, probably a small quarry. I
led my squad to the opening of the pit, hoping to escape
the deadly barrage. Looking through the narrow roadway
leading to the quarry, I noticed three or four shell craters
inside the pit. The shell holes were made by mortars, for
they were close to the farthest wall. Enemy artillery shells
would have landed in the middle or the side closest to us.
None of the shells being fired in the present artillery barrage were landing inside the pit. This led me to believe that
when setting up the guns in their present location, the
Germans took a few practice shots to zero in their mortars
on the quarry. They probably hoped we'd seek cover there,
it being the only logical place for protection. The Krauts
were crafty warriors and had successfully used this strategy on us before.

I backed away from the opening and led my squad about
fifty yards to the right of the pit. We took cover as best we
could in a small ditch leading from a house located on top of
the hill. I noticed men from B Troop also seeking cover. A
few of them ran into the pit. My supposition had been correct, for before I had a chance to go and warn them of what
might happen, the German mortars opened up. My heart
went out to those troopers trapped inside the quarry.

There was nothing my squad could do to help the
doomed men. As I watched, I saw a wounded soldier trying to drag his body away from the entrance to the pit.
Crawling on my belly, I went to his aid. If I could get him
into a jeep and make a run for it, maybe we could make it
down to the little first aid station at the bottom of the hill.

One thing for certain, lying out there in the open, he'd never survive the next barrage.

I looked at my jeep and saw water running out of the radiator, the result of a large piece of shrapnel. With both front tires flat, my vehicle was useless. Even if I could get the wounded man into a vehicle, the sound of the engine running would make it impossible to hear the incoming shells, putting us in greater danger. My only hope of getting the soldier down where he could receive medical aid was to carry him. The wounded trooper, Private Bob Ackerman, from B Troop, grew up in Illinois, and like me, was considered to be one of the youngsters in the squadron.

With artillery fire slackening for the moment, I slung my rifle across my back and lifted Bob up in my arms. I'd taken only a few steps when I heard the German guns open up again. As gently as I could, I lowered him to the ground and lay beside him. When I picked him up the second time, he whispered, "Let me lay. Save yourself, it's too late now."

The shells were now landing in the very spot where Bob first fell. It's a good thing we moved down the slope or we'd have been cut to ribbons. Every time I lifted Bob up to carry him, the shells seemed to follow us. When we were halfway down the hill, I became so concerned with getting him to safety that I forgot to listen for the sound of the enemy guns firing in the distance. A shell landed so close, it's a wonder we both weren't killed. God must have been walking beside us, leading the way through the flying shrapnel, just like he'd divided the waters of the Red Sea when Moses led his people out of Egypt. I kept praying for Him to spare my buddy's life.

As we approached the bottom of the hill, Bob spoke to me. His last words were, "I won't make it."

I looked down and saw that his eyes were closed. Later, I recalled how for just a fleeting moment, the dirt that smeared his young features reminded me of a dark storm-cloud hovering over a deathly, snow-white face. Bob's life-blood flowed slowly from his wounds onto my shirt, and dripped on my trousers.

I tried to console him by saying, "You'll make it, old buddy, for we don't have much farther to go."

If only there had been someone to give me a helping hand, but no one else remained on the side of the barren hill. They'd all taken cover. Except for the exploding shells, we were alone. I kept talking, trying to comfort him and give him hope. Though I was exhausted, the only thing that seemed to matter was to reach the first aid station and get help for my comrade. When Bob didn't open his eyes or respond to my chatter, I figured he'd passed out from pain.

At last we reached the bottom of the hill. There to our left stood the small white hospital. Except for shrapnel marks on the outside walls, it remained miraculously unscathed by the enemy shells. I quickened my pace and headed for the entrance of the building. Like tender arms swinging wide, begging to embrace me, the doors swung open. Two nurses rushed to my side, motioning me to bring my buddy inside. They had watched me carry the lifeless soldier off the hill. The shorter of the two nurses, a beautiful young girl with coal-black hair, placed both of her arms under Bob's legs and lifted them up. She guided me to a table in the middle of the room. My spirits rose, for we'd finally made it to safety.

The French nurse examined him, then turned and looked up at me. Biting her lower lip, tears began running down her cheeks. She placed her arm around my shoulder and in a voice filled with tender emotion, whispered, *"Votre comrade, il est mort."*

I couldn't speak French very fluently, but managed to understand her words. "Your comrade, he is dead."

I sat down on the floor and let my shoulders sag in defeat. Unashamed, I let the moisture from my flooding eyes plow furrows in a dust-stained face. I blamed myself for not leaving my buddy on top of the hill where he fell; he had begged me to. Maybe I could have found a medic to come and treat him. Then I realized that, lying there in the open, the shells would have torn his body to pieces.

Slowly, I raised up off the floor. I felt like a tired, washed-out old man, not only from being physically exhausted, but because of the mental strain. I had to deal with the burden of not knowing whether I'd made the right decision in trying to save Bob's life.

With my rifle still slung across my back, I stood next to him and squeezed his hand. Like the embers of a dying campfire, the warmth in his hand was slowly fading. Later, I wished that I'd said a prayer, but at the moment, I knew the time for praying had passed. Carrying Bob down the hill, I'd asked God for help, but he must have had other plans. A lone tear fell onto my fingers when I lifted them up to make the sign of the cross. I turned to the compassionate sister of mercy standing at my side. Touching the sleeve of her bloodstained white uniform, I squeezed her arm and said, *"Merci,"* then I walked outside.

I realized that Bob died in my arms shortly before we reached the first aid station. Working my way up the hill, I rejoined my squad. When one of my men asked about Ackerman, I just lowered my head and said, "He's gone."

What good would it do to elaborate on what I had done. I'd failed to save his life. After the African Campaign ended and we'd been sent back to a rest area, I wrote a poem about a number of our combat experiences in Tunisia. I dedicated it to Private Bob Ackerman of B Troop. The story of About Face Hill and the other battles of the campaign are combined into the poem. I could put my feelings down on paper, but couldn't talk about them.

### LET'S BOW OUR HEADS A MOMENT

*We all have buddies, you and I,*
*Who've shared our campfire's glow.*
*I will tell you of my comrade,*
*'Tho it fills my heart with woe.*

*The campaign was nearly over,*
*The fighting almost done;*
*We'd risen early that morning,*
*Long before the rising sun.*

> We had pushed the Jerries backward,
> I'd say, a mile or two,
> But they were firing eighty-eights,
> And they got their armor through.
>
> Our Sherman tanks stopped their big drive,
> We couldn't ask for more.
> Then we silenced three machine guns,
> Stopped a forty-seven's roar.
>
> Before midday, the Germans left,
> To make another stand.
> Dear God, they'd surely made us pay
> With our blood, to win this land.
>
> Not far ahead, there loomed a hill,
> They no doubt would defend.
> We never seemed to get a rest,
> Would the fighting ever end?
>
> Our men were tired and sorely beat,
> With ammo running low.
> We reached the bottom of the hill,
> How we made it, I don't know.
>
> We swore we'd make the Germans pay,
> For all the men we'd lost.
> Our leader said, "Don't spare a man,
> Take that hill at any cost."
>
> When we reached the top, exhausted,
> A smile was on each face.
> We'd driven Jerry from the hill,
> Though he'd almost won the race.
>
> When the earth began to tremble,
> There was no place to hide.

*The eighty-eights began to burst.*
*If we stayed there, we'd have died.*

*So we picked up our machine guns,*
*And helped the wounded too,*
*Then we headed down for cover,*
*There was nothing else to do.*

*Just before we reached the bottom,*
*I heard a distant call.*
*I turned and looked back up the hill,*
*And I saw a soldier fall.*

*I just knew I'd have to reach him,*
*Before the next shell fell.*
*I crept toward the top again,*
*'Twas my buddy, I could tell.*

*When I reached his side, I whispered,*
*"We'll make it down somehow."*
*He only muttered, "Let me lay,*
*Save yourself, it's too late now."*

*We reached the bottom of the hill,*
*Where medics worked on him.*
*I watched his life's blood drain away,*
*And just knew his chance was slim.*

*Shrapnel ripped the mangled body,*
*Of that strong, brave young man.*
*I knelt and said a silent prayer,*
*"God, please save him, if you can."*

*I guess the Lord had other plans,*
*For my pal's now at rest,*
*But he'll always be remembered,*
*By us men who loved him best.*

*We have all lost many comrades,*
*Who've found a lasting peace,*
        *When they gave their lives for freedom,*
*In the hope that wars would cease.*


        *Let us bow our heads a moment,*
*In prayer for those who died,*
        *Fighting proudly for the country,*
*We all look upon, with pride.*

                              *North Africa, May 1943*

Later that summer, when medals were awarded for the North African Campaign, a soldier from B Troop received the Silver Star for supposedly carrying Private Ackerman off the hill at Ferryville.

After the award ceremony, Corporal Louis Dakai, from Gary, Indiana, approached me and asked, "Fred, why didn't you speak up and tell them it was you who carried Ackerman down off the hill? I lay in the ditch alongside of the road and watched you struggle through those bursting shells. I saw you carry him into the little French first aid station."

"Does it really matter now?" I asked. "My coming forward and saying I carried him wouldn't bring him back to life. If another person wants to take credit for something he didn't do, let the guilt rest upon his shoulders. My conscience is already troubled, for I feel that I didn't do enough to save Bob's life. Please, don't ask me to talk about what happened that day, I'm trying hard to forget."

For many years, I never mentioned the incident to anyone because it only brought back sad memories. I could only release my feelings of despair by writing them in a poem.

After I'd left Bob Ackerman in the French aid station and rejoined my squad, the artillery barrage tapered off. Troops B and C moved out of Ferryville and headed down the road toward Bizerte. We continued our reconnaissance for the 1st Armored Division. That evening we made camp south of the village of El Azib in a grove of trees. We were only about fifteen or twenty miles south of Bizerte.

The Sherman tanks of the 1st Armored formed a defensive perimeter around our bivouac area.

The German army in North Africa couldn't possibly hold out much longer. Fighting with its back against the Mediterranean Sea and almost completely surrounded by Allied troops, they intended to make a stand and go down fighting. Somewhere up ahead would be a line of defense chosen to their advantage. In the art of war, the Germans were a brilliant fighting machine. General von Arnim now commanded all the German troops in North Africa, including Rommel's Afrika Korps. Hitler had recalled the "Desert Fox" to Germany because of Rommel's ill health. In a last desperate attempt to delay his inevitable surrender, von Arnim rallied all his available forces.

That night we slept peacefully inside a circle of tanks. It reminded me of the early pioneer wagon trains that crossed the Western plains, when they stopped and made camp for the night. For once we had a good night's rest and didn't have to dig in machine guns or send out patrols. Before it got dark, our troop commander called our platoon together. Spreading his map on the ground, he outlined our mission for the following morning.

"At 0600 hours," he said, "the 3rd Platoon will move out through the 1st Armored Division and proceed northeast on the road toward Menzel Djemil. Your mission is to determine where the Germans have established their line of defense. As you advance down the road every quarter of a mile, the radio operator in your scout car will relay your exact location back here to our command post. If we lose radio contact with you and hear the Kraut's artillery start firing, we'll know you've found the enemy. From the map coordinates you've sent back, we'll be able to pinpoint the Germans' defensive position and give you artillery support. The 1st Armored tanks will be standing by, ready to come to your rescue."

Sergeant Maher, from Indiana, was head of our troop maintenance crew. That evening he brought up my jeep that had been disabled at Ferryville. He'd fixed the flat tires and installed a new radiator. Though there were several shrapnel holes through the body of the jeep, to my surprise, my old guitar still remained in one piece. It had a couple of strings missing and a small hole in the bottom, but otherwise it could be repaired. Because there were no extra mortar barrels available to replace the one we'd burnt out at Djebel Ichkeul, my squad became a machine-gun squad.

We put bags of sand on the floor of our jeeps to give us added protection in case we ran over a mine. After loading extra boxes of ammo for the machine guns mounted in the back of the jeeps, we cleaned our weapons for the morning's mission. I still carried the 1903, .30-caliber Springfield rifle. The short-barreled Thompson submachine gun I kept inside my vehicle, and only used it on night patrols.

The next morning, Bert Gentry would be manning the .30-caliber machine gun in the back of my jeep, and Henderson, from Illinois, would be driving. Henderson was a quiet, likable fellow who kept pretty much to himself. He performed any job assigned to him extremely well, and never complained. Bert, the happy-go-lucky fellow of my squad, loved his wine, women and song. How I wish I had his carefree attitude about life. Even after he'd consumed his share of wine, you'd swear he'd never touched a drop. He could really hold his liquor. Bert always had a smile on his face and, like the majority of the Southern boys, maintained a close relationship with God.

We felt secure that night, resting inside the perimeter of tanks, but I lay awake a long time thinking about the coming battle. On tomorrow's mission, I knew we'd have no support of any kind, not until we made contact with the Germans. If, or when, they surprised us, could we hold on long enough until help arrived? As on every other evening, and especially those nights when I knew we'd face the enemy the following day, I asked God to watch over me and give me courage. Finally, I fell asleep.

Sergeant Joe Mammone, from Oneida, New York, led our 3rd Platoon section made up of jeeps and a scout car. Shortly before 0600 hours, we moved out of our bivouac area and headed toward the perimeter of Sherman tanks. It was an exceptionally beautiful May morning. As on so many other occasions when advancing into the unknown, we couldn't begin to predict the outcome of the battle. Little did we realize that before the sun went down over the western horizon, we would witness and be a part of one of the last major tank engagements of the North African Campaign.

Less than seven months before, Hitler's Afrika Korps had been the pride of the German military machine. After its defeat by the British at El Alamein in October 1942, Rommel retreated across Libya and into southern Tunisia. The German forces now controlled only two major cities in Tunisia, the ports of Tunis and Bizerte. The outcome of the conflict was inevitable, for Allied airpower had crippled the German supply lines coming from Italy to Africa. The Afrika Korps, though critically short of fuel, food and ammunition, would never be lacking in courage or superb fighting ability.

With our vehicle engines idling, we watched the minute hands on our synchronized watches move closer to 0600 hours. A couple of minutes before our departure, a colonel from the 1st Armored Division came out through a grove of trees and looked at our small column of vehicles. Sipping on a cup of steaming hot coffee, he walked over to me and asked, "Where are you fellows heading for in such a big hurry, Corporal?"

"Our orders are to move out on the road leading to Menzel Djemil at 0600 hours, contact the enemy, and establish the location of their line of defense," I said.

Squinting his eyebrows in a surprised look of disapproval, he said, "Without tank support you will be annihilated. It's suicide to go out there alone. Why don't you wait until we get our tanks moving so we can back you up?"

He'd only made a suggestion, not given us an order, but I figured that we'd already received instructions from our troop commander and shouldn't question them. "Thanks for your concern, Colonel," I said, "but we have our orders. It's our job to be your recon."

Without answering me, he shook his head in disgust, then

turned around and walked back to his tanks. He probably thought, "Let this kid find out for himself." Many times since the incident happened, I wish I'd been more like our captain at About Face Hill. He defied his superior officer and showed compassion for his men. Instead, I possessed traits similar to our colonel. He forced the men of C Troop to make a choice between life and death.

I had to live with the haunting conversation that took place between Henderson and me after the colonel departed. If I'd only reported back to our captain and told him what the 1st Armored tank commander had suggested, my conscience would have been clear.

Henderson turned to me and said, "Fred, let's go back and ask the captain if we can't wait for tank support before we move out. You heard the colonel say it would be suicide to go out there alone. With only three jeeps and a scout car, we're headin' into a death trap."

Though I knew Henderson spoke the truth, I also knew the reason why we had to go out alone. "I'm sorry, but we were given orders and I intend to follow them. We have to find out where the enemy intends to make their stand. That's part of a recon unit's job. Like you say, we might be drawn into a trap, but it's better to lose a few vehicles than have a complete tank unit annihilated. If that happens, the fighting power of the army will be weakened."

I knew better than to think Henderson was a coward. He'd proven his fighting ability at About Face Hill. At the time, I didn't seem to understand that no man with an ounce of brains should knowingly commit suicide, just to prove he is a brave man.

Our little column of vehicles moved slowly forward to keep its appointment with destiny. Sergeant Joe Mammone moved to the point position with his scout car. Every quarter of a mile, little Martinez, the radio operator, kept our commanding officer and the tank unit of combat command informed of our progress. In and out of the wadis we drove. No one broke the silence with idle chatter. All eyes were searching the terrain ahead. The tension mounted and my hands sweated as I gripped the walnut stock of my rifle. When would the Germans hit us?

I glanced over my shoulder at Bert Gentry sitting in the back of the jeep and saw his right hand trying to compress the steel handle of the machine gun. The desert tan that usually covered his face seemed to have faded, making the stubble of his beard become more pronounced. Beads of sweat trickled out of his coal-black hair and remained motionless above the barrier of wrinkles on his forehead. His troubled eyes had lost their familiar smile. As with everyone else on the patrol, the suspense took its toll on Bert's nerves. Still, no one uttered a word. We waited.

The distance lengthened between us and the 1st Armored Division tanks, our only hope of survival. They were miles behind us, still warming their engines at the oasis. Coming in contact with the enemy would almost be a relief. Anything seemed better than the suspense and anxiety we were experiencing. Our taut nerves were ready to snap.

The only noise breaking the desert silence was the constant drone of our vehicle engines. They sounded like a swarm of bees searching out a new hive. To our left, a cool breeze began to blow off Lac de Bizerte, but we knew that when the shadows disappeared from the wadis the sun would bring warmth to the land. The dark woolen clothes we wore would make us perspire, then we'd envy many of the British Tommies, dressed in their light-colored shorts. Their exposed legs enabled them to take advantage of the slightest breeze.

Up ahead and to our right loomed a large hill. It looked to be 400 to 500 feet high. The road crossed a deep wadi in front of the hill. By the time Sergeant Mammone's scout car reached the bottom of the wadi, my jeep, bringing up the tail end of the column, was about halfway down the slope. We no longer had to wait and wonder in suspense; we'd reached the climax. The world around us exploded! The Germans had patiently waited until we were down in the depression in front of them, then sprung the jaws of the trap around us. It seemed as if every Kraut gun in Africa opened up on us. The Germans had a turkey shoot, for, like shooting at a single line of those birds walking in the wild, the German gunners began firing at the rear of our column. No one could escape or retreat through their deadly fire.

The moment the firing began, out of the corner of my eye I saw Henderson's hands turn the steering wheel to the left to swing the jeep off the road. He never completed the move, and became the first casualty of the patrol. Bert Gentry dove off the back of the jeep with his rifle slung across his back. I rolled out of the disabled jeep into the deep ditch alongside the road. There was nothing we could do for our buddy Henderson. He'd been killed in the first burst of fire. The exploding artillery shells and whining machine-gun bullets almost deafened us. The Krauts were literally looking down our throats, cutting the 3rd Platoon to ribbons.

Bert and I took cover in the ditch on the right side of the road. Luckily, it was at a slight angle to the enemy's field of fire, which came at us from about a two o'clock angle. Off to our right on top of the hill, we could see infantrymen firing down at us. As long as the Krauts didn't use mortars, we might be able to survive. The shells from the 47- and 75-millimeter antitank guns and the 88-millimeter artillery pieces barely missed the top of our heads. They hit on the road behind us. If only we could hang on long enough for help to arrive.

The Krauts didn't think it necessary to come down the slope and finish us off and suffer casualties in the process. They knew we were doomed. There was no possible way to escape from the trap.

We had to let them know it would be costly for them to come after us, so I began firing at the German soldiers who exposed themselves. I emptied two clips of ammo before I realized that Bert, who I knew had reached the safety of the ditch, hadn't fired a single round. I was almost certain he'd not been hit. Looking over my right shoulder, I saw him kneeling a few feet away. He held his hands clutched together chest-high with his face raised to the smoky heavens. For a brief moment, I couldn't figure out what he was doing.

Above the noise of the exploding shells, I heard his voice cry out. "Dear Lord, get me out of this mess, and I promise I'll never touch another drop of liquor as long as I live."

As loud as I could, I yelled, "Bert, will you shut up. If you want to pray, do it while you're firing that rifle. We've got to keep them from coming down here. If we don't, you'll never live to see another bottle of liquor."

After my harsh reprimand, Bert came back to reality. From then on, he did his share of the firing and made me proud to have him in my squad. The two of us kept easing our heads over the top of the ditch, looking for targets to shoot at. I could see all of the demolished 3rd Platoon vehicles at the bottom of the wadi and wondered if the other men were still holding out.

The II Corps artillery observer had undoubtedly followed the map coordinates Martinez kept radioing back to our command post. I knew that the artillery gunners were chomping at the bit, just waiting to hear the sound of enemy artillery. In a matter of minutes after the Germans began firing at the 3rd Platoon, our artillery opened up with their 105- and 155-millimeter guns. The tables had finally turned. Now it was our turn to watch the Krauts get plastered with shells.

A short while after shells began landing on the enemy positions, between shell bursts we heard the drone of engines. The 1st Armored Division tanks were coming to our rescue. Though I couldn't see them from down in the wadi, I knew they were barreling across the open plain behind us. The Krauts continued to keep us pinned down, trying their darnedest to finish us off before reinforcements arrived.

About the time I thought we were done for, I looked down the wadi to my left. Through the smoke and dust, I could make out the outline of a 1st Armored tank coming into the wadi. It began firing at the German armor on the forward slope of the hill. With American tanks firing from behind us, and Germans shooting in front of us, all the shells crisscrossed above our heads. It was worse than being in front of a sow grizzly bear trying to protect her cubs from a pack of hungry wolves. Many people watching the scene on the newsreels back in the States would probably say, "What a thrilling sight."

To the participants of the battle, it can only be described as "horrible," like trying to escape from the fiery depths of hell. To be caught between two opposing armies on a battlefield, with shells coming from both directions, is beyond description.

Just before our Sherman tanks reached the side of the wadi where we lay, a single jeep, which must have been traveling in front of the tanks, came over the crest of the road behind us. The driver saw the remains of our vehicles in the bottom of the wadi and slammed on his brakes. He came to a stop directly opposite where Bert and I lay in the gutter. The soldier could have been a member of the 1st Armored Division recon unit. He shouted at me, but I couldn't make out the words above the noise of battle. Not thinking clearly, I leaped out of the ditch and ran toward him.

Upon reaching the side of his jeep, I shouted, "Get out of here. They have this spot zeroed in; it's a death trap!"

Before I finished yelling the word "trap," a 47-millimeter or larger shell hit him. In the next instant I was almost blinded with flesh and blood. The projectile didn't have a point-detonating fuse. It must have been a delayed-action or an armor-piercing shell. It didn't explode until it hit the far side of the wadi. The soldier's head disintegrated, leaving nothing above his shoulders but spurting blood.

I dropped to the roadbed next to the jeep, wondering if I'd also been hit. I felt no pain, just warm flesh and blood on my exposed face. I rolled into the ditch and cleared my eyes with my shirt sleeve. The jeep driver's foot must have slid off the brake pedal and released it, for I turned my head in time to see the jeep drift slowly down the slope. It was a scary and awesome sight to behold. The driver's hands still clutched the steering wheel in a death grip. The vehicle traveled for about thirty feet, then veered off into the right gutter, coming to rest against the bank.

Many times throughout our lives, an incident happens

that produces such a lasting effect that a permanent picture is imprinted in our brain. Over the years, the characters stay so lifelike, you'd think they were painted only yesterday. No matter how hard we try to erase the vision, it remains forever, a haunting memory. So it was with that headless soldier clutching the steering wheel of his jeep. Maybe it is God's will that we never forget these events; that way, we'll always remember how horrible war really is. When the guns are silenced, nobody wins.

Before I had time to react to the terrible nightmare, a mortar shell landed next to me on the road. A strange feeling came over me. I thought I'd lost my left leg, but when I looked down, I saw it remained attached to my body. I began to realize how confused my mind had become over the past several minutes. I couldn't understand how I'd escaped being hit, when the shell decapitated that unknown soldier as I stood next to him. If the shell had been fitted with a point-detonating fuse and exploded on impact, I'd have been killed.

All the training I'd received, preparing me for combat, hadn't a thing to do with the way my life was spared today. If the bullet that killed Henderson had been a few inches further to his right, I'd have become a casualty instead of him. Why had God spared me? A short while ago, I gave Bert heck for praying. At the moment, there wasn't time for me to get down on my knees, but I took a second to look up in the heavens and say, "Thank you Lord."

The tanks were now on both sides of the road in the wadi and smoke lay thick over the battlefield. The smell of burning powder bit into my nostrils and made me cough. Nearby, I saw two medium tanks from the combat command knocked out of action.

As if on a prearranged signal, the German artillery and machine guns became silent. I looked up at the side of the hill where the road disappeared, and I saw a white flag appear. The 1st Armored tanks gradually stopped their firing and came to a halt. Save for a couple of tanks that idled their engines, a deathly silence settled over the battlefield. The stillness gave me an eerie feeling, like standing in the middle of a cemetery full of open coffins, waiting for the dead to either float up into the heavens or come back to life.

A few minutes before the white flag appeared, death, with a come-hither look on its face, had tightened its arms around the men of both armies. Now, I saw a ray of hope. The white flag hovered above us like a dove perched on top of the hill. I almost expected it to fly down through the smoke and destruction, bearing an olive branch.

Bert and I looked at each other, hoping the flag meant the end of the battle. We stood up in the ditch and stretched our aching muscles, then walked down the slope toward the battered remains of our 3rd Platoon vehicles. With so many men lost and most of our equipment gone, the 3rd Platoon of C Troop was virtually nonexistent.

I reached the bottom of the wadi and spoke to Joe Mammone and the survivors. Checking the two bandoleers draped across my chest and the ammunition belt around my waist, I found them all empty. Only three shells remained in my 1903 Springfield rifle.

All eyes were focused on the top of the hill. The white flag still fluttered in the breeze that blew off Lac de Bizerte. As we watched, the man holding the flag moved slowly over the crest of the hill and started down the slope toward us. A lone soldier moved from out of the front row of men and took the lead. He marched ahead of the flag bearer. We could see a column of men emerge from behind the hill. They walked four or five abreast, almost covering the width of the road. The length of the column seemed endless, numbering in the hundreds. When they got almost halfway down the hill, I could tell that the man in the lead wore an officer's hat. Most of the other soldiers had helmets.

Gazing up at the historic event taking place, I couldn't believe that the time had come for these men to lay down their arms. I'll never understand what prompted my next actions, for I was in a trance. Some unknown force seemed to control my movements. I stepped out of the ditch onto the road, and began walking up the hill to meet the defeated army. Joe Mammone and the rest of the men must have thought all the shelling had affected my mind. Cradled in the crook of my left arm lay my bolt-action Springfield rifle. My right hand grasped the foregrip.

As a young boy, when squirrel hunting I'd carried my muzzle-loading rifle this same way. In those days I enjoyed reading stories that told about the defeat of the great armies. I used to fantasize that I was one of the soldiers watching when the defeated general handed his sword over to the victor. Never did I dream that someday I would play a part in such an event. The distance shortened between me and the oncoming column. It was as if I walked from between the pages of a history book, where I witnessed other armies that over the centuries had surrendered in the vicinity of this very hill. At one time or another, this area had been ruled by the Phoenicians, Romans, Vandals, the Byzantine Empire, the Moslem Empire, and then the French. Finally, the day had come when the latest conquerors, the Germans, were forced to relinquish control of the land.

As I drew near the marching men, I couldn't take my eyes off the German officer in full dress uniform. Even in defeat, he retained the proud military posture of a well-disciplined German officer. Farther back in the column, I noticed many Italian soldiers. When I stopped a few paces in front of the officer, he raised his hand and the column gradually came to a halt. Looking me straight in the eye, he reached down and lifted the P-38 Walther pistol out of the rigid, black leather holster at his side. Grasping the barrel with his right hand and extending his arm to its full length, he pointed the pistol grip toward me.

At the end of the Civil War, General Grant performed one of the most honorable gestures a victorious general ever made. He refused to accept General Lee's sword when he surrendered at Appomattox Court House. Being one of the lowest-ranking noncommissioned officers in the American army, I had no such finesse. I held no ambitions of military grandeur, or of ever becoming a living legend. At the moment, all I saw was a beautiful German pistol being offered to me. I figured that if I didn't take it, some armchair officer behind the lines would latch on to it. I took a step forward, then reached out and accepted the gun as humbly as I could. "Thank you," I said.

A magnificent pair of 10 × 50 German Dienstglas field glasses were slung around his neck. Knowing these would also be confiscated when the interrogators questioned him behind the lines, I sheepishly pointed to them. He removed his hat and lifted the leather strap attached to the glasses from around his neck. After handing them to me, he replaced his hat and assumed a military stance.

I never learned what rank the officer held in the German army, but the large field glasses he gave me were issued only to tank commanders.

I couldn't converse with the officer, for I understood very little German. Most of the words I knew weren't appropriate to say to a general about to surrender; they would have insulted him. My appearance held a lot to be desired, and I could tell the officer didn't seem overly impressed with me. He probably expected to surrender his force to a distinguished American officer.

My clothes, face and hands, caked with dirt and dust, were splattered with dried flesh and blood. The sleeves of my shirt showed no indication that I held any rank. Since being promoted to squad leader in southern Tunisia, I'd never had an opportunity to sew on my corporal stripes. To the general, I must have been a sorry-looking excuse for an American soldier, especially one acknowledging the surrender of such a large number of soldiers from the Afrika Korps. In contrast, the officer standing before me was immaculately dressed. I presumed that he'd changed uniforms to impress his captors. If he did, then he'd have to wait until he reached the officers behind our lines.

After turning my back on the officer and facing the wadi below, I raised my right arm, then lowered it slowly in front of me, giving the horse cavalry command of "Forward, ho." From a War Department document, I later learned that the prisoners we'd taken numbered over 800. When the column came abreast of Joe and the survivors of our 3rd Platoon patrol, they joined us. Together, we led the prisoners down the road toward Ferryville. Because our vehicles had all been destroyed, we walked along with the prisoners.

A few days previous, I'd lost my mortar. The jeep, damaged in the shelling at Ferryville, was now gone, along with the guitar that I'd carried since my days at Fort Riley, Kansas. All of these losses were material and could be replaced. When you are touching elbows with a buddy and he is killed, nothing can ever take his place. When a tragedy like that occurs in combat, there is no time to stop and express your emotions. If you do, you could wind up dead. When a comrade is wounded, that is an entirely different story.

Only when the action slows down and the adrenalin flowing through your body returns to normal, does the full impact of what really happened in the battle begin to register. All I could think about were the last words Henderson ever spoke to me the morning we left the protection of the 1st Armored Division. "Fred, you heard what the colonel said, it will be suicide to go out there alone."

Over and over, I heard those words until they almost drove me insane. I couldn't confide in anyone or tell them how guilty I felt. From then on, I vowed never to accept another promotion. Having responsibility on the battlefield meant that I had to make the decision whether a man lived or died. A squad of eight men seemed even too many to be responsible for. As a youngster, I'd been a loner. Oh—how I wish I could be a boy again.

Just imagine how some officers must feel with the fate of so many men resting on the decisions they make. When an officer gives an order, it doesn't necessarily mean that he hasn't a conscience, only that he's been taught and trained that to win a war, men must die. Risking your own life doesn't have the same aftereffect on your mind, as when you order another man to follow you, knowing that he too might die. To have him carry out your orders, then see him killed, is a hard thing to live with. It's a good thing the war kept us so busy that we didn't have time to probe into the innermost depths of our conscience. Only after the conflict ended, and a man had time to search his soul, would he realize the full impact of what happened to him during the war. Wounds of the body oftentimes heal faster than those of the mind.

After turning the prisoners over to the proper authorities, we teamed up with the 2nd Platoon and rode along in their vehicles. We advanced down the road past the abandoned German 47-millimeter antitank guns and the 88-millimeter artillery pieces that only a short time ago dealt so much death and destruction. These were the same guns that tore our 3rd Platoon to pieces.

Beyond the crest of the hill, we came upon a strange sight. Slumped over the carriage of his 88 sat the rigid, and headless, body of the German gunner. All I could think of at the time was the irony of the situation. One of our soldiers had lost his head in the battle, but the hands of fate evened the score by doing the same horrible thing to a German soldier. God works in strange ways.

I felt relieved that we were able to get the prisoners safely behind the lines without any of them being needlessly slaughtered. In the previous battle of Djebel Ichkeul, most people would say the officer assigned to our troop should never have given the order that no more prisoners be taken. A person has to put himself in that officer's crazed state of mind when he gave the order. He had just seen his best friend killed. In a sense, he'd gone insane, and wasn't strong enough to overcome his feelings of hatred and act rationally like a civilized human being. If the German people would have realized Hitler was insane when he declared, "Humaneness is a mixture of stupidity and cowardice," maybe there wouldn't have been a World War II.

An incident similar to the one that happened on Djebel Ichkeul took place a few days later, when a man in one of our troops saw his brother killed. After the battle, when the Germans responsible for the man's death surrendered and were being marched behind the lines, something snapped in the surviving brother's mind. He leaped up on a vehicle mounted with a machine gun. Before anyone could stop him, he emptied a box of ammunition into the marching column of prisoners.

War caused many young soldiers from both sides of the conflict to perform acts of violence that shocked the civilized world. Some of the incidents were never published in the papers or revealed to the public until years after the war. Many of the soldiers' minds were tortured with guilt. Their lives were ruined forever, for it became impossible for them to discuss the war. Others found they could ease their conscience by confessing to another person some of the horrible things they'd done. Only then would they begin to find peace within themselves, even though the guilt would remain.

Troop C raced toward Bizerte along with Troop E and their light tanks. The following report to the Cavalry School, written by Lieutenant Colonel Candler after he returned to the States, mentions C Troop's last combat mission in the African Campaign: "The ground for about five miles in front was flat, pockmarked by mud and shell holes, and covered by the fire of German weapons on the high ground to the south and east. Two of Carr's medium tanks were hit. The squadron, Troop E (less two platoons,) and Troop C (all in order) bounded all the way across. It was the nearest thing to a mechanized charge I've ever seen." The German artillery gunners were so confused by all the vehicles charging them that they surrendered.

With the final phase of the African Campaign over, the only material things I possessed were the clothes on my back and the weapons and equipment I carried. The memories and experiences of the campaign I would just as soon forget, but I knew it to be an impossibility. Rommel's Afrika Korps had furnished me with all of my personal weapons, except the 1903 Springfield rifle slung over my shoulder. If it could talk, each piece of equipment I'd acquired had a story to tell.

The day after Mother's Day, with the campaign finally over, we entered Bizerte, then proceeded on to the city of Tunis. While inspecting an airfield outside of Tunis, I saw an undamaged airplane on the runway, a Messerschmitt

109 (Me-109). With my dagger, I cut the swastika off the aluminum tail of the plane for a souvenir.

We traveled back to Mateur, where we were deloused, then drove across the northern coast of Tunisia to St. Ain Relhel, Algeria. There we received new clothing, equipment, and replacements for the men we'd lost. After the squadron reorganized, we headed east again to visit the city of Algiers. The small dip of ice cream we received from the American Red Cross became the highlight of our visit to the capital of Algeria. Though we tried to put the experiences of the war out of our minds, I guess the army wanted to keep us psyched up about combat. Our spirits took a nosedive when we were shown a war movie called *Wake Island*.

On May 30, 1943, we traveled to the town of St. Louis to participate in a ceremony honoring our fallen comrades. While there, Bob Hope and his cast from the USO entertained us. When the combat troops from Tunisia visited Oran and Algiers, they were surprised to see all the soldiers behind the lines wearing light-colored khaki clothes. Still in our woolen olive drab uniforms, we never got the opportunity to wear lighter clothes until after we returned to the States.

In a large, natural amphitheater-type arena, the 91st Recon attended a gathering of all the combat troops from the campaign. We listened to General Patton make a speech. He congratulated us for the part we played in defeating Hitler's Afrika Korps. He also destroyed any illusions we had of going home in the immediate future, saying, "Until Hitler is defeated, you are going to stay over here and fight, and die."

Colonel Candler, our squadron commander, received orders to return to the States. Training recon units for the campaigns soon to be fought in the European Theater of Operations would be his new assignment. Our colonel's battle experience and the tactics he'd learned in fighting the Germans in Africa would prove invaluable in the years ahead. The men in the squadron were proud of their colonel, especially those in Troop C. I'll always carry a picture of him in the back of my mind, out in front of our troop, charging up About Face Hill through smoke and bursting shells. He personally led us in our first real victory of the war.

The new commander of the 91st Recon was Colonel Ellis, a former observer for 5th Army headquarters during the African Campaign. The short, rough-speaking man would have his job cut out for him when he tried to fill the shoes of Colonel Candler. I remember part of Colonel Ellis's speech when he took command of the squadron. He told us, "You cannot rest on your laurels."

After he lectured us, we traveled west along the coast to a training area to prepare for an upcoming invasion. We camped next to the elite troops of the American army, Darby's Rangers. They were organized and patterned after the British Commando units. In Africa, the Rangers proved they could perform the impossible.

During the latter part of May and through most of the month of June, we trained our new replacements. Corporal Joe Montoro, the 2nd Platoon mortar squad leader, received sergeant stripes when he replaced Sergeant Stamps, who was missing in action. I transferred out of the 3rd back into the 2nd Platoon and took command of Joe's mortar squad.

Most of the men in the squad were close buddies of mine. George Johnson, from Middleburg, Maryland, became my first gunner and jeep driver. George Rogers, from Cleveland, Ohio, one of the most rugged men in the squad, always went into combat loaded down with crossed bandoleers of ammunition and extra hand grenades. Although twice wounded in combat, George showed no fear. The odds seemed to be against him though, for he eventually got killed in northern Italy. Paul Yenser, my old friend from Pennsylvania, had become an expert at handling explosives. Paul would also lose his life in Italy, as would another boy in my squad, Jack R. Smith.

Joe Montoro had trained his mortar squad well, and I inherited a fine group of men. Our platoon sergeant, John P. Smith, from Vinson, Oklahoma, was one of the finest

soldiers in the squadron. He took command of the 2nd
Platoon at About Face Hill, after all three of C Troop's platoon sergeants refused to follow our colonel. Staff Sergeant
Smith later received a battlefield commission in Italy and became an officer. Ted Plasse, from Woonsocket, Rhode Island, and William Roscoe from Wrightstown, New Jersey,
were replacements. Like the other men in my squad, they
soon became exceptional fighting men.

When I'd been promoted to corporal and transferred to
the 3rd Platoon mortar squad at the beginning of combat in
Tunisia, I had a very difficult time. Even though all the fellows were good soldiers, I considered myself incompetent to
lead a group of men that I hardly knew. Now that I'd rejoined the men I originally trained with, I swore that I'd
never leave them again. Getting wounded and being sent
back to a field hospital became my greatest fear. I dreaded
the thought of someone else taking over my squad, and then
when I returned to duty, being sent to a different platoon, or
maybe even another troop. It was much easier to be a private
than a noncommissioned officer. I never minded taking orders from a superior. I envied the life of a loner, for he had
no responsibilities and only himself to worry about.

After our squadron received replacements for the men
we'd lost, the army upgraded our equipment. The old
Springfield rifles of World War I vintage were replaced by
the new gas-operated M1 Garand rifles. Once again, I carried my favorite weapon, a 1928 Thompson submachine
gun. Two pouches on my belt held a total of six magazines
of ammunition, with each magazine holding thirty rounds.

Most of the radio operators and vehicle drivers were
issued .45-caliber, Model 1911 semiautomatic pistols. I'd
fired this pistol in simulated cavalry charges when I trained
in the horse cavalry, and barely qualified as a marksman.
The officers in our outfit carried six-shot revolvers with a
special clip that used the same .45-caliber ammo as the
1911 pistol and our Thompson.

An order came down from army headquarters forbid-
ding any soldier from carrying German equipment. The

German Schmeisser MP40 (burp gun) fired so much faster than our Thompson, that many of us would have liked to carry one. You could easily tell when a burp gun opened up at night; its rate of fire was much faster than our slow-firing Thompson. It drew returning fire, or a grenade, from any American soldier in the vicinity.

I took the P-38, 9-millimeter Walther pistol that I had received from the German officer who surrendered at Bizerte, and fitted it into an American .45-caliber pistol holster. With the flap of the holster fastened, no one could tell I carried a German pistol. The German fluorescent compass I'd confiscated from a prisoner, I kept concealed in my right shirt pocket. The left pocket of my shirt held the steel-covered Bible. My large Kraut wristwatch, with its fluorescent hands, couldn't be seen underneath my shirt sleeve.

When not training for the upcoming invasion, I often visited a nearby village. I bartered a couple of cartons of cigarettes for a custom-built holster made out of goatskin by an Arab cobbler. The small 7.65mm German Saur pistol that I had the holster made for never left my person the rest of the time I spent overseas. I even slept with it strapped to my body, for it fit snugly under my left armpit. My bone-handle dagger, made in Berlin, I carried in a special sheath strapped to my right leg. It remained concealed beneath my woolen trousers. I removed the bottom half of my pants pocket so the hilt of the knife remained accessible to my grasp.

In the early part of the war, all the equipment carried by the men in Rommel's Afrika Korps had been precision-made by German craftsmen, not manufactured in the satellite countries that Germany conquered.

The 10 × 50 Dienstglas field glasses created a problem at first, but because of the nature of my job, our squadron commander gave me written permission to carry them. The glasses were far superior to any issued by the American military. During the Italian campaign, the paper of authorization I carried proved invaluable. It helped keep the glasses from being confiscated by a high-ranking American officer, who thought his rank could get him something that his fighting ability couldn't.

All of my clothing and personal belongings, left behind the front lines when we went into combat, were lost on the trip from French Morocco to southern Tunisia. I didn't even have a jacket to wear if the weather turned cold. Combat jackets were in short supply, but I did manage to obtain a new shelter half and a wool blanket. All of our white underclothes were exchanged for olive drab ones.

Even though we took atabrine tablets to prevent malaria, Sergeant Joe Montoro and a few other men contracted the disease while we trained in Algeria. Down in the barren desert country of southern Tunisia, we learned to survive on a canteen of water a day. Up north, along the coast, the water situation improved. Quite often, we swam in the Mediterranean Sea. Under a cloudless, blue summer sky, we learned firsthand why travel posters referred to the large inland sea as "The Blue Mediterranean."

In between training exercises, I wrote a few poems. For a short while, we learned to relax and bask in the sun. I missed playing my old guitar, and hadn't been able to find another one to replace it.

Since arriving in Africa, everyone listened to "Axis Sally" broadcasting propaganda across the German airwaves from Berlin. Born in Portland, Maine, Sally's real name was Mildred Sisk. In the evenings, anytime we could get near a radio in one of the scout cars, we enjoyed listening to the music she played to make us homesick. Little did she realize that, unintentionally, she boosted our morale.

Before our tour in Africa came to a close, we had an opportunity to visit the ancient city of Carthage, located only three or four miles from Tunis. What a wonderful experience to have the opportunity of seeing the remains of one of the most famous cities of ancient times. How I wished the old ruins could talk and tell us of the soldiers, sailors, traders and merchants who once lived there, or had been a part of its history. Until its capture and destruction by the Romans in 146 B.C., the occupants of

Carthage ruled over a great empire of the Mediterranean. The Romans rebuilt the city, but when the Arabs conquered it in 698, they left it in ruins.

While walking through the tombs and ruins of Carthage, I happened to meet my old buddy Bert, from the 3rd Platoon mortar squad. I've often heard it said that "Time heals all wounds, and has the power to make sad memories fade, even though they may never be forgotten."

I knew there hadn't been enough time for Bert to forget about our last battle. Only a few short weeks ago, when he and I were trapped along with the 3rd Platoon, Bert had knelt in the gutter alongside me. He made a promise that if God spared his life, he'd never touch another drop of liquor. With the threat to his life over for the time being, Bert held a bottle of spirits in his hand. Lifting it high in the air, he proposed a toast. "Here's to us, Fred, and to what we went through."

He smiled and joked, like the friend I knew of old. Judging from the ruddy hue of his tanned face, I could tell he felt no pain. I completely understood and upheld the reason he'd reneged on his promise. Bert lived for today and felt that he'd better live life to the fullest, for who could predict how many tomorrows any of us would live to see.

We knew we were about to engage in a large military operation when our training ceased and we readied our equipment for battle. The Ranger battalion training next to us moved out in full combat gear, which indicated a major campaign ahead. We were told that before going into combat, there would be religious services for those wishing to attend. I went to church with Al Jerman, our 2nd Platoon radio operator. I'd never been to Catholic Mass before, but felt at ease kneeling next to a buddy who prayed for our protection and guidance in the days ahead. In the coming months, we would travel north through land predominantly inhabited by Catholics. The country was laced with the remains of once beautiful cathedrals built by Sicilian and Italian craftsmen.

In the harbor of Bizerte, we boarded LSTs and headed for

Sicily. We learned that we were now attached to General Allen's 1st Infantry Division, a part of the newly formed American 7th Army commanded by General George Patton. Less than a year ago we'd sailed across the Atlantic, our destination a mystery. While crossing the Mediterranean, we also had time to think and wonder what fate held in store for us. Even though we were now seasoned veterans on the eve of the coming battle, the same old feelings of tension and anxiety returned. Once again, we asked ourselves "What will tomorrow bring?" If only fate would reveal the predetermined events that faced us, but then again, maybe it's best we didn't know.

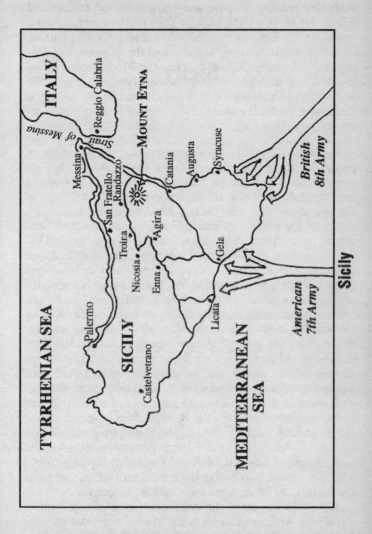

# CHAPTER VI

# Sicily

On July 10, 1943, Operation Husky, the invasion of Sicily, began. A detachment from Troop A of the 91st Recon landed with the 1st Infantry Division at Gela on the southwest shore of the island. Troop C didn't participate in the operation until after the beachhead was secured.

All of the officers in Troop C except one shavetail lieutenant were replacement officers who'd joined the 91st after the end of the African Campaign. We had lost our three platoon sergeants and all but two of our buck sergeants in Tunisia. The squad leaders and the two remaining sergeants advanced in rank to form the nucleus of the troop's noncommissioned officers. A large percentage of the enlisted men in the troop were also replacements. For this reason, Troop C didn't take part in the initial landings on D-day. After embarking from our LST at Licata, we moved inland along the winding mountain road and headed for Villarosa. There we rejoined our squadron.

General Alexander commanded all of the Allied forces in the Sicilian campaign. Sir Bernard Montgomery, also a British general, led the Canadian and British troops that made up the 8th Army. General George Patton commanded the newly formed American 7th Army. Capturing the port city of Messina, located only two or three miles across the strait from the toe of Italy, became the main military objective.

Rommel's defeat of the Americans in southern Tunisia during the African Campaign left Montgomery with a very low opinion of the fighting ability of his American allies. The fighting around Kasserine Pass was the "Yanks'" first real baptism of fire at the hands of the seasoned Afrika Korps. The British came to their rescue and saved the day.

Montgomery was impatient with the Americans but he had a short memory. He either forgot or didn't want to remember many of the tactical blunders the British troops made when they first entered combat in France and Belgium. By the time he and his army reached Dunkerque in May 1940, they were experienced veterans. Only through the courageous efforts of his countrymen with their flotilla of boats was he able to save a third of a million men and live to fight another day. During that early phase of the war, his troops were much like those of the Americans at Kasserine Pass.

If our military field commanders in southern Tunisia had been more like General Patton, the outcome would have been different. Patton didn't arrive from French Morocco to take command of the American forces in Tunisia until a few days after the battle. Before the end of the campaign, he forged the demoralized American II Corps into an efficient fighting unit.

Montgomery's forces landed in Sicily on the southeastern coast of the island south of Syracuse. With any luck, the British general figured to travel along the coastal road and reach Messina in short order. The Americans landed on the west side of Sicily. To reach Messina, they had to travel through the mountainous interior. Patton's role in the campaign was to mop up the western end of the island and secure Montgomery's left flank. Montgomery, though a brilliant general, meant to gain all the glory for himself. He had no intention of sharing it with the incompetent, inexperienced Americans.

Certain roads were assigned to Patton's sector of the island. When Montgomery ran into stiff resistance along the coast, without consulting his superior, General Alexander, or Patton, the commander of the 8th Army moved his forces into the Americans' zone and took over some of their roads. Patton became very upset and flew to North Africa to question General Alexander about Montgomery's inconsiderate tactics. Alexander sided with his fellow countryman.

Although Montgomery had raised the hackles on the back of Patton's neck, the commander of the 7th Army caused no further fuss. He decided to take full advantage of the situation Montgomery had promoted. He led the 45th and 3rd Infantry Divisions, along with the 2nd Armored Division, in a wild race to cut the island in half. In less than two weeks he captured Palermo, the capital and largest city in Sicily. This put a feather in his cap, but the aggressive American general wasn't satisfied; he wanted to show Montgomery that he was wrong about the fighting capabilities of the American soldier. Patton wanted to beat his rival to Messina.

With the 1st Infantry Division spearheading the drive and the 9th Infantry in reserve, the two infantry divisions of the 7th Army headed across the mountainous terrain in the center of the island. The race between two great generals had begun. The 91st Recon had the job of reconnoitering for the 1st Infantry.

The temperature hovered around the 90 degree mark, making the dust from the unpaved roads cake on our faces. We continually tried to cough up the parched earth that filled our throats and nostrils. When we lost contact with our kitchen truck, the Sicilian peasants gave us water and shared what little food they had.

Many of the islanders had a friend or relative living in the United States. Sergeant Joe Montoro could speak Italian and became our emissary and interpreter.

Very few mounted patrols were larger than a platoon, and sometimes they consisted of only a squad. We tried to locate the roadblocks and ambushes ahead or capture a prisoner to obtain information about the enemy's plans. I very seldom knew about the missions assigned to the rest of the platoons in the troop. It seemed that each troop operated in a world of its own, sometimes being miles apart.

In later years, whenever I talked or wrote about my experiences, I only mentioned the men I came in daily contact with. Many times each platoon seemed to be fighting its own private war. When the conflict ended, each squad had a different story to tell.

The 91st Recon was assigned the task of capturing the town of Gagliano in central Sicily. Before the engagement ended, Sergeant Gerry Kisters from Troop B, though wounded five times, knocked out two machine-gun positions. He later received the Congressional Medal of Honor for his actions and became the first soldier in the European Theater of Operations to receive both the Medal of Honor and the Distinguished Service Cross.

Sicily seemed to be one continual roadblock after another. The Germans used demolition charges to blow up the masonry bridges built by the talented Sicilians. Afterward they placed a few men with automatic weapons, and sometimes a mortar, to cover the area we had to cross. If we couldn't knock the roadblock out or bypass it, we called in the 1st Infantry to complete the job. We always knew that not far down the road we'd encounter another roadblock and have to repeat the process all over again.

As the month of August approached, the towns of Agira and Nicosia fell into American hands and the 1st Infantry reached the outskirts of Troina. Our 2nd Platoon had the honor of reconnoitering the town, which by all reports was very weakly defended. Information received from the prisoners we captured stated that Troina's garrison intended to withdraw and leave only a token force to delay our advance.

Staff Sergeant Smith led our section of the 2nd Platoon on a patrol up Highway 120 to our destination, Troina. The road wound through a valley leading into the town. With all the stone bridges destroyed, our jeeps had a difficult time crossing the dry creek beds. After driving down into the creek bottoms to bypass the rubble, we discovered that the banks on the opposite side were often so steep we could hardly climb out of them.

When we were about a mile from the town, we noticed two or three shell craters next to each demolished bridge. It took a little longer to proceed around these areas. The craters told a story. As at Ferryville in North Africa, we knew that when the Krauts retreated and set up new defensive positions, they zeroed in their guns on certain key locations we had to travel across. After taking a few test shots to establish their range, the German gunners waited for their unsuspecting prey to enter the trap they'd set. The craters made by the test shots tipped us off as to their intentions. Knowing that the 88-millimeter artillery pieces had an effective range of a little over a mile, we figured we were getting close to the enemy.

As we advanced around these shell craters, much to our surprise, we drew no artillery fire. This seemed strange as we knew we were under observation. We wondered if the Krauts were waiting for tanks to follow us, as they would afford the German gunners more important targets. Our nerves were on edge. Above the noise from our jeep engines, we tried to listen for the sound of a mortar or artillery piece being fired in the distance, but the surrounding hills remained silent.

Everyone knew that it would take only a few seconds, once we heard a mortar fire, for the whine of the shell to pass over our heads. Even worse, we dreaded to hear no whine at all, just an ear-piercing shriek that increased in pitch until it became so loud you thought the sound would penetrate the very depths of your soul. If the high-velocity 88s opened up, there would be no warning. Those shells traveled at 2,688 feet per second, over twice as fast as the speed of sound. When they landed, the ground exploded and threw up clouds of disintegrated soil. A second later you'd hear the delayed sound of the incoming projectile. With over 20 pounds of shrapnel flying through the air, if a man was standing when a shell landed next to him, he didn't have much of a chance. No one ever took an artillery barrage lightly, for even if you used every survival trick in the book, your life remained in God's hands.

Nothing happened as we moved cautiously through the valley. Our little column of jeeps crept down Highway 120 and approached the last small hill in front of the town.

Just before reaching its crest, we stopped our vehicles behind a high bank that shielded us on three sides.

Sergeant Smith dismounted and came back to my jeep. "Corporal, pick two or three of your men and come with me," he said. "We better advance the rest of the way on foot. I have a feeling we're inside the jaws of a trap."

In a small notebook inside my shirt pocket, I carried the names of the men in my squad. After returning from a patrol, I always checked off the names of the men who accompanied me. I showed no partiality in combat, for every man had to take his turn. Ted Plasse, one of the new replacements, was the first man I called forward. This would be his first patrol, but so far, he'd proven to be a conscientious soldier. George Porth, the next man on the list, was an old hand at going on patrol.

In staggered formation, we followed Sergeant Smith. After working our way around the bend in the road that led to the top of the hill, we came to a halt. Directly in front of us, situated high on a cliff, stood the picturesque town of Troina looking like a tranquilized vulture resting atop its mountain perch. I expected to see it wake up, then swoop down with projectiles clutched between its talons and devour us.

When were the Germans going to open fire? Had they retreated as the prisoners had told us? We all knew that to be wishful thinking, for the telltale shell craters were beside the blown-out bridges.

Once again we began moving down the road toward the town. Our nerves were as tight as a circus performer's high wire. After going about fifty paces, we reached a point in the road that the Krauts must have agreed was to be the limit of our advance. The vulture on the hilltop came to life. From that moment on, we knew it intended to protect the nest it sat on, the town of Troina. The wings of the great war bird were stretched over the hills on either side of the town, and we could hear them begin to move. They flapped so hard that the valley echoed with the sound of distant thunder. Feathers of hot steel were hurtled toward us from beneath those wings.

It was every man for himself as we scrambled for safety. The deep gutters that carried runoff from the mountains during the rainy season saved us. It's a good thing we didn't have far to retreat. After the first shells landed, we lost sight of each other. The dust stirred up by the shells exploding on the parched soil and the roadbed acted like a smoke screen. By crawling in the gutter, we managed to make it around the bend of the road where we got behind the high bank that concealed our jeeps. The incoming shells hit on the bank above us or else exploded harmlessly below on the far side of the road.

Sergeant Smith's foresight saved our hides. If we'd left the jeeps out in the open, every one of them would have been destroyed. After we got over the initial shock from the devastating barrage, we took a breather, then crawled back to the top of the rise. We were lucky that no troops came forward to attack us. Even though the firing slackened, we were able to pinpoint the location of many of the artillery pieces. They continued to harass us from positions that formed a large arc around the town.

Our mission had been accomplished, for we'd found the latest German line of defense. Troina would most certainly be the next major battlefield in Sicily. If the Germans intended to just use delaying tactics to slow our advance, we'd never have encountered the heavy artillery they were using. The big guns would have pulled out long ago, and they'd have left only automatic weapons and mortars.

Breaking radio silence, Sergeant Smith called the captain and gave him our exact position. Getting out of the trap the Germans set for us became our immediate concern. We knew we were in serious trouble, for every one of those demolished bridges and culverts we'd crossed were zeroed in with artillery and mortars. By letting us advance almost to the town, the Krauts knew we'd have a rough time retreating. Our bodies were wringing wet, and not all the sweat was caused by the 90 degree temperature.

Sergeant Smith figured that if only one vehicle at a time raced back across the area exposed to enemy artillery, the

Germans would concentrate all of their firepower on that lone jeep. Instead, he said we would drive back down the hill, leaving about 100 feet distance between vehicles, then make a mad dash across Troina's "Death Valley." By giving the German artillery observers so many targets to shoot at, we just might be able to confuse them. This same tactic had worked at the close of the African Campaign, east of Lac de Bizerte. Troop C made its famous mounted cavalry charge that day, which was later written up in an official War Department document.

I looked at my jeep driver, George Johnson, and said, "George, before the war, you were a milkman in Maryland. From some of the stories you've told me, you were pretty darn good at your job. When it comes our turn to move out, don't drive this jeep like you did that milk truck. Don't worry about breaking any glass bottles of milk. Make believe you're carryin' a load of cream that has to be churned into butter."

George and I were scheduled to bring up the rear of the column. Before starting out, everyone secured anything in their vehicle that might bounce out when we hit rough terrain. Sergeant Smith took the point position and raced from behind the bank that concealed us. When he got about 100 yards out, the second jeep followed. As soon as the artillery observers spotted what we were doing, they gave the signal for their gunners to open fire. The intensity of the shelling increased until it looked like someone had lit a string of Chinese firecrackers and thrown them into the valley.

By firing so many shells, the Krauts were actually helping us escape. The valley began to look as if a sandstorm was passing through. Because George and I moved out last, we were never visible to the Kraut observers. Only by keeping next to the gutter could George tell that we were still on the roadbed. At each blown-out bridge that we approached, shells exploded close to their prearranged targets. The noise was deafening. How my milkman buddy ever managed to drive between the bursts, I'll never know.

A couple of times, George almost got the jeep stuck in

shell craters. At one point he had to drive down a dry creek bed until I found a spot suitable for him to climb out. Because he'd reached the outside limits of the dust stirred up from the shelling, an observer spotted us. George's foot pressed the gas pedal to the floorboards as the gunner tried to zero in on us. The Krauts must have thought George was driving a milk wagon pulled by an old gray mare, for their shells kept falling short. They underestimated the jeep's speed and also the capabilities of a man used to driving in the city traffic of Baltimore, Maryland.

Having grown up in the 1920s and '30s, I well remember the fast getaway cars the moonshiners used to deliver their liquor, but no bootlegger ever had a better driver than George. Once we reached the protective cover of dust and it swallowed us, the artillery observer could only guess our location. The jeep wound up with a large shrapnel hole in the hood and a leaky radiator. Miraculously, thanks to George's superb driving, we never received so much as a scratch.

The Germans weren't the only ones watching the wild dash of the crazy American cavalrymen. When we reached the head of the valley and crossed over the hill to safety, two jeeps were parked there. The high-ranking officers in them were anxiously awaiting our report.

Like a sow bear protecting her cubs, Sergeant Smith remained in his jeep until the last vehicle limped to safety. Only after George and I pulled in alongside him did he dismount and walk over to our captain. I watched the two officers get out of their vehicles and move toward him. They were both generals. On the shoulder of one officer, I noticed a patch with a big red "1," the insignia of the 1st Infantry Division. With two stars on the front of his helmet, I knew the officer had to be General Terry Allen, commander of the division.

When I walked over and stood beside Sergeant Smith, the other general approached the group. He wanted to hear the report. None of us had to be told the name of this general. We'd seen him in Africa. He wore cavalry boots and breeches, like the ones many of us wore in the horse cavalry. On his hip he carried an ivory-handled pistol. Only one person we knew of dressed like that in Sicily: General George Patton, our 7th Army commander.

General Patton had hoped to drive right through the town of Troina without much trouble. He then expected to continue east on Route 120 to Randazzo and proceed northeast to Messina. If he could accomplish this fast enough, he'd be able to outflank General Montgomery and his troops. The British and Canadians moving north along the east coast of Sicily were running into stiff resistance south of the active volcano, Mount Etna. We could see the 10,741-foot-high smoky mountain standing in incredible beauty about 30 miles away.

Our recon report showed that Troina had to be the pivot point in the German line of defense that extended across the northeastern section of the island. Once Troina fell, the enemy facing Montgomery would be forced to retreat or else be trapped.

The 1st and 9th Infantry Divisions moving up through the mountainous country of central Sicily had come to a screeching halt. The 3rd and 45th Infantry and the 2nd Armored Divisions were performing miracles along the northern coast. The 3rd Infantry even made an amphibious landing behind the German lines. Patton didn't care which of his two forces reached Messina first, just so one of them got there ahead of his rival, Montgomery. His ego had to be satisfied no matter what the cost.

Sicily became a contest between two great generals, each trying to make a name for himself. Not only did they want to win battles, they wanted to win a personal victory that would be recorded in their grandchildren's history books. The poor foot soldiers in both of the Allied armies bore the brunt of the game their commanders played. When the contest ended, no matter which general won, it would be the foot soldiers who paid for the victory with their blood.

Standing beside Sergeant Smith as he made his report, I could have reached out and touched General Patton. For once he remained silent; the anger came later. As the sergeant's story unfolded, telling of the location of the guns surrounding Troina, I noticed the expression change on General Patton's face. He had listened to the intensity of the shelling we'd received and witnessed our race across the valley.

I'd heard tell of Patton's impatient and highly emotional nature but never witnessed it before. I didn't realize how irritable he could become, not until he learned that his hopes of an easy and early victory were shattered. Not just a victory over the crack German 15th Panzer Grenadier Division that faced us, but a victory over his rival, General Montgomery. Patton was determined to prove to the world that the American soldier shouldn't be treated like a second-class fighting man.

General Allen and General Patton left after hearing the disheartening report. On August 3, General Patton stopped at the village of Nicosia, just a few miles down the road from Troina. There in the 15th Evacuation Hospital, his temper almost cost him his army career.

General Patton had a great deal of respect for the wounded soldiers in his command. When he questioned a soldier in the hospital who showed no outward sign of being wounded, the general exploded. He slapped the young soldier in the face, cursed him, and booted him in the pants. Though he wore no bandages, the soldier suffered from battle fatigue and had a temperature of 102 degrees.

Did Patton take his frustrations out on that soldier from L Company of the 1st Infantry Division because he'd learned that his 7th Army couldn't advance rapidly through Troina? A week later, on August 10 in a field hospital, Patton slapped another soldier several times. Many people, upon learning about the incidents, were of the opinion that Patton should have been admitted to the hospital and treated for his own emotional problems.

Patton sometimes acted like a god in front of his men, but he was only human. Like most of us, he too became stressed out when things went wrong. Thus far in the campaign, his 7th Army had surpassed all expectations of the task given them, but that didn't satisfy Patton's ego. After being rebuffed by Montgomery earlier in the campaign, he'd set his own goal. Patton wanted the 7th to be the first Allied army to enter Messina. Things had to go his way, or else. None of us will ever know the pressures this goal placed upon him. Patton wanted to share the center of the stage with no one, not even his subordinate generals. It must have been heartbreaking to have his dream so close to being fulfilled, then be told that final victory might slip through his fingers.

General Eisenhower severely reprimanded Patton for the way he acted in the field hospitals. We are fortunate that Eisenhower let him continue to use his superior knowledge of tank warfare and command an army in Europe. If Patton had returned to the States, we'd have lost the services of probably the most controversial, but also the greatest general the United States produced in World War II.

To become a successful leader in battle, a good warrior must put aside any feelings of animosity or compassion he has toward his fellow man. Down through the ages, most generals have been trained to achieve victory at any cost. General Montgomery's antagonistic attitude toward the Americans stirred up Patton's emotions of pride and love for his fellow countrymen. Patton probably felt that his own character had been attacked. This remained the main cause of conflict between the two great military leaders.

It didn't take long for the 1st Infantry Division to move forward and get into position to attack Troina. The battle proved to be one of the toughest engagements the Allies encountered in Sicily. After the campaign ended, we learned that the newspapers back in the States reported that Troina fell the same day Troop C made its report to General Patton. How we all wished the optimistic newspaper headlines had been true.

On the first of August, the 1st Infantry Division gave A, B and C Troops of the 91st Recon the task of attacking a couple of the hills surrounding the town. As usual, every troop had a different objective and never came in contact with each other. The infantrymen of the "Big Red One" bore the brunt of the attack. The 91st played only a minor role in the battle.

Once again our vehicles were left behind the front lines,

and we became dismounted cavalry. As Troop C advanced up its assigned hill, a shell hit close to me. The concussion knocked my helmet off. When my head cleared, even though I felt no pain, I looked down at my left leg to see if it had been hit. When would I ever get over the feeling I was going to lose it?

Since the African Campaign, I'd learned that to survive, a person must think and act like a cat. Your reflexes need to be tuned to a high pitch, and you continually have to listen for an artillery piece firing in the distance. Unless it is an air burst, if you don't hit the dirt a split second before a shell lands, chances are you'll never get a second chance. Once a shell explodes, the shrapnel sprays upward and out, much like the branches on a tree. If you aren't lying flat on the ground under those branches, it is too late.

The last shell that exploded caused me to remain for a few moments where I'd dropped to the ground. After my head cleared, my eyes focused on a shiny metal object that lay in the spot where my face pressed the parched soil. I picked up the piece of metal, and upon further examination saw that it was a religious medal. It contained a picture of the Madonna. Not being a Catholic, I never realized the name of the medal I'd found. I knew that if I hadn't landed in that exact spot, I probably would have been killed, for there were shell craters all around me. After placing the medal in my shirt pocket, I continued my advance along with the rest of the platoon.

Most of the men were exhausted and thirsty before we were halfway up the hill. With the heat so intense, we thought we'd never make it to the top without water. Most of our canteens were empty. One of the fellows in my squad found a stagnant pool of water, the remains of a dried-up spring. He lay down, submerged his face in the warm liquid and quenched his thirst. After he finished drinking, I crawled over to the puddle, which by now was stirred up and muddy, and put my face into the slimy mess. The water stank almost as bad as the overflow from our old outhouse back home. At least it was wet, and that's all

Army Pictorial Service photo of The Recon Scout,
Fred H. Salter—Italy, 1944

Fred in his Sunday go-to-meetin' hat—1941

Jake and Fred
The trapping partners make "hillbilly music"—1940

# Fred in the Horse Calvary

"Sittin' on
the old top rail"

Cavalry mounts
and stables

Inspection

Ten-minute break

A cavalryman's noblest companion

Headin' for the water trough

Empty manure wagons

Enjoying a Sunday break
from Stable Police

The waterin' trough

Full dress uniform

A pose for the folks
back home

Cleaning machine guns on the Troop Street

Recon chow hound

Gaeta, Italy, May 19, 1944. Medics Manley and Gentry attending "Pop" Haggerty at the blown-out bridge.

Kneeling:: George Johnson (Fred's driver). Standing, left to right: Ray Matazewski, Vic Molinski, Fred, and Charley Hester

Maj. Gen. Geoffrey Keyes awarding the Silver Star to Cpl. Fredrick H. Salter for gallantry in action on the Fifth Army front in Italy. Corporal Salter is with a reconnaissance squadron.

that mattered. I swallowed my first mouthful, but when I took the second gulp, I felt a couple of soft squirmy objects slide down my throat. When I looked down into the puddle, I noticed it contained dozens of large, juicy leeches. I'd reduced their numbers.

It is interesting, when you think of some of the strange thoughts that flash across a person's mind at a time like that. I thought of the Bible story of Jonah and the whale, and out loud I said, "Well, Jonah, I hope you have a good trip before you come out the other end. Don't stop along the way."

Under different circumstances, I probably would have been upset. At the time, all I cared about was getting relief for my parched throat in the 90 degree heat.

When we reached the top of the hill, all of us were played out. Not only were we fighting the Germans, but also the elements of the hot Sicilian summer. We wasted no time in digging in our machine guns and setting up our defensive positions. Al Jerman, who'd taken me to a Catholic Mass back in North Africa, dug his foxhole next to mine. I told Al about the medal I'd found on the ground next to where my head rested.

After examining the medal, he said, "Fred, that's a miraculous medal, it probably saved your life."

How it got up on the side of the mountain overlooking Troina remains a mystery. I attached it to the chain around my neck that held my dog tags. All through the war, I carried the medal. The tiny symbol of faith made a believer out of me.

It would be six more days before Troina fell and the Germans retreated toward Randazzo. Troina had been defended by the German 15th Panzer Grenadier Division. They lost an estimated 1,600 men in the battle.

On August 7, as we moved slowly through the town, the stench filled the air with the smell of death. After six days of lying in the 90 degree and higher temperatures, the bodies of the dead animals and fallen soldiers from both armies were bloated, almost to bursting. Blowflies covered the corpses, and when I saw them feasting on the flesh of my fellow humans, I almost vomited.

The town lay in ruins. Most of the inhabitants who hadn't fled from the battle took refuge in the cellars beneath the stone buildings. Those civilians not buried alive crawled out from beneath the mass of rubble they'd once called home. Some survivors brought their dead friends and relatives with them and began to dig graves.

The battlefield remained silent, as if God had never given man the capability to hear, only gave him two eyes to look upon the world of horror and senses to smell the stench of death. The solitude seemed only a time for mourning, making you realize that war has no victors.

I came upon a sight I will never forget, a father and mother burying their infant child. I can still see the tears flowing down the dust-stained face of the heartbroken mother as she hugs her dead child to her breast. What words of comfort could a young soldier say to the parents of that child to help ease the pain?

Like thousands of other families in war-torn countries, that poor family became the innocent victim of a war that both sides would lose. Even though we would eventually wind up the victor, thousands of mothers in America would hold to their bosoms the precious memories of their sons lost in combat just as that poor Sicilian mother held her only child to her breast.

After the Sicilian campaign ended, I wrote this poem about Troina.

### AFTER THE SMOKE HAD CLEARED

*Many tales have been told of battles,*
*Of bloodshed and horrors of war,*
*How men struggle to kill one another,*
*For the cause they are fighting for.*

*There are stories untold in the headlines,*
*Of the crippled, helpless, and aged*
*Who are caught between two great armies,*
*While a battle is being waged.*

*We were after a town on a mountain,*
*"No-Man's-Land," the valley between.*
    *Both armies brought up more artillery*
*Than all other battles had seen.*

    *For six days artillery kept pounding.*
*Day and night the doughboys fought hard.*
    *Overhead, the planes strafed and dive-bombed.*
*The valley, with craters was scarred.*

    *Down among the fields and the meadows,*
*Which once had been covered with grain,*
    *Lay the bodies of slaughtered cattle,*
*And the trampled wheat, red with stain.*

    *The six days of conflict had ruined*
*Many years of sweat and hard toil.*
    *It not only destroyed the buildings,*
*But the crops, the cattle, and soil.*

    *Our forces pushed into the valley,*
*And we passed the ruins and dead.*
    *Where once there stood bridges and churches,*
*Lay huge piles of loose rock instead.*

    *The worst scene of all was a mother*
*With tears streaming down her sad face*
    *That fell on the curls of the dead child*
*She held in her arms, wrapped in lace.*

    *Her husband beside her was digging,*
*A grave for the child she held there,*
    *For it had been caught in the cross fire,*
*Crawling from its shelter for air.*

    *When you read of bombings or battles,*
*Don't just think of the soldiers there,*

> *Remember, there might be young children,*
> *Who hardships of war also share.*
>
> *The young children like all the soldiers,*
> *And when they call, "Bonbon," and wave,*
> *A young man just can't be refusing*
> *To throw them the candy he's saved.*
>
> *I'm thankful that God spared our country,*
> *And the bombs aren't falling back home*
> *Where our loved ones and all the children*
> *In peace, o'er the hillsides can roam.*

After the battle of Troina, the 9th Infantry Division relieved the 1st Infantry. The vehicles of Troops A and B of the 91st Recon were brought forward, and the two troops reconnoitered toward Randazzo. Troop B had the honor of entering the town ahead of the other Allied forces. They linked up with the Canadian troops of the British 8th Army on the right flank.

The 2nd Platoon of Troop C was given the mission of traveling over the mountains north of Troina. There were no roads in this sector of the island. We were instructed to establish an observation post overlooking the sea and spy on the Germans fighting General Patton's forces along the northern coastal road. Patton wanted to know the results of the Allied naval shelling being carried out against the retreating Germans. When the 3rd Infantry Division's recon reached our position, we were instructed to make contact with them.

Patton intended to learn all he could about the enemy's defenses and their troop strength. If at all possible, he wanted to continue making amphibious landings along the coast behind the enemy's lines. He was still determined to win the race to Messina.

The 2nd Platoon started out on its assigned mission, mounted in jeeps and Tom Thompson's lone scout car. We traveled over terrain unfit for a Missouri mule, let alone a vehicle. Once again, Joe Montoro's proficiency in speaking the Italian language saved the day. Joe became friendly with a native who knew a trail over the 5,000-foot-high mountains that led to the northern coast.

As we wound our way over the rugged terrain, the low-hanging clouds saved us from being detected by the Germans. Many times we had to dismount and push Tom's scout car up the trail. Our Sicilian guide led us over the crest of the mountains, and before long we descended the slope leading to the coast. We knew if we were forced to retreat, it would be impossible to take our vehicles back over the treacherous terrain. It was Friday, August 13, 1943, a fateful day for anyone superstitious. We wondered if it would turn out to be our unlucky day.

Before we reached the bottom of the forward slope, we spotted a small town up ahead. It overlooked Route 113, the main road that ran along the seacoast. Our guide told us to remain hidden, while he went forward to see if there were any enemy troops in the vicinity. A short while later he came running toward us, waving his arms for us to go back over the mountains. He said there were 400 Germans stationed in the town.

Our guide wasn't the only person excited and scared, for we knew we couldn't retreat. If worse came to worst, we'd go on the defensive and use our machine guns and mortar. Hopefully, we might be able to hold the Krauts off until Patton and the 3rd Infantry Division advancing along the coast came to our rescue.

Against his better judgment, Al Jerman, our radio operator, broke radio silence and contacted our rear command post for instructions. When II Corps headquarters learned of our whereabouts, they told our captain that we'd read the wrong coordinates on our map. We couldn't possibly be where we claimed, for the location we'd given would put us 20 miles behind the German lines.

After rechecking our position on the map and giving the captain the name of the town in front of us, II Corps relayed this message over the radio. "If at all possible, remain hidden and send out patrols. Keep us informed of German troop movements on the coastal highway."

Throughout the whole campaign, the Sicilian people were very cooperative with the Americans. Though Italy still remained allied with the Axis powers, the peasants were always sympathetic to our cause. The townspeople kept our position secret from the Germans in the area. Later that night they brought us food, water and wine.

As soon as we learned about the large force of Germans in the town, Sergeant Smith picked out a good defensive position on the hillside, and we set up our machine guns. Thanks to the Sicilian people, Friday the 13th reversed its tradition of bad luck. It turned out to be one of the luckiest days of our lives. August the 14th might be a different story, for if the 400 Germans suspected we were in the vicinity and they attacked, it would be impossible to hold our position for any length of time. We were too far behind the German lines to expect reinforcements to reach us or to be resupplied with ammunition. None of us slept that night, for we expected the worst; it never came.

The Italian and Sicilian people are world famous for their dramatic performances and acting ability. The following morning, a group of these would-be actors, pretending to be German sympathizers, approached the German commander stationed in the town. They informed him that a large force of American infantry had left Troina, and were seen heading over the mountains. They told the worried officer that the Americans intended to attack his unit from the rear, then link up with General Patton's army. The German commander realized he would be trapped if Patton kept advancing and a sizable force cut him off from the coastal road.

The townspeople were trying to avoid a conflict, for they didn't want their town to become a battleground and be destroyed. This is the main reason the Sicilian informers staged such a good bluff.

When a German patrol returned, and reported having seen the forward elements of an American scouting party above them on the side of the mountain, the German commander immediately prepared to evacuate the town. What the Germans had spotted were a couple of men from our platoon gathering information about the American navy shelling of the coastal road. A short time later the entire German force retreated without a shot being fired.

We kept our vehicles camouflaged and continued to observe the Germans retreating toward Messina. Many Italian soldiers threw down their rifles and returned to the town. They exchanged their army uniforms for civilian clothes furnished gladly by the townspeople. The Italian soldiers, even though they looked well fed and clean, were sick and tired of war. All they wanted to do was go home to their families.

When we saw Patton's forces advancing along the coast, we left the town and followed the retreating Germans. The Krauts continued to fight an orderly withdrawal along the coastal road. This enabled the bulk of their army to get safely across the Strait of Messina into Italy. Patrols from the 3rd Infantry Division entered the city of Messina on the evening of August 17th. Much to the disgust of General Montgomery, the Americans arrived there only a few hours ahead of his gallant British troops. After 38 days of fighting a well-organized and stubborn German army in mountainous terrain and sweltering temperatures, the British 8th and the American 7th Armies conquered Sicily.

Montgomery, Britain's brilliant and greatest general, was largely responsible for the defeat of the Afrika Korps at El Alamein. His fellow countrymen also came to the rescue of the inexperienced American II Corps in southern Tunisia. After this event took place, Montgomery held a very low opinion of the American soldier, and his judgment wasn't easily reversed. Everyone now hoped that after seeing how well the "Yanks" had performed in Sicily, he would change his attitude and consider them equal to his own troops. One thing for certain, he would never again underestimate the fighting ability of his rival, General George Patton.

A couple of days after leaving the northern coast, the 2nd Platoon rejoined Troop C. Once again, the troops of the squadron were reunited. We traveled to Randazzo, then visited the active volcano, Mount Etna. The squadron proceeded northwest along the coast, driving through Termini on our way to Palermo.

In the capital city, we listened to Patton make a victory speech, much like the one we'd heard after the African Campaign. General Eisenhower ordered Patton to apologize to his troops and the hospital personnel for his inappropriate behavior when he slapped the two soldiers in the field hospitals. In his self-important way he did apologize, but he never humbled himself in front of his men. After the ceremony, we were scheduled to reorganize our squadron in the vicinity of Castelvetrano, south of Palermo.

On our travels to the new bivouac area, we enjoyed watching the Sicilian people harvesting grapes. Young children walked around on top of the carts loaded with the fruit fresh from the vines. They stomped the ripe grapes with bare feet that were covered with the powdered soil of Sicily, making the bright-colored juices ooze up between their toes. Maybe this age-old practice was responsible for the Italian wines having such a distinct, down-to-earth flavor.

The Sicilian people are very artistic, and all of their carts are painted with beautiful designs. Though hard-working, the majority of the people are poor, partly because of the sparse rainfall for growing crops. The soil on the western side of the rocky island, after having been cultivated for centuries by one conqueror after another, isn't well suited for crops. The volcanic ash deposited on the eastern part of Sicily during the eruptions of Mount Etna helps to make that area very fertile.

Before reaching Castelvetrano, we swam once again in the beautiful blue waters of the Mediterranean. For the first time since leaving the States, we were served fresh meat and hot dogs. A ship loaded with fresh food had just arrived at the port of Palermo.

Upon arriving at our bivouac area, we received new equipment and replacements. Our squadron once again returned to full combat strength. During the remainder of our tour in Sicily, we trained and ran patrols along the northern coast. We remained on the lookout for landing parties trying to sabotage or spy on the Allies' preparations for invading Italy.

Our first day in Castelvetrano, we held a big party to celebrate the end of another campaign. The townspeople furnished us with wine and companionship. By early evening, nearly everyone in the troop "felt no pain."

Tom, my buddy in the 2nd Platoon, must have contracted a severe stomach or intestinal disorder, for he continually expelled gas. We figured that maybe the combination of hot peppers and wine he'd been consuming might have something to do with his problem. No matter what type of food he ate, it all seemed to ferment. Now, gas is lighter than air and usually rises, but my friend's gas wasn't the kind to head skyward and make him belch. When large quantities of it are produced in a container with more than one outlet, as the pressure builds up, gas seeks an opening with the least resistance.

Tom's gas defied all the laws of physics and traveled south, eventually being expelled out the lower end of his torso. I have to admit, the gas didn't smell quite as bad as that made by the sulfur and molasses my mother fed me every springtime for a tonic. Even so, the volume produced could very well have filled a balloon capable of spying over the enemy's lines. During those trying days my buddy suffered with the problem, I sometimes wondered how he ever stayed on the ground.

The 2nd Platoon had moved its gear and bedrolls into a large building with a concrete floor. With everyone in a fun-loving mood, a group of the fellows started making bets that the gas Tom kept generating would burn. He had consumed just enough wine to cloud his thinking, so he readily consented to participate in the experiment. It was almost dark when one of the fellows had our good buddy drop his trousers and bend over. One of the men produced a cigarette lighter to use as a torch, and everyone gathered around to witness the end results of the test.

Tom knelt on the concrete floor and bent over in a horizontal position with his hands on the floor. He reminded me of a Civil War cannon, loaded and primed, with its fuse about to be lit. While waiting for him to generate a fresh supply of gas, we discussed the possibility that the alcohol content of the large quantity of wine he'd consumed might make the expected explosion volatile. With everyone's mind befuddled from alcohol, we decided to continue with the project anyway. To be on the safe side, we pointed Tom toward the front door and opened it just in case he took off like a rocket. At least he wouldn't hurt himself, that is, unless the wide shoulders of his six-foot-three-inch frame hit one of the doorjambs on the way out.

After waiting a few minutes, when no gas erupted from the rear of our human cannon, Keith Royer and I decided to help nature speed up the process. We knelt down on each side of Tom. With our hands clasped beneath his belly, we pushed forcefully upward on his stomach. Almost immediately, a swishing sound came from his mouth, like air escaping from a balloon. When our clasped hands began to vibrate and we heard a rumbling noise above them, we knew that we'd succeeded in making his stomach and intestines release their latest accumulation of fermentation.

With one hand resting atop the rear end of the cannon, and the other holding the lighter in front of the fuse hole, the torch holder became impatient waiting for Tom to generate gas. Not realizing the dangerous spot he was in, the very moment we put upward pressure on Tom's stomach, the torch holder bent his head down to see if there were any obstructions in his end of the operation. That mistake almost proved fatal.

Before any gas could escape, a lone piece of semihard fecal material blocking the lower intestine had to be removed. The sudden pressure we'd applied on Tom's stomach did the trick. Like a cork popping out of a bottle of champagne, the round cannonball-like obstruction shot out the fuse hole and hit the torch holder smack dab on the forehead. You'd have thought the projectile had a point detonating fuse attached to it, for on impact, it exploded. It's a good thing Tom wasn't constipated, or the torch holder would have been a goner.

Unlike a gun that shoots flame out the muzzle end, this cannon backfired out the breech. A blue flame, about three feet long, shot out the rear end of the cannon and burnt the eyebrows off the inebriated torch holder. The poor fellow's forehead looked like a preacher had just baptized him in the basement of an outhouse with the only material available. By the looks of his eyebrows, you'd have sworn he stuck his head too close to the fire and brimstone spewing from the gates of purgatory. If the experiment had killed the torch holder and Tom, how would the army have explained their deaths to the next of kin? Our two buddies would have been killed in action, but what type of action? Maybe the government report would have read, "Killed in action by cannon fire."

The only other casualties of the operation were a few singed hairs around the fuse hole and the reproductive organ of our buddy. The experiment ended, reminding me of a firecracker that failed to explode, one that just hissed and fizzled, then petered out.

Everyone whooped and hollered with joy, even Tom. With the pressure released from his stomach, he felt relieved, but the pain from his singed bottom hadn't had time to register in his brain. It's a good thing an internal explosion didn't occur, for we could easily have lost one heck of a good comrade. Later, none of us could agree on how far forward the rocketlike flame had pushed Tom across the slippery concrete floor. At least he didn't fly out through the door.

Once again, we were all beginning to relax, trying to forget the hardships and sorrows of the last few weeks.

A few minutes after completing the comical experiment, our laughter was interrupted by the sound of a machine gun firing on the outskirts of town. The excited townspeople who had helped to make our celebration possible came running to us for help. They told us that either the "Black Hand," or a secret organization like the Mafia, had captured a stockpile of automatic weapons and an ammunition dump. The villains were terrorizing the town.

Our 2nd Platoon officer called us together and said we would have to silence the machine gun. With our weapons slung over our shoulders and a few hand grenades hanging from our belts, the slightly inebriated members of the 2nd Platoon marched to the edge of town. We could still hear the machine gun firing on the opposite side of the large olive grove.

Our lieutenant, like most of the men in the platoon, still remained under the effects of the wine he'd consumed. He could hardly maneuver, but he said, "Corporal Salter, take my flashlight and one man from your squad. Go out in the middle of that olive grove. Take protection as best you can behind a couple of tree trunks. Give the rest of us ten minutes so we can divide up the platoon and get ready to attack that machine gun from both sides. When you think we've had enough time to get in position, shine your flashlight around the olive grove and draw their fire. Leave the rest up to us. We'll move in on them from each side and wipe that gun out."

I will always believe that our lieutenant picked me for the job because I remained one of the only squad leaders in the platoon still halfway sober.

I didn't have to look in my notebook to find out the name of the next man on my roster scheduled for patrol duty. William Roscoe, from Wrightstown, New Jersey, a fine young boy and a conscientious soldier, had joined our outfit as a replacement after the African Campaign. I tapped Bill on the shoulder and said, "Roscoe, it's your turn."

Roscoe looked dejected and sad, but his voice showed no sign of fear. I knew he wasn't thinking of himself when he said, "Fred, please pick someone else for this mission. At mail-call today I received a letter from my wife. She just gave birth to a baby boy. I'm a father now, Fred, and I want to live to see my son. We're being ordered to go out there and commit suicide."

When Roscoe told me his reason for not wanting to go on the mission, I understood how he felt. My heart went out to him, but regrettably, not my conscience. For a moment, I hesitated, then I realized we'd been given an order by a superior officer. My thoughts flashed back to a similar incident that had happened only a few months previous. In Tunisia, another man in my squad, Henderson, had spoken almost those exact same words.

"Dear God," I thought, "please don't let the same thing happen again."

I had a difficult decision to make, but someone had to go with me. I said, "I'm sorry Roscoe, let's go."

Most of the men in our outfit were single and, like me, they never realized the pressures and responsibilities resting on a married man's shoulders. With a wife and son back in the States waiting for his return, Roscoe, like most married men in combat, had a family that was forever in his thoughts. I often wondered how married men could put their lives on the line day after day and still keep up their courage. Like Roscoe, most of them did.

Roscoe and I survived the crazy mission assigned to us that night. That episode reminded me of the many life-threatening decisions I'd made concerning the fate of other men's lives. It was probably just as hard for our lieutenant to give me that stupid order as for me to pick Roscoe for the job. Many of the commands given by a few of our superiors were difficult to obey. Most of the time I never held ill feelings against our lieutenant for an order he gave me in the line of duty. He was an excellent combat officer and I respected him. Someone had to make decisions and give the orders, but "rather him than me."

While we were bivouacked at Castelvetrano, I suffered my first attack of malaria. My fever never reached the point where I became delirious, but I wound up with scabs all over my body caused by the high temperature.

Decorations were awarded in Sicily for deeds performed above and beyond the call of duty in the African Campaign. Joe Montoro, Charles Atherton, from Calhoun, Kentucky, and I were cited for knocking out a German 88-millimeter gun. It had held up the advance of the 1st Armored Division during one of the tank battles in northern Tunisia. The Bronze Star later replaced the award.

On one occasion in Sicily, Sergeant Ogg from the 3rd Platoon called for mortar support. He ordered our guns brought forward to knock out a machine-gun nest that had stopped our advance. The mortars and their shells were too heavy to pack very far on our backs in the rough terrain. Unless we could drive a jeep close to where the guns were to be set up, we very seldom used them.

The casualty list for the Sicilian campaign hadn't been as high as in Africa. After one engagement with the enemy, one of my buddies, a machine-gun operator nicknamed Shorty Miller, showed me his helmet. The lead scout car in the 1st Platoon had encountered a roadblock. The Germans began firing a 20-millimeter cannon at the vehicle. One of the bullets entered the front side of my friend's helmet and came out the back, never touching his head. For a few days following the incident, Shorty still had a terrific headache. The impact of the bullet almost knocked him unconscious. If the shell had been a half inch closer to his skull, the war would have ended for my friend. Close calls such as that were not uncommon during combat.

The Sicilian Campaign turned out to be one continuous roadblock after another on the narrow mountain roads. It took only a couple of Germans to blow up a bridge and halt a large column of advancing soldiers. A well-placed machine gun overlooking the rubble made it extremely difficult to proceed.

Arthur Taliferro, one of the scout car drivers, lost his life in Sicily as his vehicle approached one of these roadblocks. He took a direct hit when he raised his head above the turret of the scout car.

In Sicily, a comical incident happened to Pop Haggerty

from our 2nd Platoon. Pop got his nickname from being the oldest man in the platoon. To us kids, anyone in his thirties was ancient. Pop liked his wine and always managed to have a bottle handy, even when we were on the front lines.

One day while we lay concealed, trying to figure out the best way to eliminate a troublesome machine gun, Pop thought he might as well have a drink to quench his thirst. With a scorching hot sun overhead, we lay in the gutter alongside the road, pinned down by the gun hidden somewhere above us in the rocks. No one noticed Pop take a bottle of wine out of his pack. We saw him roll over on his back but didn't realize his intentions, not until he raised the bottle up in the air so the liquid could flow down his parched throat. Pop happened to tip the bottle up a bit too high where it became visible above the top of the ditch. The bright Sicilian sun, reflecting through the reddish wine, attracted the attention of the machine gunner. It probably seemed like an excellent target.

Pop took his tongue away from the opening of the bottle to let the wine trickle down his throat. At that moment, the machine gunner squeezed off a few rounds and made a direct hit. The glass shattered just above the neck of the bottle. Another inch lower and Pop would have lost a hand. If the bullets had only sheared off the bottom of the bottle, some of the precious liquid might have been saved.

The German machine gunner probably had a good laugh and must have thought, "If I can't have a drink, then you can't have one either."

If you've never seen a mad Irishman, you should have been there the day the Krauts spilled wine all over our Irish buddy. Pop seemed more concerned about losing a good bottle of wine than about almost losing his hand.

We enjoyed our rest period at Castelvetrano and the patrols that took us along the coast of the island, but "Times, they were a changin'." General Eisenhower disbanded the 7th Army. The 1st Infantry Division, along with General Patton, made ready to depart for England. General Mark Clark, stationed back in North Africa, became commander of the American 5th Army, which would soon invade Italy.

When General Patton left, we lost a great leader and one of the most dedicated soldiers in the entire army. People read and listened to news reports back in the States telling of the victories gained by their husbands, sons and friends under the leadership of General Patton. These patriotic citizens praised his achievements to "high heaven."

Far behind the front lines, the tactical decisions and plans for the campaigns were being made by high-ranking officers. These men determined the strategy to be used in achieving a victory. They knew that a price in lives had to be paid in order to gain that victory. "We will lose so many men taking our objective," they figured, "but the cost will be worth it."

Were they correct in their assumption that losing a few men is a small price to pay for gaining an important piece of real estate? You might not totally agree with their way of thinking, especially if you were a foot soldier participating in the battle to conquer that property. You were only concerned with the question, "Will I become one of the expected casualties?"

Put yourself in the shoes of the soldier who carries the gun into battle, the man or young boy continuously under fire day after day, sometimes week after week. Only then can you begin to understand the difference in thinking between an infantryman and a high-ranking officer who only occasionally visits the front lines. That officer can come to the battlefield and experience firsthand the shelling and a few of the horrors of war, much the same as the foot soldier. There is a great difference between the two men. If the going becomes rough, the officer knows that he can return behind the front lines for a reprieve, knowing that the foot soldier will carry out his orders.

After a man spends a certain amount of time under fire, he often reaches a breaking point. The length of time that a soldier can endure the shelling and the physical and psychological stress of combat before he finally breaks, differs with each man. When a foot soldier reaches the limit of his physical and mental endurance, an officer from head-quarters, who has not experienced the same battlefield conditions, might not have sympathy for him. The officer might not understand that the battle-weary infantryman, whether he be an enlisted man or combat officer, is not a coward, but just another human being who has given his all, with nothing left to give.

When General Patton slapped one of those combat soldiers in the field hospital in Sicily, maybe he didn't realize that the man had reached his breaking point. As a combat soldier, I remember only too clearly the time I almost reached mine. Unlike a general visiting the front lines, thousands of men who were in my position didn't have the opportunity to turn their backs on their comrades in the foxholes and return to safety.

Along with "The Desert Fox," General Erwin Rommel, and the British general, Sir Bernard Montgomery, General Patton was one of the greatest generals that ever took part in modern warfare. Though I disagree with much of his way of thinking, I am proud to tell my children and grandchildren that I once served under General George Patton, the man who lived up to his nickname, "Old Blood and Guts."

We all dream of living in a world free from wars, but that is an impossibility. Usually, the persons responsible for starting wars don't have to do the actual fighting. They don't have to look a man in the eye, wondering whose blood will be spilled first by the bullets from the guns they are carrying or from the cold pieces of pointed steel gripped in their hands. Maybe if nations sent the men into battle who promoted wars, the common soldier wouldn't have to suffer for the fanatical ideologies of men like Hitler.

Italy surrendered to the Allied powers on September 3, 1943. Many military strategists could see the logic in Winston Churchill's policy of attacking the weak underbelly of Europe. England lost a great majority of its young men in the trenches after they crossed the English Channel into France during World War I. In the terrible months ahead, the German soldier, the mountains, and Mother Nature's unbelievably harsh elements put doubts in the minds of the men sent to carry out Churchill's policy. The terrain of Italy turned out to be a dream come true, but only for the army defending that boot full of mountains. Getting a toehold on that boot became the next objective of the Allies.

**Italy**

# CHAPTER VII

# One More Hill

The landing craft hit the beach with a jolt. A moment later, we leaped into the shallow water. At long last, we'd set foot on the mainland fortress of Europe. Those of us who survived the coming winter would be scarred for life. The physical or mental wounds many of us received came from one of the most bitter campaigns of World War II, the battle to conquer Italy.

The 91st Recon attached to II Corps of the 5th Army didn't participate in the Allied landings at Salerno, a town about 30 miles southeast of Naples. Instead, we crossed the Strait of Messina, landing at the very toe of Italy's boot near the town of Reggio, Calabria. We followed the route taken by General Montgomery's 8th Army up through southern Italy. After winding our way past blown-out bridges and concrete pillboxes, we made contact with the U.S. VI Corps. By the time we reached them, the American forces were bogged down at the Volturno River, north of Naples.

While stationed overseas, American GIs were issued a pack of cigarettes a day, but I didn't smoke. A couple of days before we crossed the Strait of Messina, I traded all of the cigarettes I'd saved in Sicily for an old, battered guitar. After wrapping it in a piece of canvas, I strapped it on the back of my jeep. Once again I was content. Except for my harmonica, we'd been without a musical instrument around the campfires for almost five months.

The guitar couldn't withstand the constant rain of southern Italy's autumn weather, and within a couple of weeks it fell apart. We found the climate in Italy much dif-

ferent from the dry air of North Africa's Sahara Desert
and the plains of Tunisia.

Sergeant Maher and his maintenance crew came to my
rescue. Because most everyone in the troop enjoyed singing,
the sergeant and his men offered to help repair the guitar.
With the main body of the instrument completely destroyed,
the only parts salvageable were the strings, the neck as-
sembly, and the tail piece. One of General Montgomery's
soldiers heard of my plight and donated a large metal
ammunition box to our worthy cause of rebuilding the guitar. The lid on the metal container, when clamped shut,
made the unit waterproof. The box was just a shade smaller
than the body of the original guitar. Sergeant Maher bolted
the neck of the old guitar to one end of the ammunition
box, then soldered the tail piece that held the strings in place
to the opposite end. Even without a hole in the top of the
box to help amplify the sound, no one could believe the fine
tone quality of the finished product. Best of all, we no
longer had to worry about the weather destroying it. The
slightly metallic sound might not have been quite as mellow
as a wooden guitar, but no one complained.

By now, we'd been overseas for almost a year. During
that length of time, I'd written quite a number of poems.
All of them, and the words to most of the other songs we
sang, I kept stored inside of the waterproof guitar.

The people in southern Italy were very poor. What food
they had grown and stored from the previous harvest, the
Germans confiscated. Any extra food we GIs could obtain,
we shared with the undernourished children. Behind the
front lines, whenever our troop set up its kitchen, we dug a
garbage pit to bury the scraps we didn't eat. At mealtime,
against army regulations, Captain Maple, our troop commander, let the starving civilians enter our bivouac area.
Instead of dumping the scraps left in our mess kits into the
pit, we emptied them into the tin cans carried by the starving Italians.

The cold rains of autumn kept us drenched to the skin.
With the Italian winter not far away, most of the time we

were chilled to the bone. Though we were issued rain slickers and long, cumbersome overcoats, I needed a combat jacket. Since I had lost mine in North Africa, the supply sergeant had been unable to get me another one. If only I'd thought about the coming winter when we traveled up through Sicily, I could easily have taken a jacket from a wounded or dead soldier. In the 90-degree-plus temperatures, keeping warm was the farthest thing from my mind. I never realized that certain articles of clothing and equipment were in short supply.

In Sicily, I'd picked up a couple of heavy wool, dark purple German army blankets. I'd rolled them up in my canvas shelter half and used them under my blanket for a mattress. Sleeping on the bare ground could get mighty uncomfortable, even after scraping a hollow in the ground to lay your hip.

One afternoon in the late autumn of 1943, we were bivouacked behind the front lines near the Volturno River. Taking advantage of the lull, everyone kept busy repairing and cleaning their equipment. The sun came out for a change, and I thought, "Now is a good time for me to make a vest out of those old German army blankets." I borrowed George Johnson's combat jacket to use as a pattern, then traced the back and the two front pieces onto the blanket. I'd marked out two pieces of each pattern so that I could double them up and make a warmer vest. After cutting all the material out, I sewed the pieces together.

Back in the States during basic training, we'd been taught how to sew. The instructor even showed us how to darn socks, for the army realized that up on the front lines, we'd probably have to be our own tailors.

After a few pricked fingers caused by a heavy needle in the inept hands of a GI, I finally managed to sew all the pieces of the vest together. I even attached a high collar to keep my neck warm. The finished product wasn't the best-looking job, but at least it would keep me from freezing. After trying it on to make sure it fit, I proceeded to make buttonholes. As a substitute for store-bought buttons, I rolled up inch-and-a-half-wide strips of leather, making a roll about a half inch in diameter. They looked just like buttons that the frontiersmen and early pioneers used on their buckskin jackets. The work became so interesting and rewarding that I never noticed I had an audience until a shadow moved across the soggy ground in front of me.

Upon looking up, there to my surprise stood Captain Maple and Major General Geoffrey Keyes, commander of II Corps. I became so excited that the leather button I'd just finished fell out of my hands. Sitting on the ground Indian fashion with my legs crossed, I made a move to untangle them. Before I could rise off the ground and salute, General Keyes put his hand out and said, "Don't get up, soldier. Keep on with what you're doing. Tell me, what are you making?"

This was the first time I'd ever seen a high-ranking officer, especially a general, pass up an opportunity to have a soldier from out of the ranks snap to attention and salute.

Nervously, I said, "In combat in northern Tunisia near the end of the African Campaign, I lost all of my equipment, including my personal belongings and my jeep. My driver, Henderson, was killed that same day. Since landing in Italy, our supply sergeant hasn't been able to get hold of any combat jackets. The nights are getting colder, and even though I have a heavy overcoat, it is too bulky and noisy to wear on night patrols. That's the reason I decided to make a vest."

The general studied me for a long moment, then glanced down at the crude vest I'd made out of those dark purple army blankets. Later, I thought of how much he reminded me of General George Washington at Valley Forge during that terrible winter of 1777 and 1778. Washington had also been a caring general.

I looked up into General Keyes' face, and I'll never forget his expression. His eyes were slightly moist. If the lines surrounding them, and those rippling across his forehead and radiating from the corners of his mouth, could have spelled out a single word, it would have been "compassion," for that's what he showed me. As corps commander, having the responsibility of leading thousands of men into battle, he took the time to look after the welfare of his combat soldiers.

Turning to Captain Maple, he said, "Captain, send your supply sergeant over to II Corps headquarters. Have him tell the officer in charge that I have personally ordered a combat jacket be sent over here for this soldier. If there are no jackets available, tell him that I've instructed my executive officer to take one from one of my officers at headquarters."

I laid my roughly made vest down on the ground, then stood up and saluted, saying, "Thank you for your kindness, General."

General Keyes had wandered into our bivouac area on an unannounced inspection tour of our troop. That's the reason no one had been prepared for his visit. That evening I wore a combat jacket after having been without one for almost six months. The jacket wasn't new, for there were small holes on the top of the shoulders, indicating that officer's insignias had been removed. Even though I now had a jacket, I saved my handsewn blanket vest and used it many times in the weeks ahead.

There is an irony to the story of the vest, for it, too, was destined to suffer the same fate as the jacket I lost in Africa. Before the end of winter, the vest, along with all of my personal belongings, was blown to smithereens by an artillery shell during the battle for Cassino. Maybe the Germans figured that if they couldn't have those purple blankets to keep them warm, no "Yankee" soldier would benefit from them either.

After the general departed, I wiped moisture from the corners of my eyes. Some of the water ran down my cheek and hit my upper lip. I reached up with my tongue and touched it. When I discovered that it left a salty taste in my mouth, I knew the droplet hadn't come from the cold rain that had started to fall. How I wished that I could have been as great a leader as our general. I respected most officers, for I figured they had to live with their conscience. They had the responsibility of holding a man's life in their hands. The outcome of their decisions determined whether that man lived or died. The lives of a squad of eight men seemed so many for me to be responsible for. Maybe that day along the Volturno River, General Keyes tried to make peace with his own conscience and atone for some of his wrong decisions. Would I ever be able to make peace and heal my soul?

The Italian mud proved to be an ally to the Germans. With our vehicles continually getting bogged down, they were practically useless. We wore rubber overshoes over our combat boots, but they weren't high enough to keep the mud from flowing over the tops and into our shoes and socks. Sometimes the suction of the mud became so great we could hardly lift our feet. It seemed as though we were being pulled toward the center of the earth by a tremendous vacuum.

A foot soldier walked, ate, and slept in the mud. Many of them took their final breath in it. Oftentimes when we were on the front lines, the mud in the foxholes became so bad we thought death would be a welcome relief. As we lay shivering in the wet, cold, coffin-like foxhole of mud, we wondered which was worse, the never-ending exploding shells or the dreadful Italian winter.

If one of us got diarrhea, which was almost a certainty, our troubles were compounded. Many times we'd be pinned down by the enemy, making it impossible to raise our heads out of the foxholes for fear of getting them blown off. With no other place to relieve our bowels, except inside of the foxhole, you can imagine what the living conditions were like. A soldier didn't have to fall asleep to experience a nightmare, for he lived one every day. Trying to survive the harsh winter with no roof over our heads made us realize what all soldiers have known since the beginning of time: "War is hell."

When we were behind the front lines, two men slept beneath a pair of shelter halves buttoned together to make a six-foot-long pup tent. Surrounded by a sea of mud, the tents continually leaked if we touched the underside of them. We dug shallow trenches around the outside of the tents to divert the water, but still couldn't keep it from running under our blankets.

When back in a rest area, George Johnson and I shared a pup tent. We played cards, our favorite games being gin rummy, cassino, and hearts. Many times we played by the light of a candle. If no candles were available, we wrapped a wick around a piece of coiled wire and placed it upright in a tin can full of light oil. The crude lamp didn't furnish much light, but anything was better than spending the long winter evenings in total darkness.

Dry firewood wasn't too plentiful, so we began cutting down the olive trees. With most of the wood unseasoned, we had a difficult time making it burn. It's a wonder there were any olive trees left in Italy by the end of the war. At the time, we were only concerned with trying to keep warm.

Our bivouac area also served as our outdoor laundry room. After building a fire with olive branches, we'd heat a five-gallon bucket of water. When the water started to boil, we put our dirty clothes in the bucket, then stomped the clothes up and down with a pick handle to get the dirt out of them.

Whenever possible, I attended church with Al Jerman. The miraculous medal I'd picked up on the battlefield in Sicily influenced my renewed faith in God. There were very few atheists in the foxholes. I began to believe there had to be a divine power watching over me, mostly because of all the narrow escapes I'd experienced. It couldn't be just luck that saved me so many times. I would still need a lot of help if I expected to survive, for the end of the war was nowhere in sight.

A couple of times I attended church services in a town called Santa Maria. Before the war passed through the town, the cathedral must have been beautiful. Now only the walls of the building remained. The altar and the back of the church were the only things untouched by the shells. With freezing rain falling, we knelt and gave thanks to God, asking that he protect us in the battle ahead.

When not up on the front lines, we trained for night patrols. I felt safe out in the darkness. The main fear I had while out on patrol came from the thought of possibly crawling, stepping or tripping one of the "bouncing Betty" antipersonnel S-mines that leaped in the air. The Schu mines, which were made mostly out of wood, were almost as bad. This mine would blow your foot off, or if it exploded when you were crawling, you could lose your hand.

The 91st Recon moved up to the front to take part in the attack on the Mignano Line. We led mules up trails on Mount Sammucro that would have discouraged mountain goats. The mud, mixed with the snow we encountered, made climbing the treacherous paths almost an impossibility. When the incoming shells exploded nearby, the poor mules were ripped to pieces. They didn't understand they had to get down on the ground in order to survive. During the month of December, we hauled ammunition and food up the mountains to the first Special Service Forces. On our return trips, we carried the dead and wounded. There were mountains with names like Monte Rotondo and Monte la Difensa. Monte Sammucro was 1,205 meters, or 3,940 feet high.

The 143rd Regiment of the 36th Infantry Division fought gallantly on the Mignano Line. After the German defenses finally collapsed, the 143rd required 1,100 replacements to bring it back to full strength. On December 12, the 504 Paratroopers took over Mount Sammucro from the 143rd. Troop C of the 91st Recon then became attached to the paratroopers. The 33rd Rangers also fought on Sammucro.

Monte la Difensa was finally taken by the first Special Service Force made up of Americans and Canadians. This outfit distinguished itself as one of the toughest fighting units in the entire American 5th and British 8th Armies.

We had Christmas dinner of 1943 on the Mignano Line. I opened up a can of type-C hash, the same menu we'd been served a year earlier in North Africa. The only difference between the two meals: we ate this year's dinner with hands numbed from the freezing rain and snow. Huddled together on top of a 3,000-foot-high mountain in Italy, we shivered beneath the soggy army blankets draped over our shoulders. Our teeth chattered between cracked lips as we whispered "Merry Christmas" to one another. Memories such as these are what bind men together.

The town of San Pietro had been named after the patron saint, Peter. All the time we spent on an observation post overlooking the village, we felt sorry for ourselves, that is, until we looked at the infantrymen. They had it far worse than we did and fought with a courage and determination that made you realize the truth in General Patton's words when he said, "The American soldier is as good as any soldier in the world."

We often wondered how Patton would have handled the situation in the rugged mountains of Italy. We could only guess, then shudder at the thought. He could never have used tanks in some of the rugged terrain. With his strong determination to defeat the enemy, it wouldn't have surprised us if he tried to take the tanks apart and had us haul the pieces up the slopes, then assemble them atop the mountains. Even with all the modern technology used in the war, the final task of clearing these mountains of the enemy fell upon the foot soldier.

Since joining the American forces at the Volturno River, we hadn't used our vehicles in combat. They were only needed when the enemy retreated and it became possible to drive on roads or trails. With the terrain in the enemy's favor, every foot of frozen mud and rock the Allies gained became a costly piece of real estate. Throughout the winter of 1943–44, and up until the following May, our squadron continued to fight as dismounted cavalry.

We often became disillusioned and had our feelings hurt by many of the army's policies. The combat infantrymen, which also included the men in an infantry division's recon units, were entitled to wear the Combat Infantryman's Badge. This allowed them to receive a well-deserved five dollars extra each month. The 91st Recon, because we were an independent cavalry unit of II Corps, weren't eligible to wear the badge even though we performed recon duty for both armored and infantry divisions. Many times, we were put in the front lines to fight alongside the infantry.

It is almost impossible for anyone to imagine what a combat infantryman had to go through in Italy, especially during that record-breaking cold winter of 1943–44. Ernie Pyle, the war correspondent, witnessed it firsthand and wrote about it. Bill Mauldin, the famous cartoonist, an infantryman himself in North Africa and Italy, also portrayed life as it really happened. One of Bill Mauldin's first drawings in Africa made fun of us cavalrymen. He drew a cartoon showing an old horse soldier standing beside a jeep with a flat tire. Mauldin sketched the cavalryman with a pistol in his hand pointed at the vehicle, getting ready to put it out of its misery. Mauldin was poking fun at the old cowboys and horse soldiers on the Western plains who shot their horse if it had a broken leg. Ernie Pyle and Bill Mauldin showed the folks back home the real war.

After the Mignano Line broke and the men of C Troop returned to the valley below, we wrote new words to an old song. One evening as we sat around the campfire singing, Al Jerman added the line, "Those 88's are breaking up that old gang of mine" to the song, "Those wedding bells are breaking up that old gang of mine." We wrote different words and had them depict the travels, hardships and adventures of the 91st Recon since it landed in North Africa. We called our marching song,

### THE ROUGH AND READY RECON
*(Sing to the tune of "Those Wedding Bells Are Breaking Up That Old Gang of Mine.")*

CHORUS        *We're the rough and ready Recon,*
*We've fought in foreign lands,*
*In Italy and Sicily,*
*And on Tunisian sands.*

*We've been used as quartermaster,*
*We've fought as doughboys, too,*

*We've been M.P.'s, pack trains, engineers,*
*Ain't a job that we can't do.*

VERSE        *Tell your Maw and your Paw,*
*You left the States in '42,*
*Write your pal, tell your gal*
*You won't be home 'til this war's through.*

CHORUS       *When the Yanks march into battle,*
*Us Recon boys you'll see.*
*We'll wipe the Jerries off the map,*
*Then Europe will be free.*

*We've got tanks and 37's,*
*75's and mortars, too.*
*We Recon boys are fighting for*
*The Red, the White, and Blue.*

VERSE        *There goes Hans, there goes Fritz.*
*Shaggin' down the pass.*
*Take close aim at their frame,*
*And bore them a new——, Yes,*

CHORUS       *Hear the General say, "Move forward,*
*Gotta find that 88.*
*We'll draw their fire, then find their range,*
*And use the 91st as bait."*

*Hear machine-gun bullets whistle,*
*Hear those 47's whine.*
*The 88's ain't slowin' down,*
*Those Recon pals of mine.*

In the last two lines of the chorus, we started out singing, "Those 88's are breakin' up that old gang of mine." We soon changed the words. The reality of their meaning touched us too deeply. The German 88-millimeter artillery weapon proved to be one of the most accurate, deadly and feared guns in the European Theater of Operations.

After the United States entered the war, Germany developed an electrically operated six-inch multiple rocket launcher. The gun had a demoralizing effect whenever we heard it fired. Much like the Stuka dive bomber, the sound it produced put the fear of God into its victims. The Germans called the six-barrel gun a *Nebelwerfer*. The inventive Krauts made holes in the sides of the shells so they screamed when they came hurtling through the air. No other sound on the front lines terrified us more. It alerted us to the fact that death and destruction poured out of those six barrels.

Chills raced up and down your spine, and a soldier's stomach muscles tightened whenever he heard the *whoop, whoop, whoop* of the shells leaving their barrels. The screaming that followed echoed back and forth between the mountain valleys, sounding like someone opening and closing a door leading to a torture chamber. For this reason, most of the soldiers called the shells "screaming meemies." Our outfit also nicknamed the gun, "the six-barrel pipe organ playing the 'Purple Heart Blues'." After the shells exploded, many a soldier received the Purple Heart, the medal given for being either wounded or killed in action.

On the second of January, 1944, Troop C marched through the Liri Valley that lay north of San Pietro. Our mission: to protect the left flank of Task Force "A." We stared in awe at the total destruction of the villages we passed. Every building had been reduced to a pile of rubble. Not a tree remained untouched from the shelling. We were preparing to take part in the attack on the area in front of Monte Porcha and Monte Trocchio. These two mountains were the last obstacles held by the Germans south of the Rapido River. They had to be taken before the town of Cassino could be attacked.

After being supported by a heavy barrage from our artillery, we pushed off into the darkness. On our left flank were the British forces, and on our right, a regiment of the 36th Infantry Division and a unit from the 1st Armored

Division. Captain Maple led us into battle as dismounted cavalrymen. Our attack lasted throughout the night. After advancing as far as possible just before dawn, we dug in on top of a knoll. At the time, we didn't know its name, but later we called it "Hill 69."

The Germans fought stubbornly, but performed a well-organized retreat to new positions. We were glad when the captain gave us the order to set up our machine guns and get ready for defensive action. The men began digging their foxholes in preparation for the counterattack almost certain to follow. Before I had a chance to get my foxhole started, Captain Maple sent word for me to report to him immediately. When I reached the spot where he intended to dig his command post, I had to wait until he'd finished talking on a portable radio. He was in contact with our commander behind the front lines.

After putting down the receiver, he said, "Corporal, I'm in trouble. I've contacted headquarters and told them we are digging defensive positions and that we intend to hold every inch of ground we've taken. They've asked for our exact location and want the map coordinates so that the new line of defense can be established at corps headquarters. Throughout the night, we advanced quite a distance. We've lost contact with the forces on our flanks. I don't know exactly which hill we are on, and I can't give headquarters our location. I've stalled them by saying that I'll report our position after we dig in and secure our front.

"Take one man with you and move out through our left flank. If you don't make contact with the British, move over to our right flank and get in touch with our infantry. I'll have all the machine gunners alerted to be on the lookout for you. Hopefully, they won't get trigger-happy, and you'll make it back safe. First off, see if you can locate the British and get map coordinates so I can make my report. I'll keep delaying headquarters as long as possible. Good luck."

I returned to my squad and told Sergeant Montoro the mission I'd been given. The captain had already contacted the 1st Platoon and told them to send a man to accompany me on patrol. As I stood talking to the sergeant, PFC Jim Ross tapped me on the shoulder and said, "I'm ready, Fred. Let's go."

After picking up extra ammo and grenades, Jim and I wasted no time in moving out through our left flank into the gray light that comes just before dawn.

It is just as dangerous to be moving around in front of your own lines as it is to crawl along in front of the German trenches. Even veteran soldiers who are in defensive positions will often fire at something moving out in front of them. Many times it is too late if you hesitate to shoot at a silent shadow, especially after the Kraut that made the shadow has hurled a potato masher into your foxhole.

Jim Ross and I moved out about 300 yards to the left of our troop. Each time I crept forward, Jim covered me. I'd wait until he moved up to within a few yards of my position before starting out again. Though this might seem a slow method of advancing, we found it the best way to protect each other. At least one man remained concealed if the Krauts began firing. Moving around in No-Man's-Land was always a hair-raising experience. With the coming of dawn, the light increased and we were able to distinguish objects. Almost ready to move forward, I saw a movement about 100 yards to our left. I put my hand out in front of me, pointing out the direction of the danger to Jim. I lowered my arm and motioned for him to get down. We waited.

One of the most important lessons of survival when on patrol is to have patience. I'd learned that tactic as a young boy while hunting. A deer, when approaching a field where it intends to feed, never ventures out into the open without first surveying the area. An old buck will remain hidden for a long time when it is wary of an enemy. Oftentimes he lets the does and fawns throw caution to the wind and venture out into an opening ahead of him. He would never have survived so many hunting seasons without being overly cautious.

Almost ten minutes passed and finally our patience paid off. Something off to our left moved again. This time I could barely make out the top of a helmet. Moving it carefully lest it crack, I parted the frost-covered brush in front of me. While watching the unsuspecting soldier turn his head, I noticed his helmet resembled those issued by the U.S. Army before Pearl Harbor. British troops still used that type of helmet. I waited a moment to make sure that the sides and back of the headgear weren't lower and flared out like the German helmets, then I motioned Ross to move into a depression and stay down. After he got in position, I crawled to my right into a hollow about a foot deep.

You don't get many second chances when you make a mistake out in front of a machine-gun nest, whether it be manned by friend or foe. I tried to make sure that if we were mistaken for Germans, we wouldn't get killed in that first burst of fire. At least, being down below the surface of the ground, we'd have a little protection. I was positive the soldier couldn't reach us with a grenade.

Now, if I could only make that British soldier realize we were an American patrol. The "Tommy" probably had a Bren or Vickers machine gun pointed in our direction. If he had any doubts about our identity, he'd shoot first and ask questions later. How I wished I'd worn my helmet for identification, but all I had on was my wool knit cap. I took it off and put it over the end of the barrel of my Thompson submachine gun. Slowly, I raised it up in the air and yelled, "We're Yanks don't shoot."

I called out the password we'd been given the night before, hoping the British had the same one as we Americans. When no response came from the "Tommy," I shouted, "We are Yanks, I have to talk to you."

Any second I expected to draw a hail of machine-gun fire. Instead, the unmistakable accent of a British soldier drifted across the frost-covered ground. "If you are a Yank, stand up and put your hands above your head."

I hated to leave my Thompson lying on the ground, for without it I felt as naked as a molting rooster. I'd no other choice but to give in to his demand, so I stood up and reached for the cold Italian sky.

I walked toward the soldier, and when I got within a few

feet of his machine-gun nest, he smiled and said, "You can't blame me for not taking any chances, can you, Yank?"

I called out to Ross, and said, "Pick up my Thompson, will you, Jim, then join me."

We'd made it safely inside the British lines, and I let out a sigh of relief. I explained to the Tommy that it was urgent we talk to his commanding officer. "I have to tell him that we are positioned forward of the British lines," I said.

The soldier immediately motioned for one of his comrades to take over his gun position. With Ross following me, the three of us crept about one hundred yards to the rear, stopping behind a stone house. Incredibly, the two-story building remained intact. Its roof, untouched by shell fire, could protect the occupants from the harsh elements. The soldier led the way up a pair of rickety stairs to the second floor and introduced us to his commander. The officer stood up, and without waiting for me to salute he grasped my hand. Squeezing it hard in a genuine greeting of comradeship, he asked, "What can I do for you, Yank?"

Taken back by his warm reception, I hesitated for a moment, then said, "After last night's attack, our troop has dug defensive positions slightly forward and about 300 yards east of your right flank machine gun. Our captain isn't sure of our exact location, and corps headquarters wants to establish our position on their charts. Can you help us?"

The officer led me to the window opposite the front lines. In the early morning light, he unrolled a topographical map and pointed to his exact position. I copied down the coordinates he gave me. Crossing the room to the side nearest C Troop, he stayed back from the window and pointed to the hill we Americans now occupied. I asked if I could take another look at his map. Studying it for a moment, I found our hill, then memorized its location. After thanking him for the information he'd given me, I asked, "Sir, what British outfit have I contacted?"

Proudly, he replied, "The Welsh Sherwood Foresters and the Durham Light Infantry."

Smiling from ear to ear, I said, "I'm part Welsh. My father flew in the RAF in World War I."

When I mentioned that I'd visited England and Wales as a young boy, the commander called to his fellow officers. Placing an arm around my shoulder, he said, "What do you know, we've got a bloody Welsh Yankee in our midst."

Walking over to a canvas knapsack, he produced a bottle of rum. Pouring about three fingers of the liquor in a tin cup, he offered it to me, saying, "This calls for a drink."

When I raised my hand and said, "I don't mean to offend you, Sir, but I can't drink with you right now," he seemed a little upset. After I explained how important it was for me to get back to my unit with the information he'd given me, he understood.

He told one of his fellow officers to go out to their forward positions and tell the men to prepare to move closer to C Troop's left flank. "Wait until our Yank friend has time to report to his commanding officer before you make the move," he said. "As the Yanks would say, we don't want anyone getting trigger-happy."

Before saying "So long," I told the Welsh officer, "I'll probably see you this evening. I know the captain will send me out to make contact with the troops on our flanks after it gets dark."

As I prepared to leave the building, he told me not to walk in front of the window facing the enemy lines. He didn't want the Krauts to know he was using the stone house as a command post. We shook hands, and I thanked him again for his hospitality and the valuable information. My newfound Welsh friend sent one of his men to accompany Jim and me to the perimeter of their defenses. Within a few minutes, we came in behind the front lines of C Troop.

By now it was broad daylight. As I approached Captain Maple, I noticed the tired and worried look on his face. He hurried toward me and asked, "Did you have any luck, Corporal?"

I didn't reply to his question. Instead, I said, "Unfold your map, Captain." After he squatted down and spread the map on his lap, I pointed to a semicircle of contour lines drawn close together that indicated a hill. "There's where we are, Captain."

When I showed him the Welsh infantry unit's position and told him they were going to close the gap between our two forces, his face broke into a smile. He shocked the livin' heck out of me when he said, "Salter, if you were a girl, I'd kiss you."

The expression on my face probably told him that I was a "hick from the sticks." I didn't know how to react to the captain's comment. No one had ever said anything like that to me before. I didn't relish the thought of a man kissing me on each cheek like the Frenchmen do when they greet each other. Even though I knew the captain was a macho fellow, I took a couple of steps back. Ross and I looked at each other, then we started to laugh. We realized the captain had only been trying to tell us how much he appreciated the job we'd done. Now he'd be able to relay the information we'd obtained to his superiors.

He walked over to the portable radio and transmitted a message to headquarters. As if he'd made a slight oversight in his timing, he apologized for not having contacted them sooner. While he talked, he motioned for me to wait there until he completed his call.

When he finished his report, he said, "All the other squads on the hill have machine guns, but because we don't carry the mortar when we are used as infantry, I want you to be on steady night patrol. Get your squad situated and have them support the other machine-gun squads. Afterward, get some rest. At dusk I want you to contact the Welsh infantry and deliver a message. By the time you've completed that mission it will be dark, then you can make a sweep out in front of our lines. Your main objective will be to observe and listen for enemy activity, especially the sound of troop movements that could signal an enemy buildup and possibly a counterattack."

Though dead tired, I had a feeling of accomplishment, for Ross and I completed what I thought to be a successful patrol. To me, that type of work afforded more of a challenge than being in charge of a mortar squad. It pitted a man's wits against a cunning enemy. Its success didn't depend just on how accurately you could fire a gun.

Not having to carry the heavy 81-millimeter mortar into combat when we were dismounted made me very happy. It took three men to carry the base plate, barrel, and bipod, for each piece weighed almost 50 pounds. A mortar shell weighed from 6 ½ to 11 pounds. It was almost an impossibility for an eight-man squad to carry their own gear, a firearm, plus mortar ammunition up the rocky cliffs and steep terrain. Unlike the infantry, the recon mortar squads weren't issued walkie-talkies until later in the war. The forward observer had to be within earshot or sight of the mortar crew. When we were on mounted recon duty with our vehicles, we didn't have a problem setting up the mortar and using it successfully. The infantry had a 60- as well as the larger 81-millimeter mortar. They were fortunate, for their 81-millimeter mortar squads were in a separate platoon.

After receiving my latest assignment from the captain, I checked on the men in my squad, then dug a foxhole below the crest of the ridge. Throughout the day we took a terrific pounding from the German artillery. The Krauts intended for us to pay dearly for the ground we'd taken. From the intensity of the shelling on our left flank, I knew our Welsh comrades were also experiencing a rough day.

Late that afternoon I reported to Captain Maple. He instructed me to make contact with the Sherwood Foresters and report any new developments. The note he handed me to give to their commander I presumed thanked the Welsh officer for the information he'd furnished us that morning. After completing that mission, I was to begin my night patrol across the front of our lines.

Before I left, the captain said, "I've already alerted the 3rd Platoon machine-gun nest on our right flank that you'll be coming through their positions sometime before dawn."

I had studied my topographical map that afternoon

and knew that our right flank ended next to the railroad bed at the base of the hill we were defending. The railroad bed paralleled Highway #6 going from Naples through the Liri Valley and on to Rome. The Germans had pulled all the rails and ties, but the roadbed remained in good shape.

The captain knew that I preferred to work alone whenever possible. I felt pleased that he had confidence in me. Without having to worry about a partner, I could set my own pace.

I moved west and came in behind the Sherwood Foresters' main line of defense. The first soldier I contacted recognized me from the morning's patrol. I told him that I had a dispatch for his commanding officer. We started walking through the trees that reminded me of a graveyard of naked scarecrows. That day's artillery barrage had devastated everything aboveground. As we moved along, I anxiously awaited my upcoming meeting with the Welsh commander. After he learned that my father migrated to America from the British Isles, he had welcomed me with open arms.

The soldier led me past the ruins of the two-story stone house that, on my previous visit, had served as their command post. A pile of rubble was all that remained. We proceeded on to a dugout where he said his commanding officer had established headquarters.

The British Tommy informed me that during the morning's heavy artillery barrage, the stone house had been destroyed. When I inquired about my friend, the commander, the soldier told me he'd been killed in the barrage. I became very depressed and didn't ask any more questions. Even though the friendly officer had held a high rank in the British Army, he treated a lowly squad leader from another country as an equal.

When I met the new Sherwood Forester commander, he greeted me very cordially, but through no fault of his, the feelings weren't the same. I didn't seem in the mood to strike up a conversation. After I handed him the dispatch from Captain Maple, he gave me a sealed report to carry back. He wished me well and told me to be careful.

Not wanting to carry a document on patrol with me and take a chance of having it fall into enemy hands if I were killed or captured, I made my way back to C Troop. By the time I handed the envelope to the captain, darkness had settled over the lines. I moved out through our left flank to begin my patrol.

Taking my time, I crawled about one hundred yards out in front of our lines. Not knowing the distance to the German lines, I figured this to be far enough, at least until I had some indication as to the location of their defenses. Sooner or later, one of their men would become careless and reveal his position. Within the hour, I picked up the low tones of talking off to my left, but I contacted none of their patrols.

A man has to learn to be patient when listening for movements of the enemy. I knew how imperative it was that headquarters be made aware of a troop buildup in front of a specific area. Once they learned the exact location of an increase in troops, they could reinforce that sector and prepare for a counterattack. So far, this patrol remained uneventful.

Daylight had almost arrived by the time I completed my mission and crawled through the 3rd Platoon machine-gun nest. Even though the enemy shelling might disturb my sleep when I finally had a chance to lie down in my fox-hole, at least the tension would ease and I'd be able to relax. The strain of the last 24 hours had not only affected my body, but also my mind. Tired, cold, and with the front of my body covered with mud, I made my way to Captain Maple's command post to make my report.

When I finished, he said, "Get a couple of hours' rest, Corporal. This afternoon I'm going to send you to the rear to bring up half of the scout car and jeep drivers. The remaining drivers are to be left with the vehicles. We need a few extra men to reinforce our position here on Hill 69."

That morning the shelling became almost unbearable, even worse than the previous day. At the height of the barrage, one boy, who'd recently joined us as a replacement, leaped out of his foxhole. He dropped his rifle and frantically waved both arms above his head, shouting for God to make the firing cease. Screaming, he ran toward the incoming shells, never stopping until a soldier in the foxhole next to him leaped up and tackled him. Even after the men dragged the poor fellow behind the hill, he continued to cry out. What a pitiful sight, to witness a comrade go berserk from the shelling that never seemed to end.

The hill literally shook from the heavy pounding. As I lay trying to get a much needed rest, shrapnel cut a small tree down that stood next to my foxhole. To keep it out of the mud, I'd hung my Thompson submachine gun on the lower branches of the tree. The gun landed on top of me. After every barrage ended, because of the intense shelling, Sergeant Smith shouted roll call and checked for casualties.

Shrapnel cut Al Jerman's radio antenna in half. He taped it together, so he could make contact behind the lines.

Early that afternoon I left Hill 69 and returned to where the vehicles remained hidden. I gave the officer in charge the captain's message. The men scheduled to move up to the front were glad they didn't have to move out until after dark. Little did they know the fate that awaited them on Hill 69.

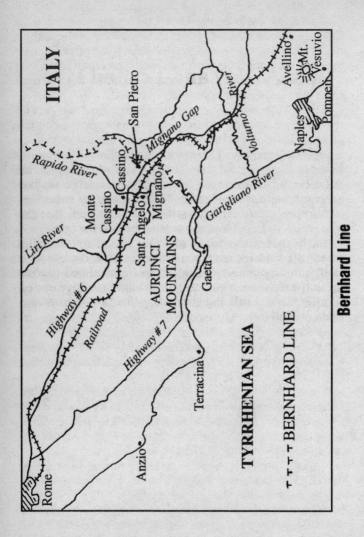

**Bernhard Line**

# CHAPTER VIII

# Twisted Hay and Twisted Lives

When the last ray of light vanished from the cold winter sky, we started our trek toward Hill 69. Because we were moving under cover of darkness during the last phase of our march, I left the frozen fields of mud and traveled down the old railroad bed. Before it reached the right flank of our troop, the railroad bed went through a cut in a high hill. The banks on either side of this cut were almost perpendicular. Only an occasional harassing shell exploded as we passed through, and we suffered no casualties. After leaving the cut, we turned left into a deep ravine that led to our right flank. "I'd hate to go through that railroad cut during daylight," I thought. "The Kraut artillery observers are looking directly into it."

Around 0400 hours, we reached the troop defensive positions, and the vehicle drivers reported to their respective squads.

When I reported to the captain, he said, "Salter, from the latest reports, the Germans have counterattacked the troops on our right flank. Our comrades have suffered heavy casualties. The top brass back at headquarters figures the enemy will hit our sector next."

I knew the captain wasn't confiding in me just to hear himself talk; he had something else on his mind. I had an idea that I'd be busy the rest of the day.

"I want you to return to the rear area immediately," he said. "Bring up your jeep with the trailer attached. Load the jeep down with your mortar, a couple of machine guns, and all the .30-caliber ammunition possible. The trailer is already filled with mortar ammo, but load more on for the machine guns. Have as many men as possible carry a box of ammo or a mortar round." My mind raced ahead when he told me the mission I had to accomplish. There were less than two hours of darkness left. I wondered if he expected me to bring the jeep and other equipment through during daylight or wait until that evening.

His next words answered my question and my heart sank. "You will have to get the men through to us as soon as possible so we can be prepared for a night attack. There is only one way any vehicle can reach our position without becoming bogged down in the mud; that is through the cut in the railroad bed. Once you reach this end of the cut, you can run the jeep and trailer down into the ravine to your left, and you'll be safe."

It sounded so easy when he said, "If you get that far, the men from the troop can haul the guns and ammo up the hill."

As he spoke, I knew that the strain of having to perform such a life-threatening mission must have shown on my face. I never questioned his decision, as I could tell he hated to send me, but the fate of the troop rested on his shoulders.

"We need reinforcements if we intend to hold this hill against a counterattack," he said. "When you get back to the vehicles, tell the officer in charge to send the remaining jeep and scout car drivers along with you. If the troop's vehicles have to be moved, the men in headquarters platoon will have to drive them."

His last words to me were, "It will be daylight when you come through that railroad cut, and no one has to tell you how rough it's going to be. All I can say is, good luck."

Knowing how bad he felt, I just said, "Thanks, Captain." Then I made ready to move out. I realized he had no alternative but to send me on the mission. The phase of the assignment that worried me was the last couple of hundred yards we had to travel through the cut. Looking directly into the barrel of that German "88," I knew we'd be as vulnerable as a raccoon caught in a chicken yard.

Once again I retraced my steps down the railroad bed.

Only an occasional shell landed, none of them very close. I still had about an hour of darkness protecting me from enemy observation.

The extra-thin, moccasin-like soles of my combat boots served me well when on patrols, but they weren't much good for warmth. After having walked continually through frozen mud the last couple of days, my feet were so numb I could hardly feel them.

I'd traveled about halfway back to where our vehicles were hidden when I smelled smoke. If only I could place my frozen feet next to a fire, it would be wonderful. I wondered where in the heck that smoke came from. The first light of the approaching day penetrated the darkness, and off to my left I saw the outline of a small hut. When I approached it, I noticed the low slanted roof remained intact, a miracle this close to the front lines. There were no windows in the stone shed, but a wisp of smoke drifted out from beneath the pole rafters.

I didn't have to be overly cautious this far behind the front lines, so I walked over to the hut and pushed on the small door. It sagged on its leather hinges, and the bottom scraped the dirt floor inside the shed. A faint glow came from one corner of the hut. As my eyes became accustomed to the dim light of the interior, I noticed the smoldering fire.

Much to my amazement, there on the floor, propped up against the far wall, sat a little Italian lady. Weatherbeaten and wrinkled, she looked as old as time itself. Two small children, not more than seven or eight years old, sat next to her. I guessed the old lady to be their grandmother. Dumbfounded, I stood and watched for a moment as the children took handfuls of dried grass and brush from a pile in the center of the room. Ignoring my presence, they carefully twisted the hay into bundles about an inch in diameter. After tying each of them together with a piece of grass, they stacked the bundles in a neat pile against the stone wall. I couldn't believe what I saw. They were burning twisted hay to keep warm.

Opening the conversation, I said *"Buon giorno"* to the shy grandmother and the timid children. Without waiting for a reply to my greeting, I sat down next to the fire alongside the children. Spreading my hands in front of me, I warmed them over the tiny flame. In my broken Italian, I tried to make the old lady understand that my feet were frozen. After taking my boots and socks off, I proceeded to rub my feet and warm them over the heaven-sent fire.

Without saying a word, the grandmother grabbed my socks and hung them on a stick close to the fire. Afterward she took a boot in each hand and held the tops of them over the flame, letting the smoke and heat warm the insides.

The children weren't afraid of me, but I could see the sadness in their eyes when they looked up into my face. Their gaunt features and bloated bellies told me they were starving. Since we began the attack on Hill 69, I'd saved all the candy and packets of hard crackers from my cans of type-C rations. I took the candy out of my ditty bag and handed it to the children. When the hungry youngsters saw it, for the first time since I entered the hut, they showed emotion toward me. The smiles that lit up their faces touched me so deeply that it would have been real easy to break down and cry. I looked into those sunken eyes and at the two frail bodies with skin stretched over nothing but protruding bones. I thought to myself, "How lucky the youngsters back in the States are not to experience the hardships of war like these children."

When I offered the old lady the few pieces of hardtack crackers, the look of gratitude showed through her eighty or ninety years of wrinkles. The movement of those age-old lines thanked me much more than spoken words. She didn't eat the crackers, but folded them into the corner of her tattered shawl. I knew that as hungry as she must be, after I left the children would be fed, probably the first solid food in many a day. I vowed that on my return trip to Hill 69, I'd stop and give them more food.

Those poor Italian peasants suffered far worse than us soldiers. If we survived the war, at least we had a home to return to even though it might be thousands of miles away. In contrast, most of the Italian homes were blasted into a pile of rubble. A great number of the former inhabitants would never survive the conflict.

Around many a campfire, I'd often sung an old cowboy tune called "The Little Old Sod Shanty on My Claim." The song told how the early settlers on the Western plains burned twisted hay to keep warm. I'd never really thought about the words that I sang until I saw these two youngsters performing the same task to keep their war-twisted bodies warm. The lives of us soldiers were also being twisted just like that hay. When peace came, would our lives ever get straightened out? Inside a humble peasant's hut, in the midst of one of man's senseless struggles for power that no one wins, I learned the true meaning to the words of the song.

After a few minutes elapsed, my feet started to burn and tingle. I knew that the blood was beginning to circulate in them. I kept rubbing them until they came back to life. Many days would pass before they ever felt comfortably warm.

In a humble gesture of appreciation and love. I hugged the children. With my few words of Italian, I tried to thank the broken remains of a war-torn family for sharing the warmth in their hearts and the warmth of their primitive home. Families such as theirs had populated and farmed this once peaceful and fertile valley. When the guns were silenced and forged into plowshares, the valley would bloom again. The thorns of war would leave permanent scars, not only on the land, but in the hearts of the survivors.

With sadness in my heart, I walked outside the hut and returned to the world of hatred and senseless killing. When I closed the door, I turned an emotional page in my book of life. From that moment on, I carried treasured memories of a side of war that people seldom witness or even hear about, memories that a soldier never forgets.

Before dawn removed the cover of darkness from the tops of the snow-covered mountains on the west side of the valley, I arrived at C Troop's rear command post. George Johnson, my jeep driver, and George Porth, my second gunner from McAlester, Oklahoma, helped load the machine guns and extra ammo in the jeep.

The trailer with camouflaged netting draped over it, though already loaded to near capacity, had room for a few boxes of 30-caliber ammo. Later in the day, I would regret not having removed my personal belongings from the trailer, especially the guitar made out of a British ammunition box. In all the confusion, I just plain forgot about it. I did remember to gather up all the extra cans of type-C rations I could find so we could give them to the starving grandmother and the children in the stone hut.

As soon as we had the jeep loaded, we started for the front. Behind the lone vehicle, in a staggered column, marched the remaining drivers from the troop. I'd previously told the men that when we reached the south end of the railroad cut, we'd stop and take a break. From that point on, anyone on the roadbed would be under the hawklike eyes of the enemy artillery observer.

"George Johnson, Porth and I will make the run through the cut with the equipment and ammo," I said. "The rest of you will proceed around the left side of the railroad bed and come in behind Hill 69. Even though you'll probably be exposed to enemy fire for a short distance, you'll have a much better chance of survival than if you try to go down the old railroad bed. The steep sides of that cut make it a death trap during an artillery barrage. Many of the shells explode on the high banks above your head. When the Krauts see our jeep and trailer trying to get through, we might create enough of a diversion that the artillery gunner won't bother your column. Stay dispersed anyway."

Within the half hour, we arrived opposite the stone hut where three starving victims had shared their hospitality and brought my frozen feet back to life. I halted the column for a moment, then ran to the hut. When I opened the door, the squeaking of the leather hinges startled the old lady. She sat on the floor with her arms wrapped around the sleeping children. Her tattered shawl lay draped over the shoulders of the little girl. The dying embers of the twisted hay still gave off a little warmth.

I never uttered a word, but placed the box of food inside the hut next to the door. Pointing a finger from the box toward her and the children, I let her know the contents were for them. Afterward, I closed my left eye and twisted my right cheek with the thumb and forefinger of my right hand, making the Italian gesture for "Good." The grandmother's features came to life. She squeezed the wrinkles together, which deepened the furrows on that ancient old face. The faint smile made the highspots on her cheeks brighten up the scraggly white hair that surrounded them. As I closed the door, she whispered, *"Grazie,"* the most appreciative "thank you" I've ever received.

Our column of reinforcements proceeded on its way. Upon reaching the cut, I brought them to a halt. After pointing out the safest approach to the rear of Hill 69, I wished them good luck. They immediately started out across the frozen mud.

As I looked up at the 30-foot-high sides of the gauntlet we had to run, I knew full well the trouble the three of us were in. The possibility existed that we'd never make it to the far side of the cut. After waiting until a few artillery salvos were fired, we moved forward and peeked around the bend in the railroad bed. Looking down that corridor of death, I knew how the Hebrew prophet Jonah must have felt when he gazed into the mouth of the whale just before it swallowed him.

Though all three of us had experienced artillery fire during three bitter campaigns, this would be the closest we'd ever come to looking down the barrel of a deadly German 88. What an eerie feeling knowing that you have to advance directly into the range of that gun. Its 20-pound shells send out chunks of steel capable of cutting your body to pieces faster than a skilled surgeon can dissect you. What we proposed to do was almost like running hatless in a hailstorm, hoping against hope that none of the pellets of ice hit the top of your head.

All men in combat experience much the same feelings when they are in a similar situation. The airmen, who dive-bomb and strafe targets protected by antiaircraft (ack-ack) guns, rely on the maneuverability of their planes and their speed. Lastly, they pray that God will protect them from the bursting shells. The infantryman charges across a battlefield into the face of rifles and machine guns, whose bullets have a vampire's thirst for human blood. The infantryman has the same feelings of anxiety, fear and dependence on some greater power just like the fighter pilot.

Our present situation was no different from those experienced by thousands of other men in combat. We all feel alone in a world that rests heavily on our shoulders.

When I gave the signal, George Johnson put his foot on the gas pedal. As the jeep lurched forward and my head snapped back, I knew George had pushed the accelerator clear to the floor. George Porth, sitting on top of the load of guns in the back of the jeep, gripped the machine-gun mount to keep from being tossed out of the vehicle. With my left hand I held on to a box of ammunition. My other hand clutched the Thompson submachine gun. Silently I prayed.

The roar of the jeep's engine drowned out the sound of the distant gun. We were unable to hear the whine of the shells before they exploded. The *whoosh* came afterward. The first projectile landed far out in front of us, and we raced through the smoke and dust it created. George maneuvered the vehicle skillfully around the old shell holes in the rocky roadbed. He seemed oblivious to the sounds made by the guillotine-like pieces of steel being hurtled through the air. His experienced hands clutched the steering wheel in a deathlike grip. If a shell fragment had penetrated his body at this moment, I do believe his determination and devotion to duty would have continued to control those hands and guide us through the living inferno.

No driver at the famous Indianapolis Speedway could have performed a more skillful job than George. As he swerved through the maze of shell craters, I couldn't figure out how the short-wheelbased jeep and the trailer remained upright.

The farther into the cut we raced, the higher our hopes rose. We knew that the German gunner was having a difficult time tracking us through the cloud of dust and debris. When we saw a patch of clear sky up ahead at the mouth of the cut, for one brief moment we actually thought we might make it. "Just a little farther, Lord, and you'll have delivered us out of the belly of the whale."

The Kraut gunner gave up trying to make a direct hit on our racing jeep. Instead, he concentrated his fire near the end of the cut. Usually, a gunner's firing pattern consisted of putting one shell in front of the target, one behind, then, hopefully, have the third round land directly on the target. Just before we reached his imaginary objective, he threw the first shell in front of it. We knew the next shell was going to hit close to us. Only God knew how close.

We heard the explosion behind the trailer. Whether the extremely low angle of the high-velocity 88-millimeter shell carried the shrapnel in a forward motion, spraying it down through the cut, we never knew. None of us were hit. The trailer, which almost overturned, took the brunt of the blast. Somehow, George managed to keep the jeep from upsetting. By the time we came to a halt at the very end of the cut, the wrecked trailer was a mass of flames.

A few feet ahead and to our left lay the ravine. It might just as well have been a mile away, for the disabled trailer with its smashed right wheel kept the jeep locked in its grip. The camouflage netting covering the trailer was ablaze. The scene looked like a flaming volcano spewing out sparks, ready to erupt at any moment. We were desperate.

With the jeep's engine still running, all three of us dove for the ditch on the left side of the road. Another shell landed behind the trailer, and we knew it would be only a matter of seconds before the Kraut gunner lowered his sights to finish us off. Luckily, the next shell hit about 30 yards in front of us. We knew the gunner had our range. Maybe he just wanted to prolong our agony. Although it seemed like a lifetime, only a matter of seconds had elapsed since the jeep slid to a stop.

I yelled to George Johnson, "Get in the jeep. When I un-hitch the trailer, turn left down into the safety of the ravine."

George screamed, "Are you crazy?" But without hesitating, my old buddy leaped into the jeep. Miraculously, the engine remained running.

By the time I ran out of the ditch and dove next to the trailer hitch, the boxes of machine-gun ammunition on top of the trailer were exploding. It's a wonder all of us weren't killed by our own bullets and shells. As I put upward pressure on the tongue with my shoulder, the trailer seemed to rise off the tail end of the jeep easier than I anticipated. No wonder I didn't have any trouble; George Porth lay on the ground next to me, pushing up on the hitch. With no regard for his own safety, he crawled out of the ditch to help. When the chips were down, these two men proved to be "comrades in arms."

The instant I saw the trailer hitch clear the back of the jeep, at the top of my lungs I yelled, "Gun it, George!"

Like a flash out of a cannon, the jeep sped left, off the roadbed into the ravine. George Porth and I let the trailer hitch hit the gravel and rolled into the deep ditch. The next instant, an 88 shell landed in the exact spot where the jeep had stood. With machine-gun ammo exploding inside of their steel containers, the sky lit up like a Fourth of July fireworks display. We couldn't lift our heads out of the gutter to witness it for fear of getting them blown off.

We realized that we had to get away before the "finale" came and ended the musical composition the bullets were playing. That would take place when the mortar ammo exploded. We'd crawled a short distance and were almost out of the cut when it happened. The "grand-daddy" of all explosions sent us reeling. I'll never understand how Porth and I managed to escape being hit by falling debris. Maybe there was so much explosive material in the trailer that everything disintegrated. The smell of cordite almost choked us. After the smoke cleared, you could have put all the material left on the spot where the trailer stood into a wheelbarrow. The concussion from the blast was terrific. That alone should have killed us.

For the next few minutes we were too stunned to talk.

Finally, I said, "George, thanks for helping us. I believe you better follow Johnson, for the troop will be anxious to get the remaining guns and ammo out of the jeep. I have to go back through the cut and make sure the rest of the men have gotten through."

After what happened, I should never have considered returning through that "suicide alley." With my head still reeling from the explosion, I wasn't thinking straight.

After the next barrage slackened, I started through the cut. Before I made it halfway to the opposite end, I saw a group of British soldiers marching toward me. I surmised they were on their way to reinforce the Sherwood Foresters on the left flank of Hill 69. It was too late for me to stop them; they were already inside the cut. They should never have taken this route. The German gunner was going to have another "field day." He couldn't help but see the column of soldiers walking in the ditch on each side of the roadbed.

A moment later a shell landed inside the cut and I immediately hit the ditch. As soon as it exploded and I knew it was safe to move, I jumped up and raced forward, but not before noticing the devastation caused by the shell. It had made a direct hit between two British soldiers. The heavy overcoats they'd been wearing were blasted into shreds of dark brown wool stained with blood. Pieces of clothing were scattered over their wounded comrades and on the roadbed. Limbs and body parts were strewn about, and chunks of flesh were embedded in the loose gravel on the sides of the cut.

Under different circumstances the incident might have affected me emotionally, but at the moment my only concern was survival. I moved forward and almost reached the far side of the cut when I heard the 88 open up again. After the first shell hit, I knew this barrage would land closer to me. The gunner concentrated his fire on the far entrance to the cut. As I dove into the ditch and hugged the frozen ground, a shell landed directly alongside of me on the roadbed. If it had hit another couple of feet to the right, I'd have suffered the same fate as the British soldiers.

The next few minutes of my life will forever remain a

blank. I was knocked unconscious. When I regained my senses, I found the concussion had blown the helmet off my head. Blood gushed from my nose. It's a good thing I didn't have the strap of my helmet fastened under my chin or my neck would have been broken. Because I'd been lying below the surface of the roadbed, the shrapnel from the shell traveled over my body. Luckily, I wasn't hit, but my head felt like someone had clobbered me with a sledgehammer. For the remainder of my life, I never knew what it was like to be without a ringing sound in my left ear.

I lay still for quite a while, then crawled the short distance out of the cut to safety. All of the men I'd led up to the front were gone. Hopefully they'd reached Hill 69. It's a good thing the Germans concentrated all of their fire on the railroad bed or the story might have had a different ending.

For almost half an hour I lay back in the brush. My nose finally quit bleeding and I began to feel a little better, but the left side of my head hurt terribly. My ear buzzed and rang so loud that I couldn't hear a thing out of it. If the trailer explosion hadn't fogged my brain, I knew I'd never have returned through the cut. My only concern at the time had been to fulfill my responsibility of getting reinforcements up to the front.

Excluding my encounters with rifle and machine-gun fire, the artillery shell that exploded next to me on the railroad bed was the closest call I had had so far in the war. I tried to think positive, telling myself everything would be okay, that the hearing in my left ear would return. I broke an ice-covered puddle and used the muddy water to wipe the blood from my face. After what seemed like an eternity, I staggered back to the troop.

By the time I reported to Captain Maple, the men had already unloaded the jeep and distributed the ammunition. When I apologized for losing all the mortar ammo, he said, "We're just thankful that you saved some of the equipment and ammunition and got the reinforcements through without any casualties."

When he questioned me about the blood on my jacket,

I told him I'd had a bloody nose. There was no point in going into the details of the stupid trick I'd pulled that caused me to get hurt. After I explained about the blood, he said, "You look in pretty rough shape, Corporal. Maybe you better let a medic look you over."

I followed the captain's advice and reported to John Manley, our 2nd Platoon medic from Norwalk, California.

When I explained to John what had happened, he examined me and said, "Fred, I'm sending you back behind the lines to a field hospital. From the look in your eyes and the symptoms you have, you've suffered a concussion. I wouldn't be surprised if you had a broken eardrum."

Fear welled up inside of me, for I was dreadfully afraid of leaving the 2nd Platoon. What if I returned from the hospital to find that someone else had taken over my squad? Suppose they transferred me to another platoon, for that's what happened to me in the North African Campaign. Worse yet, what if they put me in another troop? All of these suppositions actually happened to many of my wounded buddies upon their return from a hospital.

I became so upset that in a state of panic, I gripped John's arm and said, "I can't go back to the hospital. Please, John, do me a favor. Promise me you won't tell anyone I've been hurt."

John and I had been together through three campaigns. I knew I was taking advantage of our friendship by asking him to do something against his professional judgment as a medic. I explained my fears of leaving the troop and being sent back to the hospital. I told him the psychological problems I had in Africa when I became separated from my squad and wound up in another platoon.

When I finished talking, John shook his head. As he turned to walk away, he said, "Fred, I think you are a fool, but if that's the way you want it, I'll go along with your way of thinking. I'll tell the captain that you need a day's rest from patrol duty. If something happens to you though, I'm not taking any responsibility. After having a concussion, you better not go to sleep for a while, at least not until that headache goes away."

Relieved that John hadn't forced me to receive further medical attention, I returned to my foxhole and lay down. By the time darkness settled over the front lines, the pounding in my head had subsided and I began to relax. After talking to John, Captain Maple understood the extent of my exhaustion. He knew I'd gone without sleep the last couple of nights, and that I'd had a rough experience. Some of the men in the 3rd Platoon who were dug in alongside the railroad cut had witnessed the trailer explosion. They filled the captain in on the details. He sent word to me that someone else would run my patrol that evening. As tired as I was, sleep didn't come until almost daylight.

Looking up at the fine particles of falling snow, I watched an occasional air burst. The hot shells piercing the cold Italian sky should have warmed the air. Even though many of them burst over our heads, we remained chilled to the bone. I realized that yesterday I'd almost found a lasting peace. But for the grace of God, the war would have ended for me. Having been given a few hours to relax, I had time to think about the war.

The German soldiers fought tenaciously against the 5th Army troops that January of 1944. They were fighting for time so they could complete their winter line of defense, somewhere to the north of us. When we reached it, we knew we'd find it almost impregnable. The German soldier carried into battle the motto of the Third Reich, "To serve Hitler is to serve Germany; to serve Germany is to serve God." With the mountainous terrain and unmerciful weather working to their advantage, we sometimes wondered if God might not be favoring their side in the conflict.

The winter of 1943–44 proved to be exceptionally severe. We went into battle wearing only woolen uniforms and combat jackets to ward off the bitter cold. With the wind blowing across the snow-covered mountains and then swirling down into the Liri Valley, we were continually cold. The single blanket that each of us carried on top of our backpacks provided a little warmth until it became wet and frozen.

After we'd been on Hill 69 for a couple of nights, under cover of darkness our mess sergeant and his cooks brought overcoats up to our positions. They randomly dropped a coat into each foxhole. Because these men from headquarters platoon had to leave before daylight, they were unable to see what size coat each of us received. Some fellows were given a coat entirely too big. Others struggled frantically, trying to get their arms into the sleeves of a coat too small for them. Throughout the night, between shell bursts, we traded overcoats. Even if a fellow wound up with one that didn't fit just right, no one complained. In the freezing weather, anything draped over your shoulders was a godsend.

The day after I suffered the concussion, my mental condition improved, but I still had difficulty hearing out of my left ear. The throbbing and ringing almost drove me crazy. Since I'd voluntarily made the decision to remain on the front lines, I decided to make the most of it and put my problems aside. I intended to finish the assignment Captain Maple gave me. That afternoon, I gathered my gear together in readiness for the evening patrol.

My canteen, half full of partially frozen water, had to be left in my foxhole. If I carried it with me I'd be committing suicide. To a German soldier, just itching to squeeze the trigger of his machine gun, the sloshing of ice in a canteen would echo across No-Man's-Land like waves breaking on an arctic beach.

Late that afternoon I reported to Captain Maple for my orders. Soon after dusk I moved out in front of our lines. On this patrol, I didn't have to make contact with the Welsh Sherwood Foresters. I felt sad over the death of my newfound Welsh friend, but he was only one of many that I mourned.

Captain Maple didn't put a time limit on the completion of this mission. He instructed me to make it back inside our lines before daylight. I'd made one mistake too many the last couple of days and realized that my impaired hearing handicapped me. I couldn't afford to make any more slipups.

All through the early part of the evening, I crawled close to the enemy lines. More than once, I listened to an unmistakable German accent float across the lonely wasteland of death. Like a snail with frozen slime beneath its body, I crawled through territory that neither army laid claim to. I knew that the German soldiers behind their machine guns must be cursing the cold and be as uncomfortable as I.

Not long after starting the patrol, I froze in place. The Krauts shot a flare up over No-Man's-Land, hoping to surprise one of our patrols in the open. I placed my hand over my mouth to disperse the jet stream of moisture so it wouldn't rise above the depression where I lay. If a Kraut spotted the rising steam, it would look like a miniature Old Faithful geyser in the frigid night air. When the last ray of light produced by the chandelier of death faded from the sky, I moved on, alert to every sound.

Though all of my thoughts should have been directed toward the situation at hand, my mind flashed back to stories I'd been told as a boy. I loved the tales about the Apache warriors of the American Southwest. I asked myself, "Am I practicing all the survival tricks that I've learned from them?" Only a few decades ago, they successfully fought the same U.S. Horse Cavalry that I trained with. Born to the ways of the desert, the Apaches learned to take advantage of every bush and depression in the terrain. They became a part of that landscape and used the natural obstacles to make themselves almost invisible to the invading white man. I knew I'd never be as good as those ghostlike stalkers of the desert, but I had to try or I'd never survive.

It's probably a good thing the army had young men in its ranks who were dreamers, men who should have been born a hundred years earlier. Many of us grew up worshiping trappers, frontiersmen and cavalry scouts like John Colter, Bill Sublette and Kit Carson. We idolized the Native American warriors: Cochise, Geronimo and Crazy Horse. These men fought to save a land that rightfully belonged to them. Many of us young boys enlisted in the service, then volunteered for patrol duty and became scouts, not just because we were patriotic, but to satisfy a hunger for adventure. Like the Mountain Men of the early West, we belonged to a different breed. Loners by nature, we seemed compelled to venture into the unknown. We sought a challenge that would fulfill the needs of our reckless youth. Many died seeking it, but would have it no other way.

At one point on my patrol, the Germans shot a manmade sun out of a flare gun and turned midnight into noon. Caught out in the open and unable to move a muscle, I was completely at their mercy. Hoping to blend in with a small bush located between me and the enemy, I waited for the life-giving darkness to embrace me. I lived a thousand deaths.

Just before daybreak, I decided that I better start back to Hill 69. As I moved in a direct line and away from the German positions, my face brushed against a small yellow triangular flag attached to a wire sticking out of the ground. The cloth was imprinted with a black skull and crossbones. Instantly my belly contracted away from the frozen ground and tried to reach my backbone. I realized what I'd stumbled upon. On either side of me, barely visible in the darkness, were more of those same flags. I had wound up in the middle of a minefield. I'll never understand how I got as far as I did without crawling on top of one of those mines and becoming just a memory to my family back home.

I knew I couldn't linger there much longer. Before the first light of day the Krauts would notice me. Slowly I inched my way along, asking myself, "What if the Krauts hear me, and shoot up another flare, then catch me out in the open?" I knew I'd be a goner. If they spotted anything unusual, they might just send out a patrol to investigate. If that happened, there was only one way I could think of to slow them down. I had no other alternative but to let the minefield work to my advantage.

Instead of removing all of the flags as I crawled between them, I took up every other one. I figured that if the Krauts walked through the minefield, the odds were fairly good that they'd step on a mine without a flag. Hopefully, they'd get a taste of their own medicine. During the attack against Hill

69, Clarence Luce, a buddy of mine from the 3rd Platoon, lost his life when he stepped on one of their mines.

Shivering from the cold, though wringing wet with sweat from the tension, I worked frantically to beat the approaching dawn. Finally, I reached the end of the checkerboard of death. Maybe God wasn't completely on Hitler's side after all. At any time during the game that destiny and I played with mines instead of checkers, fate could have jumped me. It would have wound up with an American scout on its side of the checkerboard. I'd have lost the contest and been out of the game forever.

The flags were the only evidence that remained of the strategy I'd used. They were tucked safely in the pocket of my combat jacket, away from the prying eyes of a German patrol. The Krauts wouldn't think anything was amiss when they came to pick up the flags before they retreated. I was almost certain that, no matter how careful they were, one of the Krauts would step on a mine in the process. The few pieces of cloth marked with a skull and crossbones weren't very much to show for a night's patrol, but at least none of the flags were stained with my blood.

After leaving the minefield, I moved along as quickly as possible, for I had an appointment with the dawn. By the time the stars winked at the darkness for the last time, I came over the knoll that separated me from our front lines. What a relief to have only a short distance to go.

Hidden from the Krauts' view, I crawled through a small depression along the edge of a patch of woods. Hearing the hum of an airplane engine, I looked up in time to see a single low-flying plane approaching from the friendly skies to the south. It flew almost directly over me at a speed slow enough so that I could make out the markings of an American plane. I could even see the pilot when he looked down in my direction, probably searching for enemy targets. He continued on his course toward the German lines, and I smiled, knowing the Krauts were in for a pack of trouble.

A moment later I became puzzled, wondering what the

crazy pilot had in mind. Above the enemy lines, he banked his plane sharply and headed back toward me in a dive. Then it dawned on me; he probably thought I was a scout for a German patrol hidden in the patch of woods out here in No-Man's-Land.

As I watched the vulturelike hunter from the heavens swoop down from the sky, I felt like a rabbit trying to escape from its menacing talons. The defenseless feeling would have been complete if I'd seen a horned beak painted on the nose of the diving plane. Even without it, I felt like I was about to be devoured.

I expected to be strafed. Instead, just before reaching my position, the plane leveled out. The pilot released what looked to be a large canister, and I watched it fly apart. The contents spread out across the sky overhead like a swarm of bees coming out of a shattered hive. Terrified, I knew what to expect. Automatically, I rolled into the deep gully to my left. If the ditch had run parallel to the plane's line of flight, I'd have been killed. Instead, the sides of the cut saved me.

The small antipersonnel projectiles were carried in a forward motion by the plane's momentum. They landed all around me. Luckily, they contained no explosives but were patterned after those that my dad had used in World War I in France. He had been in the Royal Air Force and told me that pilots often carried a sackful of projectiles on the floor of their planes. Whenever they flew over German troops, they threw a handful of the projectiles over the side of their open cockpit. Dad brought one of these "airborne darts of death" home with him from the war. He gave it to me as a souvenir. Like the one I'd just picked off the ground in Italy, it, too, was pointed, with fins on the tail end. Never did I think I'd see the day when I'd become a target for one of them. The harpoonlike projectiles would go right through a man's body. This incident was the only time during the war that I ever became a target for them.

If firing my Thompson submachine gun at the vanishing plane could have reached the pilot, at that moment I'd have felt no remorse in killing him. Instead, I shook my head and uttered words unfit for delicate ears. After I thought about it, I realized that because I wore a dark wool knit cap instead of a helmet, and had my face smeared with burnt cork, the pilot could easily have mistaken me for a German scout. Talking aloud as I looked at the lifeless syringes of death lying scattered on the ground around me, I asked, "What else can happen to me on this patrol?"

At long last, I recognized the familiar terrain directly in front of Hill 69. Moving in front of the 3rd Platoon's machine-gun nest, I positioned myself in a hollow. After calling out the password, I yelled my name. The relief crew had been alerted that I'd be coming through that morning, making my entry uneventful.

A few minutes later I reported to Captain Maple and told him the patrol had been routine with no enemy activity in our sector of the front. On the topographical map laid out before him, I retraced the route I'd taken. I pointed out the approximate location of the enemy minefield. When it came time to attack the German positions, this information would save a lot of lives. As it turned out, the patrol I'd just completed would be the last one I had to make on Hill 69.

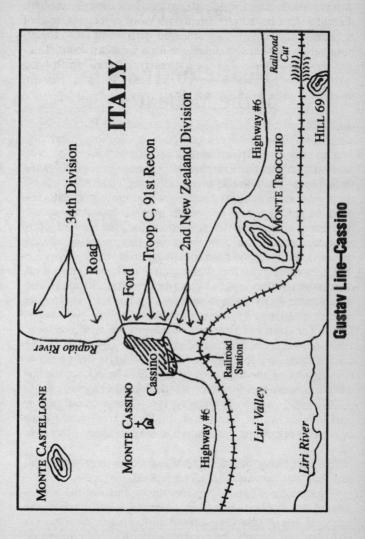

**Gustav Line–Cassino**

# CHAPTER IX

# 'Neath the Tears
# of the Monastery

The men of C Troop were scheduled to move into No-Man's-Land later that evening. After running my patrol, I returned to my foxhole and managed to get a couple of hours' sleep. As darkness approached, I crawled up to our platoon's machine gun to relieve one of the men. Corporal Raymond Still from Normangee, Texas, manned the gun. He had it positioned with an excellent field of fire. Ray was a wonderful combat soldier, a good man to have by your side.

The weather cleared that evening and, with no cloud cover, the cold penetrated our worn winter clothing. The moon came up over the mountains, and as we watched the area to the front of us, a shell burst out in No-Man's-Land. The sound of the explosion bounced back and forth between the hills. It traveled as fast as gossip from the Ladies Auxiliary the day the women caught the preacher coming out of the house of ill repute. The echoes diminished and were swallowed by the darkened canyons.

Ray and I each took a can of type-C rations out of our packs. While we ate, I asked my buddy, "How'd you like to be eating pork chops, ice cream and cake instead of this cold stew?"

"It'll probably be a long time before we ever get a meal like that, but we can dream," he replied.

Most soldiers hated the army chow, but not me. I considered our kitchen crew to be among the best chefs in the army. If the meals they served didn't satisfy everyone's taste buds, it wasn't the cooks' fault; they only prepared the food issued to them.

On the front lines, we usually ate type-C food that consisted of a can of either hash, stew or beans. Along with each of these three varieties, you received a can that contained a few crackers, a couple of pieces of hard candy, and a packet of either coffee, cocoa or lemonade. I must have been raised different from most fellows, for I thrived on the type-C. Oftentimes my buddies called me a "chow hound." I grew up in an area of the country hit hard by the Great Depression. Many families in the foothills of the Appalachian Mountains were lucky to have a crust of bread on the table. They gladly ate everything put in front of them.

Ray and I sat behind the air-cooled .30-caliber machine gun pointed into the lonely and deserted land in front of us. We memorized the shape of every rock and bush, waiting for their features to change. To pass the time away, we often whispered to each other. If we were uncertain about the identity of an object we were studying, we nudged one another and shared our opinions.

The moon drifting across the sky continually altered the shape of the shadows in No-Man's-Land, turning them into imaginary targets. Silently, we swiveled the machine gun in their direction and waited for the ghostlike objects to move. They either came to life or turned out to be figures of our imagination.

I know the conversations Ray and I shared were similar to those that drifted toward me on the night breezes as I crawled out in front of the German lines on patrol. The causes the opposing armies fought for might be different, but the tired, cold and lonely men behind the guns shared the same dreams. They painted mental pictures of their loved ones and home much the same as we did.

Later that night when we moved off Hill 69, the British took over our sector of the front. We never complained about being replaced. Most of the time we were battle weary, worn out both physically and mentally. This last battle left me with my head throbbing from the concussion I'd received. My hearing would never be normal again.

As we left the lines, one lone incoming shell burst close

to me. I didn't hear the artillery piece fire in the distance. A jagged piece of shrapnel about six inches long landed at my feet. Too exhausted to think clearly, I reached down and picked up the hot piece of metal. Immediately I dropped it, and in a daze, looked down at my blistered fingers. It was time to leave the front lines.

In the army I very seldom showed any outward expressions of my religious beliefs. Being a loner, I didn't have anyone to confide in. Every night before falling asleep, I looked up to the heavens and asked God to watch over me until the war ended. I needed His help more than ever now. My job depended not only on having a keen sense of smell and excellent night vision, but also on good hearing, which was now impaired.

When we returned to our rest area, Sergeant Joe Montoro informed me that the captain had put George Johnson and me in for Silver Stars, the decoration awarded for gallantry in action. The medals were to be given for the mission we accomplished at the railroad cut next to Hill 69. The one thing that bothered me about receiving the decoration was the fact that officers weren't giving credit to the man who voluntarily helped George Johnson and me. George Porth endangered his own life just as much as we jeopardized ours.

I approached our platoon lieutenant about the injustice to Porth. He brushed aside my arguments and said, "I'm sorry, Corporal, but we are only authorized to give out a certain number of Silver Stars. The main reason you are receiving one is that the captain wants to show his appreciation for the help you gave him running patrols on Hill 69. He can't give you a medal for the actions that took place on your patrols, for there were no witnesses to the deeds you performed. To receive a medal, another person has to verify the deed and then recommend you for the award."

My protests about the unfair situation were to no avail and landed on deaf ears. George Porth deserved a medal more than either Johnson or I. No one ordered him to risk his life. It had been my responsibility to get the equipment and ammunition to the hill. I didn't figure I'd done anything above and beyond the call of duty. Oftentimes an observer mistook stupidity for an act of bravery.

When the lieutenant refused to discuss my complaint with Captain Maple, I walked away from him in disgust. From that moment on I lost all faith in my platoon officer. My thoughts drifted back to North Africa, remembering what had happened to me after I carried Bob Ackerman down off the hill at Ferryville. I didn't do it to get a medal, for medals were unimportant. When another man received the Silver Star for the act I'd performed on the battlefield, it bothered me, even though I kept the hurt inside. I knew how Porth must feel after this recent episode of nonrecognition. Until the day I left the military service, I never understood many of the army's policies, especially when it came to dealing with the men who did the actual fighting.

I thought about the command I gave George Johnson. I had ordered him to get into the jeep and drive it to safety, even though shells were exploding all around us. If he hadn't escaped before the burning trailer exploded, or if an artillery shell had killed him, the foolish order I'd given would have been responsible for his death.

I was no better than our lieutenant at Castelvetrano, Sicily. He gave Roscoe and me a stupid suicide command. The order that I'd given Henderson, sending him to his death in one of the last tank battles in Tunisia, would haunt me as long as I lived. Though I hated to admit it, I was beginning to place little value on human life. I seemed to be caught up in the army's game of tossing men's lives around like the early Romans did when they threw the Christians to the lions in the Colosseum.

The experiences that I had endured over the past couple of weeks preyed heavily on my mind. I became depressed. All of my personal belongings were in the bottom of the trailer when it blew up, even the dark purple vest that I'd made out of German army blankets. My most prized possession, the guitar I'd made out of an ammo box, was now just a memory. The poems I'd written throughout the war were inside of the guitar. Except for the few verses that I'd sent home to my friends and family, the irreplaceable writings of the war in Africa, Sicily and Italy were lost forever.

To relax, I put my thoughts into a poem, and vowed this would be the last one I'd ever write. For over 45 years, I kept that promise. The poem tells about those days and nights we spent on Hill 69. It portrays the life of the foot soldier who fought in Italy. I called the poem,

### A DAY IN BATTLE, THOUGHTS IN A FOXHOLE

*These are the thoughts of a soldier,*
*Crouched low in his foxhole out there.*
*Though tired, half frozen and hungry,*
*From between his lips comes a prayer.*

*He prays for the Lord to spare him*
*From the bombs and shrapnel this day,*
*That He'll keep watch o'er his foxhole,*
*And guide all the bullets away.*

*He wipes the frost from his rifle*
*And brushes the mud from his hair,*
*Then carefully rolls his blanket*
*In the dark and cold morning air.*

*If water left in his canteen*
*By chance wasn't frozen last night,*
*He'll swallow a drop with his biscuit*
*And finish his hash, 'fore it's light.*

*Dawn breaks across snowy mountains*
*And the soldier dreams of his home,*
*His friends, his family, and country,*
*And the girl he's left there alone.*

*His wallet carries some pictures*
*He treasures and guards with his life.*

He smiles and looks at his family
And the girl he'd like for his wife.


All day machine guns are ready
In case of a counterattack.
The men are prepared for battle
With rifle and pack on their back.


A shell bursts up in the heavens.
The Germans are getting their range.
All of us look at each other,
We know that our luck's going to change.


An instant later it happens,
A barrage that shakes the whole earth.
Shells whistle and scream like sirens,
Then explode and throw clouds of turf.


Unending the shells come over,
'Til the sweat breaks out on your face.
The sky is smoke, dirt and powder,
And shrapnel is running a race.


It whines through the air just like bees
And cuts all your camouflage down,
Then sprays dirt into your foxhole,
While hunting you down like a hound.


You hear a lone shell come over
And closer and closer it whines.
Your heart can't pound any faster.
You're hot, but there're chills down your spine.


There comes a deafening explosion
That shatters the prayer from your lips.
You're covered with dirt and debris
And the rifle from your hand slips.

*You lay and shake for a moment*
*And wonder if you're in one piece.*
*You thank God for sparing your life*
*But beg Him to make those guns cease.*

*The barrage seems never to end;*
*Then up in the sky, planes we see.*
*They dive-bomb enemy strongholds.*
*The Good Lord has answered our plea.*

*We smile as they strafe and dive-bomb*
*Through German ack-ack in the sky.*
*Our planes have silenced the Germans,*
*And we thank them as they fly by.*

*The medics attend our wounded*
*And carry them back to the rear.*
*We stick to the hill and dig deep*
*For we know the Jerries are near.*

*Our radio on the hillside*
*Keeps contact behind our front line.*
*The shrapnel broke its antenna*
*And the men patched it up just fine.*

*All day long, blasted artillery*
*Throws shells on the hill where we lay.*
*More than once your nerves seem to crack,*
*But the men continue to stay.*

*Many times a shell comes over*
*That makes you crouch low in your hole.*
*There'll be no deafening explosion,*
*Just a dud that vibrates your soul.*

*As darkness falls over the lines,*
*Forward listening posts are all out.*

*Patrols bring back information*
*We'll use in tonight's final bout.*


*You stand guard on a machine gun*
*As bullets go whistling by*
*And dream of a plate of turkey,*
*Then lick your parched lips with a sigh.*


*Mid shell-bursts you ask your buddy,*
*"How'd you like some pork chops and cake,*
*Some ice cream and pie and chicken,*
*Or a nice big round juicy steak?"*


*But alas, your dreams are broken*
*When he hands you a can of stew*
*And says, "Quit makin' me hungry.*
*We'll get it when this war is through."*


*An hour or two before daylight*
*We pick up our roll and our gun,*
*Move forward into the unknown,*
*Dodge lead; they ain't shootin' for fun.*


*Finally, we take our objective,*
*But we've paid a price for the hill.*
*We fall to the ground, exhausted,*
*And pray for those guns to be still.*


*Like mad, we dig with our shovels*
*'Til our foxholes are plenty deep.*
*Machine guns are all in action,*
*But still, there is no time for sleep.*


*Once again, the shells come over*
*And make your adrenaline flow.*
*This is the life of a soldier,*
*It's the only life us boys know.*

> *These are our thoughts in a foxhole,*
> *While hungry and cold on the line.*
> *Someday, this war will be over.*
> *And the sun on us boys will shine.*

After our successful attack on Hill 69, Monte Porcha was taken by infantry of the 5th Army. Soon afterward, Monte Trocchio fell. This lone mountain, the last obstacle before reaching the Rapido River, stood in the middle of the Liri Valley about three miles south of the town of Cassino.

Troop C retired to a rest area not far behind the front lines. For the second time since we landed in Italy, American Red Cross girls visited our squadron. They passed out steaming hot cups of coffee and doughnuts. It seemed strange to see American girls this close to the front lines.

Because the terrain where we bivouacked shielded us from enemy observation, we were allowed to watch a movie. Very seldom did we get to attend a USO show, for our squadron was one of the many units in the army called a "bastard outfit." We were the lone cavalry reconnaissance squadron, not only in II Corps, but in the entire 5th Army. Like other small units in the corps, we never became a permanent part of a division. Whatever outfit was on the line in our sector of the front when the Germans retreated, whether it be infantry or armored, we were attached to that unit. Being a small outfit had its advantages, but when celebrities came overseas to entertain the troops, they usually visited the divisions.

January was half over by the time we moved off Hill 69 to lick our wounds, regroup and continue our never-ending training. A tenseness filled the air, and everyone had the feeling that something big was about to happen. On January 19, our premonitions were confirmed. Captain Maple called C Troop together and told us the role we were to play in the upcoming battle. On the following evening, January 20, the men of the 36th Infantry Division were scheduled to cross the Rapido River below the town of Cassino. The battle plan called for them to establish a beachhead on the far side of the river, a simple task, according to General Mark

Clark's strategists. Of course, these planners were at 5th Army headquarters, far behind the front lines.

Troop C had the honor of keeping in contact with the Germans once the 36th Division secured the beachhead. Supposedly, the Krauts would evacuate Cassino, retreat up the Liri Valley with their tail between their legs and head for Rome. General Clark, commander of the 5th Army, must have been living in a dreamworld to think General Kesselring's army would give up so easily. The Germans spent weeks building fortifications in preparation for just such an attack.

Our vehicles were loaded and ready to pull out at a minute's notice. I'd received another small trailer to replace the one destroyed in the battle of Hill 69. Anxiously, we awaited news from the 36th Infantry. For the first time in the Italian campaign, we were going to revert to mounted cavalry. Apprehension etched the faces of the men.

On that fateful night of January 20, the sky lit up brighter than 1,000 volcanic eruptions of Mount Vesuvius. All along the front, from the Tyrrhenian Sea on the west coast to the Adriatic Sea on the east, the ravenous appetite of the artillery pieces could not be satisfied. Their feverish mouths belched out undigested chunks of steel that refused to be chewed up until they exploded behind the German lines. The largest artillery barrage so far in the war made me wonder if the eighty-mile-wide boot of Italy might not split apart at the seams.

As H-hour approached, all eyes focused on the sky to the north. Antiaircraft, mortar and machine guns took part in the harassing fire. Thousands of tracer bullets arched across the winter sky, looking like a giant nocturnal rainbow.

Stories relayed to us by one of the recon patrols told about the swampy approaches to the Rapido River and the enemy artillery fire that covered every inch of mud on each side of it. If Troop C ever reached the far side of the river where the rainbow of harassing fire ended, we never expected to find the legendary pot of gold. In its place, we'd probably find helmets full of tears, stained red with blood from men of the 36th, for they were given an impossible task.

The Germans were entrenched in the most sophisticated fortifications that any defending army could hope for. They used Italian labor to reinforce natural caves, construct concrete bunkers, and build their defenses. The winter line was destined to find a place in the history books not yet written. It became known as the famous Gustav Line. On that cold winter night in January, none of us ever dreamed that almost five months would pass before any Allied force breached the line.

If ever a battle sapped the strength, sucked the blood and tore the living soul out of an army, Cassino was that battle. It challenged the pride and manhood of almost every nation that fought for the Allied cause in Europe. It made fools of the military strategists of the nations who attempted to conquer it. The rains and melting snows flowing into the Rapido River carried the life's blood of thousands of youths from both armies out into the Mediterranean Sea. In the end, Cassino would fall. Ironically, the beautiful Benedictine monastery overlooking the scene also became a victim of one of the most devastating battles in the history of modern warfare.

The 36th Infantry Division had to launch a night attack because the Germans controlled the surrounding mountains and literally looked down their throats. The fate of the Benedictine monastery, perched atop 1,700-foot-high Monte Cassino, became one of the most controversial topics throughout the Christian world. Contrary to what the Germans claimed, many of the Allied soldiers believed they were using the abbey as an artillery observation post.

On the evening of January 20, under cover of darkness, the infantrymen and engineers hauled rubber rafts and thirteen-foot-long wooden boats to the river. The majority of the boats never made it through the deep mud to the water's edge. The village of Sant' Angelo lay on the far side of the river. The 19th Engineers of II Corps tried desperately to construct bridges. Though only twenty-five to fifty feet wide, in some places the river was ten feet deep. The banks on the German side of the river were five to ten feet high, but our side was fairly level. The dams located at the headwaters of the Rapido, which the

Germans destroyed, flooded the lowlands and turned them into a quagmire. With artillery zeroed in on every foot of the river, no bridge the engineers constructed survived.

Throughout the night, we waited for orders to move forward and cross the river. Those orders never came. As hard as they fought, the brave men of the 36th were doomed. All the previous attacks made by the British on the left flank failed. General Mark Clark had previously assured General Walker, commander of the 36th, that before his men crossed the river, the left flank would be in Allied hands. He didn't keep his promise.

If the British attack had been successful, the Texas Division might have had a chance. Under the circumstances, trying to make a crossing with German firepower concentrated on one area proved disastrous. General Mark Clark should have called off the attack, but he didn't.

Segments of a few infantry companies made it across the river before all the boats, rubber rafts and footbridges were destroyed. Once the men reached the far side of the river, they were stranded. Most of those who fought so courageously to take their objective were either wounded, killed or captured. The second day's renewed attack turned out to be a repeat performance.

Troop C received orders to leave its vehicles at the bivouac area and proceed at once to the Rapido to support the ill-fated 36th. We dug a second line of defense a short distance from the river in mud the consistency of thick soup. We tried to construct breastworks in front of our foxholes, but the supersaturated mud flowed like lava and drained back into the trenches. To escape the never-ending shrapnel and bullets, we repeatedly dove into the slippery muck.

The first night we spent next to the river, we dragged a couple of shattered boat hulls over our foxholes to provide a little protection from the weather. As bad as the situation seemed to us men on the south bank of the river, we had a picnic compared to those who remained alive on the Cassino side. Not many of them would ever return.

On January 25, the Germans declared a truce that lasted over two hours. The American medics, carrying white flags, crossed the river and recovered the dead and wounded. For the first time in the war, I witnessed a truly humane incident. Even the German soldiers sympathized with the men of the 141st and 143rd Regiments of the 36th Infantry. The Texas Division suffered a total of 1,681 casualties. The German soldiers must have wondered what kind of a commander we had leading our troops. A man had to consider victory in battle of greater importance than human life or he'd never have ordered a frontal assault across a river bordered on both sides by a sea of mud, especially after the British flank attack failed to take any of the high ground. If our commander believed his cause to be that just, he should have been out in front of his troops leading them into battle. Our colonel led C Troop's assault up About Face Hill in Tunisia.

General Von Senger, the German commander who masterminded the building of the defenses at Cassino, approved the truce of January 25. In World War I and earlier in World War II, he earned the reputation of being a superb military strategist and a caring, compassionate leader. Like Rommel, "The Desert Fox," Von Senger was also anti-Nazi, hating Hitler's dreaded Gestapo with a passion.

After World War II ended, there would be a congressional investigation as to whether General Mark Clark used good judgment when he ordered the Rapido River crossing. Nearly every survivor who attempted to cross the frigid waters of the river, or who lay in the mud on its banks that fateful winter, disagreed with the congressional committee's final verdict.

General Clark, though a professional soldier, had experienced only a few weeks of combat up until October 1943, much less than many of his subordinate commanders. He was strong-willed, egotistical and too eager to have glory heaped on himself. Against the advice of his fellow officers, including General Walker of the 36th, who had fought in World War I, General Clark proceeded with the attack. Even though under pressure from higher authorities, Clark should have changed his plans. The 36th Division needed a rest, for they had been in the line continually since the battle of San Pietro.

During the postwar investigation, not wanting to see the reputation of one of their fellow officers tarnished, Clark's friends supported the decisions he'd made at the Rapido. They whitewashed their findings. Many survivors of the battle had ancestors who had fought with Sam Houston under the flag of the "Lone Star State." Their battle cry had been "Remember the Alamo." The men who survived the fighting along the Rapido River, instead of wanting to remember, tried to forget the Battle of Cassino. If they had had their way, the congressional board of inquiry's findings would have been different.

During the hearing, General Clark stated that he had expected heavy losses in the attack, but that in order to draw German troops away from the invasion forces who landed on the Anzio beachhead on January 22, the coordinated operation was necessary. The beachhead landings took place 70 miles farther up the coast from Cassino and only 35 miles south of Rome.

Troop C continued to support the remnants of the 141st and 143rd Infantry Regiments. Originally, we were dug in on the left side of Highway #6 across the river from the little village of Sant' Angelo. New orders were issued instructing us to take up positions on the east side of the highway directly in front of the town of Cassino. The British 8th Army sent troops from their sector of the front to strengthen the American 5th Army along the Rapido. Hopefully, this would relieve some of the pressure on the exhausted men of the American 34th and 36th Infantry Divisions. The New Zealand troops ordered to the Cassino front occupied the former positions of the 36th. Later, in the fighting around the monastery, which was only a few hundred yards northeast of the town of Cassino, French and British troops experienced in mountain warfare took over the 34th's positions.

Ironically, our old enemy, the Hermann Goering Parachute Division, which had fought against us in North Africa, now held the town of Cassino. Troop C moved east of Highway #6 and dug in their machine guns. Soon afterward, Captain Maple sent word for me to report to him. I had a feeling that the request meant only one thing: I was being singled out for a patrol mission.

The captain started the conversation by saying, "Corporal, there isn't any need for your mortar here in front of Cassino. We have direct contact with II Corps' artillery and can call for their support on a moment's notice."

Picking up a short stick, he drew two parallel lines in the wet ground, saying, "This represents the Rapido River." On the left side of the crude map, he made a line running perpendicular to the river and crossing it. "This is Highway #6 leading into the town of Cassino," he said. "Our left flank borders the highway and our front runs along the Rapido. The 34th Infantry Division is positioned on our right flank. The Germans are dug in a short distance back from the opposite shore. I've been ordered to send a patrol out every night, not a combat patrol, but one to gain information about the enemy."

As soon as I heard the captain's last statement, I knew the reason he'd sent for me. In the recent battle on Hill 69, I'd been given the responsibility of scouting the enemy's lines. The grave look on his face, and the humble tone of his voice, relayed the importance of the task he was about to assign me.

Deep furrows appeared on his forehead when he said, "Corporal, I am putting you in charge of those patrols. Dig your foxhole behind the 2nd Platoon's machine-gun emplacements. Inform me of its location just in case I need to get hold of you in a hurry. Each night before dark report to me for your orders. I'll tell you what sector to operate in. Most of the time your job will be to cross the river, then move along in front of the German lines. Like on your patrols at Hill 69, you are to listen for troop movements. Report anything out of the ordinary that will alert us the Krauts are reinforcing their positions in preparation for a counterattack. Make sure you return under cover of darkness. There is no way you can survive out in No-Man's-Land once it gets daylight."

This last piece of advice was most important. Off to the northeast, less than a mile from the town of Cassino on Hill 516, loomed the ancient Abbey of Monte Cassino. Perched atop the 1,700-foot-high mountain, the monastery reminded me of a gigantic ark left high and dry when the Mediterranean Sea receded centuries ago. In January 1944, it overlooked a semifrozen sea of mud. Though not a beautiful building like India's Taj Mahal, it had an air of mystery about it. Day and night it seemed to cast a spell over me. Wherever I moved, the structure held me in its grasp, not a tender caress, but a dominating hug. The dark windows in the sides of the imaginary ark were like penetrating eyes following every movement anyone made on the valley floor.

Below the abbey on Monte Venero was a strongly held German position known to the Allied soldiers as "Hangman's Hill." Behind the monastery to the northeast, covered with a mantle of winter white, lay Monte Cairo.

The captain continued his instructions and said, "Corporal, I know you like to operate alone, but most of the time I'm going to send another man on patrol with you. It's imperative that any information you obtain reach headquarters before the Germans have time to counterattack. On some patrols, I might assign a higher-ranking noncom to accompany you, but because of your experience, you will be in charge. Tonight, I want you to contact the troops on our flanks. Make sure you tell the squad leader of the machine-gun nest you intend to return through to alert his relief. Good luck, and be careful."

Captain Maple was a conscientious officer. I not only respected him, but also considered him my friend. He didn't expect more from his men than humanly possible and always seemed concerned about their safety. Oftentimes he asked for a noncommissioned officer's opinion and never made you feel inferior.

After digging a new foxhole, I checked in with Sergeant Montoro. I made sure that he knew I'd been relieved of my responsibilities as a squad leader. Afterward, I lay down to rest.

One of the new replacements, Henry Mahaney, from Farmington, Michigan, crawled over and lay on the muddy ground next to my foxhole. "Fred," he said, "you've been on a lot of patrols. What is your secret of survival? Will you teach me a few of the tricks you've learned? I'm afraid I'll never survive unless someone helps me."

I never really thought of it before, that a man had to depend on tricks to survive. I told Henry, "When you say 'tricks,' if you mean having a little knowledge of the wilderness, some common sense along with luck and a faith in God, then maybe a fellow on patrol does need to know a few. Night patrols to most men are a hazardous duty, but I've always considered the night to be my friend. If you understand the darkness and use it to advantage, it can become an ally in the completion of a successful mission. It is much safer to run a patrol at night than during the day. The exceptions are when the enemy uses flares and trip wires which are almost impossible to see."

Henry couldn't write any notes down, but he listened intently when I said, "One of the most important rules of survival is to have patience. I seldom make a move without first studying the lay of the land. Before starting out on a patrol, I try to memorize the terrain, made clear by the contour lines on a topographical map of the area. I pick out different routes leading to my objective. Though some of them may be longer than others, there is less chance of being discovered if you don't cross an open area. Unless the night is pitch-black, the distance you save could wind up being the shortest route to your grave.

"I try to improvise alternate methods of escaping from a bad situation. A plan of action is essential when the unexpected happens. It is difficult to formulate a new plan once you are trapped. Henry, you will find that patrol work is much like rolling dice, it is a game of chance and impossible to win all of the time. Sooner or later the odds will work against you. I make an effort to beat those odds by putting myself in the enemy's shoes. I try to think like a well-disciplined German soldier. Loading the dice with the knowledge I've learned through four campaigns of patrols has helped. Instead of lying in my foxhole daydreaming, when I have a few minutes to relax, I keep my mind busy."

Henry didn't question my self-taught philosophy about patrols but asked, "Fred, what goes through your mind when you are all alone out there in No-Man's-Land? How can you tell if you are close to the enemy?"

"Once you begin a patrol," I said, "you have to psych yourself into a state of mind that makes you feel you are part of the environment. It takes a great deal of practice to separate the night sounds natural to the surroundings from those caused by humans. The wind gently blowing through the brush and trees or the friendly chatter of a bird or animal can be a comfort.

"There are other sounds that alert your senses to the danger lurking close by, like the whisper of cloth or metal rubbing against a branch or gliding through tall grass. The splash of a few drops of water dripping from a man's boot or the change in the sound of water flowing over a rock in a stream can warn you that you are not alone.

"There are smells that have to be sorted out. Animals give off a different scent than humans. Even the eating habits and personal hygiene of man can produce a different body odor. Oftentimes in the dark of night, if the breeze is coming from the right direction, that smell can be detected from quite a distance. The drifting odor from a cigarette cupped unseen in an enemy's hand can warn you of impending danger. You have to constantly be aware of the direction of the breezes, for they can not only warn you of danger but also alert your enemy to your presence.

"It is uncomfortable to sit in one position for any length of time without moving a muscle, but you have to train yourself to do it. If you think you hear or smell something foreign to the environment, find out where the telltale sound or odor is coming from before you attempt to move. Detecting the faintest whisper of a soldier conversing with his buddy lying behind a machine gun is enough to save your life.

"Henry, when you approached my foxhole, you probably saw me getting my equipment together for tonight's patrol. I was checking the swivels and bands that hold the straps on my Thompson submachine gun. I have to make sure that the tape covering them will deaden the sound of metal rubbing against metal, otherwise it will telegraph my presence. The odds of survival are always in favor of the soldier lying in a defensive position. That's the reason you can't make too many mistakes while crawling out in front of him.

"Even though the blackness of night might be in your favor and you feel confident that you've taken every precaution to conceal your movements, there is one situation you have no control over. The shooting of a flare up into the heavens changes the whole perspective. As the parachute slowing the descent of the flare floats to earth, the only thing you can do is freeze in place. During those moments of tension, you pray that the camouflage precautions you've taken will conceal you until fate switches off the light. When the brilliant light in the sky first appears, I usually close my eyes and bow my head so I am not blinded. The situation is similar to staring into the flames of a campfire, then looking out into the night and expecting to see what's beyond the perimeter of light. Your night vision is gone.

"Many of the things I practice when on patrol, I learned as a boy growing up in the woods and while tending my trapline at night. When I took scout training back in the States, we were taught never to look straight at an object we were trying to distinguish in the darkness. To make things appear clearer, look slightly off to one side. It's an old night trick that really works. The darkness doesn't make you any less afraid, for death is forever present, but you have to understand the darkness and let it work in your favor."

Henry interrupted me and asked, "What about mines and booby traps, Fred, how do you detect them?"

"They are the things I fear most at night," I said. "Unless you notice the disturbed ground where a mine has been planted or see or feel a trip wire, your chances of survival are pretty slim. Before the war, when I ran a trapline, we used traps and snares to catch wild animals. Most mines are placed much the same way in a well-used path or runway, or a place where there is only one entrance or exit.

"Another thing you have to contend with when you venture out into No-Man's-Land is being shelled by your own artillery. It doesn't take much drop in elevation of an artillery barrel to have a shell land in No-Man's-Land in front of the German lines instead of behind them. When a patrol reenters its own lines, then they also have to worry about the German artillery.

"I've heard tell that the Americans are developing field glasses and rifle scopes that use infrared light. They operate by battery packs. This new equipment will make night vision possible. I'm glad that the Germans haven't perfected it yet or else our patrols would be more dangerous.

"I've noticed that you are a very religious man, Henry. Most everyone feels alone at some time or other in his life. Never is that feeling more apparent than when you're out on patrol. There is no one you can call on for help, no one except God. It is a good thing to have faith, and I'm not trying to destroy your trust in God, but you must do your share in helping Him out. Relying on God alone, without learning some of the things I've been telling you, will get you to Heaven a heck of a lot sooner than you've planned. Your life, when on a patrol, is balanced on a fine set of scales. It can be tipped one way or the other by the slightest mistake."

I very seldom held long conversations with the men in my squad. Usually, I kept my thoughts to myself, but I felt good about passing on what I'd learned to a young fellow who wanted so hard to survive. Henry had a chance to practice some of this advice a few nights later when he accompanied me on a patrol.

Corporal Nick Sanchez from St. Charles, Illinois, a squad leader from the 1st Platoon, went along with me on that first mission. Usually a jovial person, this particular night Nick realized the graveness of the task he'd been given. He became very quiet. We were ordered to contact the units on our flanks, which usually proved to be a job without incident. As it turned out, this one was routine. By the time we made our report to Captain Maple, Nick was in good spirits and smiling.

The following evening, investigating the area around the blown-out bridge on Highway #6 became my objective. Sergeant Henry Trevino, from the 3rd Platoon, volunteered to go with me. Henry had been in the regular army before the war. By the time we got ready to reenter our lines, both of us were wet and cold from the swollen waters of the Rapido River. Except for hearing a tracked vehicle changing positions next to one of the buildings on the outskirts of Cassino, the mission was uneventful.

As we approached our lines, we stopped to make sure we were positioned in front of the 1st Platoon's machine-gun nest. Early the previous evening, we told them to be on the lookout for our reentry.

I lay behind a tree the Germans had cut down over a month earlier when they made preparations against the American attempt to cross the Rapido. The Krauts wanted to have a clear field of fire and increase their odds of repulsing our attacks. Henry crawled up alongside me and whispered, "Fred, this isn't the first patrol I've been on with you. I'll never forget the day we attacked About Face Hill in Tunisia. I watched you crawl up the hill through the tall grass in front of me. You raised up on one knee beside a large boulder, then emptied a 30-round clip of ammo from your Thompson. After I saw what was left of that Kraut, I couldn't figure out why you kept squeezing the trigger. I've always wanted to ask you, what made you keep firing?"

When I didn't reply, he asked, "Don't you remember?"

Even though he'd been correct in his recollection, there were some things that a man didn't want to talk about. Episodes such as those, you tried to forget. Years later, I'd wake up nights reliving them.

A couple of nights later, George Rogers, a member of

my squad who'd been wounded twice so far in the war, accompanied me on patrol. We were told to cross the ford of the river on our right flank, work our way along the low ground in front of Cassino, then proceed to Highway #6, which bordered our left flank. I never felt at ease with George, for I knew that if we ever got in a difficult situation, he wouldn't hesitate to open fire and expose his position. Usually, I instructed the men on my patrol to use a hand grenade whenever possible rather than have the muzzle flash of their weapon give their position away.

With olive-green pineapple grenades hanging from the ammo belt around his waist and crossed bandoleers of ammunition draped across his robust chest, George reminded me of Pancho Villa, the Mexican bandit chieftain. In fact, I often called him Pancho. This particular night I told George to remove his bandoleers, for while he was crawling, they might catch on a twig and give our position away. Unlike me, George preferred to carry the new, semiautomatic M1 Garand rifle, issued to the riflemen of the troop back in Sicily. It replaced the old 1903 Model bolt-action Springfield rifle.

When we started out on our mission, the sky was blacker than Hitler's mustache, a beautiful night to run a patrol. After passing through the 2nd Platoon's machine-gun emplacement, we proceeded down to the river. With George covering me, I crossed at the ford without any problem. Moving a few yards to my left, I waited behind the three-foot-high riverbank on the opposite shore for George to join me.

We were about to climb over the bank and start crawling toward the German lines when we heard the muffled report of a flare gun. Instantly the sun seemed to catapult out of the center of the earth and hang suspended overhead. If the Germans had waited a few seconds longer to launch their flare, we'd have been caught in the open. Because the ford was the logical place to cross the river, the Krauts periodically shot flares over it. This time, they almost succeeded in catching us.

Patiently, we waited for the parachute carrying the flare
to land. Even with my eyes closed, the intensity of the light
became so bright, I was positive the flare would land on top
of us. Instead, it came to rest on the flat ground about six
feet in front of the bank behind which we crouched. After
waiting a few minutes for our eyes to become accustomed to
the dark, we moved out. As I crawled past the spot where the
burnt-out flare had landed, I crumpled the small white cloth
parachute in my hand, then shoved it in my combat jacket.
Years later, all the souvenirs I'd been fortunate enough to
save while on patrols brought back memories of the life I'd
lived on the edge of the abyss of death.

George and I spent half the night working our way west
across the swampy ground in front of the town of Cassino.
Once we reached Highway #6, we took our time crawling
along the edge of the road that led into the town. Though
we had to be careful about not making noise on the hard
surface, it was good to be on dry ground again. We kept
out of the gutter because it was full of noisemaking trash
and leaves. All the while, we listened for the sound of the
enemy.

Like a buck deer moving cautiously through strange
territory, we stopped every few feet to sort out the night
sounds. If we hadn't, we might not have heard the hard-
soled boots of a German patrol coming toward us. We
were fortunate that they were on their side of the river. If
they'd been concerned about making noise, we'd never
have had time to lie down in the gutter.

Much to our horror, the patrol of six or seven men
came to a halt directly opposite us. A couple of the men
sat down on a stone wall on the other side of the road. The
rest of them remained standing. Two of the Krauts were
within a couple of feet of where I lay. Little did they realize the prize of human flesh within their grasp. The men
began to talk in low tones. My heart skipped a few beats,
sounding like a one-cylinder Wisconsin engine with water
in the gas. I was certain the Krauts were unaware of our
presence. They'd just stopped for a break before crossing

the river to infiltrate our lines. The patrol was probably on the same type of mission as George and I, trying to obtain information about troop movements.

With arms outstretched, I tightened my grip on the Thompson submachine gun. Unable to move my head, for fear of rustling a few leaves, I raised my eyes and glanced in front of me. Only then did I notice the luminous-dialed watch on my wrist. It seemed to shine as bright as a jar full of the lightning bugs that we collected as kids. I realized that George and I were in for a heap of trouble if the patrol spotted my watch. If the gutter hadn't been littered with so much trash that rested against my arm, I probably could have pulled the sleeve of my combat jacket over the watch. With one of the German soldiers standing directly above me, I couldn't even take a deep breath for fear of disturbing the trash.

In those few short moments, when every page in my book of life flashed before me, I wondered if the final chapter would end with me compacting garbage in a gutter at Cassino.

One of the Germans sitting on the stone wall on the opposite side of the road lit a match. Like most soldiers, he wanted to smoke a cigarette while taking a break. Even though he cupped it in his hands and shielded the light, a faint glow penetrated the blackness of the night. All eyes immediately turned in his direction, otherwise George and I might have been discovered. Before the man had a chance to put the match to his cigarette, the patrol leader barked a harsh command. From the sound of his voice I knew the nicotine-addicted soldier was severely reprimanded for doing such a stupid thing so close to the American lines.

George and I were lucky that one of the men standing next to us didn't light the match or else all eyes would have turned in our direction. Someone on the patrol would certainly have spotted the outline of our bodies lying in the gutter.

Though it was the dead of winter, sweat rolled down the burnt cork that stained my forehead. It ran into my eyes. The tension became so great that I almost threw caution to the wind and swung my Thompson up at the ghostlike silhouettes. Even though the element of surprise would be ours, my better judgment told me to have patience. I knew it would be next to impossible to wipe out every man on the patrol, let alone escape afterward.

All of a sudden the Germans stopped whispering, and I wondered if they finally noticed the glow from my watch. If any one of them so much as made a move to reach down in the gutter to investigate, I knew I'd have no other choice but to use the Thompson. I kept thinking, "Be prepared to attack, before any of them can get into action." I had nothing to lose, except my life, and that wouldn't be worth "a promise from the devil" if they discovered us.

Though we felt like condemned men standing on the gallows with a noose around each of their necks, the hangman gave George and me a reprieve. Instead of the enemy walking toward me, they moved down the road in the direction of the blown-out bridge on Highway #6.

When the sound of their boots faded into the darkness of the early morning hours, I crawled back to George and whispered, "We've come far enough. There ain't no use pushing our luck any farther. Let's head back."

George and I didn't know whether the German patrol turned left off the highway and were going to cross at the same ford of the river that we intended to use. This made us overly cautious and delayed our return. It was almost daylight before we set foot on the south bank of the Rapido. With the patrol ended, I gave my mind a rest and tried not to think about the next one. I was just thankful that I'd lived through another night.

As the days passed, the monastery, looking mournfully down on our troops, shed tears of human blood down the cheeklike slopes of Monte Cassino. The age-old building must have realized that sooner or later it would die in the crossfire of two great armies. I, too, wondered how long I could beat the odds of fate and continue to survive the longest battle the Americans fought in World War II.

# CHAPTER X

# Forgive Us This Day

When the moon came from behind a blanket of winter clouds and reflected on the light yellow travertine stone of the Benedictine monastery, the building resembled a mountain lion crouched atop a hill. It seemed to watch every move that its prey made. Though we tried to ignore the eerie creature, that didn't lessen the terrible effect it had on us men dug in beneath its shadow.

The nerves twitching up and down your spine made you feel like the tawny-colored animal was about to spring out into the valley or reach down and strike you with its deadly paws. No area along the Rapido River in the vicinity of Cassino could escape the watchful eyes of the deadly cat. When the artillery and screaming *nebelwerfer* shells rained down on us from the valleys behind the abbey, the air became filled with a terrifying screaming sound. As the shells passed over the monastery, it cried out like a lion in the wild. I even started thinking and acting like a cat. I know that some of the felinelike tactics I practiced helped me survive.

We couldn't move out of our foxholes in the daytime. The fear of drawing artillery fire directed by an observer in the abbey hung over our heads like a guillotine suspended from a frayed rope.

The day after George Rogers and I ran into the German patrol on the outskirts of Cassino, I lay in my foxhole half asleep. A single air burst exploded a short distance away. The explosion came so unexpectedly that I never had time to roll over onto my stomach and hug the bottom of the foxhole. A piece of shrapnel penetrated the heavy overcoat I'd thrown over me and tore through the combat jacket I wore. I realized that I'd been hit in the chest but figured things couldn't be too bad, for I only felt a little pain. If the small jagged piece of steel would have hit a couple of inches to the left, my steel-covered Bible might have stopped it. The shell had exploded far enough away so that the velocity of the shrapnel had decreased by the time it hit me. Luckily, I received only a flesh wound, but it bled profusely.

After cutting off the tail of my heavy undershirt, I laid the narrow piece of cloth over the two-inch-long gash on my chest. When I applied pressure to the wound and lay still, it quit bleeding. For the first time in the war, I opened up the first aid kit on my web belt and put a bandage on the wound. I tied a piece of my shirt tight around my chest so the dressing would stay in place.

After I swallowed the sulfanilamide tablets that were in my first aid kit, I thought to myself, "What is going to happen to me next?" I let the wound bleed for quite a while in order to cleanse it. Hopefully, the sulfa tablets would take care of any infection. My fear of being sent back to a field hospital became so great that once again I decided not to report the incident. Because of my insecure feeling about not wanting to leave my comrades in the 2nd Platoon, John Manley, our medic, branded me "a stubborn maverick." I couldn't find fault with his description but didn't intend to change my philosophy.

That evening the captain ordered me to go west across Highway #6 and contact the troops on our left flank. On February 12, the New Zealand troops took over positions along the river previously occupied by the American infantry. When I started my patrol, I traveled behind our front lines before crossing over to the New Zealand positions. I didn't relish the thought of approaching a machine-gun emplacement from the front like I did on Hill 69.

When I arrived at their command post, the friendliness of everyone I came in contact with impressed me. I immediately took a liking to the men from "down under." They seemed so independent and nonmilitaristic. These were the same characteristics that Captain Maple said I possessed. The New Zealand officer in command treated me as cordially as had the commander of the Welsh Sherwood Foresters.

I had barely made myself known to the officer before he produced a bottle of rum. He didn't pour any of it into a tin cup; instead, he handed me the bottle and said, "Here, have a ration of rum, Yank. I know you fellows aren't issued any."

For the second time in less than a month, I politely refused a drink of rum from officers of the British 8th Army. I told the commander that I had to go out on a patrol after reporting to my captain. Not being a drinking man, I realized that it wouldn't take much rum to make me groggy and dull my senses. With my type of job, I needed to remain clearheaded. The New Zealand officer seemed to understand even though his subordinates joked with me, saying, "You are probably too young to drink."

They enjoyed kidding me, but I took it good-naturedly. I found them to be a wonderful bunch of men.

Early the following morning, after making my report to the captain, I returned to my foxhole a few minutes before the mountain lion atop Monastery Hill bared his fangs. I found that one of our cooks had left a large can of food for me. George Rogers told me that the mess sergeant ran out of type-C rations, the individual cans of hash, stew or beans. The only rations available were those packed in boxes holding enough for a squad of men. Each box contained number-ten cans of fruit, vegetables, meat and hardtack, with each item in an individual container.

The mess sergeant threw a can in each foxhole, supposedly enough food to last each soldier for a day or two. With rations in short supply, he had no alternative but to distribute the large cans. Even if the cooks were able to steal some food from another outfit, which they sometimes did, it was impossible to bring it to the front lines during daylight hours. The only drawback with the existing plan of giving a large can to each man was that the contents had to be divided up in the dark.

I returned from a rough patrol that morning. The flesh wound on my chest had become irritated from crawling and began to bleed again. Exhausted, I flopped into my foxhole. I didn't bother to open my can of food to check the contents; instead, I fell asleep. By the time I awoke, the sun was high over the mountains to the east. I took my knife and cut the top off the can of food to see what I'd be eating for the next 24 hours. Hopefully, it would be fruit. My spirits took a nosedive when I stared into that ten-pound can. It contained precooked sausage held rigid in a solid glob of white grease.

A few days earlier, I'd lost the eating spoon out of my pack. With nothing to occupy my time during the daylight hours, I carved a spoon out of a piece of wood that I'd found outside my foxhole. I used this eating utensil all the time we remained at Cassino. Upon returning to the States, I carried the memento with me as a reminder of my life on the front lines.

After scraping as much of the hard grease out of the top of the can as possible, I threw the soaplike substance over the side of my foxhole. Reluctantly, I began to eat the only food available. The cold and marbled grease-coated sausage stuck to the roof of my mouth worse than warm peanut butter. Though it was almost impossible to chew, I managed to swallow most of the chunks, hoping my stomach could furnish enough warmth to melt and separate the grease from the ground-up meat.

Throughout the day I nibbled on that can of nauseating army chow. By late afternoon, I became so sick that I vomited in my helmet and threw the slimy contents out of my foxhole. It solidified on the ground and formed a slippery mess. Many years passed before I could stand the smell of sausage without getting a sick feeling in the pit of my stomach.

The German artillery observers were just waiting for an opportunity to direct fire on anything that moved. This made relieving our bowels quite a chore. The helmet that we used for shaving and bathing once again proved useful as a chamber pot. We had no other choice but to empty our excrement over the sides of our foxholes. This was much safer than exposing our lily-white backsides to a German sniper's bullet.

The combat situation on the Cassino front reached a critical stage. General Mark Clark remained under tremendous pressure from his superiors to link up with the Anzio beachhead to the north. Clark planned to make the connection by going the shortest route possible. The German general Frido Von Senger, a veteran strategist, knew how Mark Clark's mind worked. He built his main line of defense on the assumption that Clark would take the easiest option.

The mountain range that faced us had only one main pass heading north. Highway #6, often called the Appian Way, was built by the ancient Romans long before the birth of Christ. They used huge blocks of lava laid over broken stone to build the road. It entered the narrow Liri Valley behind Cassino and headed north through the pass toward Rome. On the right, overlooking the entrance to the valley, sat the monastery of Monte Cassino. Before we could reach the town, the Rapido River had to be crossed. General Von Senger flooded the upper part of the river, turning the flatland along its banks into a sea of mud.

Sometimes, the shortest route for an army to move between two points is more costly than taking a more difficult course of travel. The less rugged terrain is often the deciding factor that determines the route a military leader will take. The frontal assaults made by the 5th Army on Monte Cassino proved to be among the biggest military blunders of World War II.

Later in the war, one of the fiercest battles fought by the Allies on the western front in Europe took place at Bastogne, Belgium. It was called "the Battle of the Bulge," and 76,890 Americans and 120,000 Germans were either killed, wounded or missing in action in the battle. In comparison, in the mountain war at the Battle of Cassino, the Axis and Allied armies together suffered approximately 350,000 dead, wounded and missing in action.

General Alphonse Juin commanded two mountain divisions that made up the French Expeditionary Corps. They were fighting in the Abruzzi Mountains to the northeast of Monte Cassino. General Mark Clark ordered him to make a frontal assault on the monastery. Juin, an experienced general, proposed flanking the German strongpoints. He said that most of the Allies' superiority in equipment couldn't be used to break through the Gustav Line. General Keyes, commander of the American II Corps that we were attached to, advocated the same strategy to his superiors. All of these proposals fell on deaf ears.

Though Juin was an expert in the ways of mountain warfare, the stubborn General Clark refused to listen to him. The frontal attack by the French troops failed miserably with extremely high casualties.

The American 34th Infantry Division was also ordered to make a frontal assault in the area of the monastery. An infantry division usually consisted of about 15,000 men. Before the brave men of the 34th were taken out of the front lines, their casualties were so great that the division became almost nonexistent as a fighting unit. The soldiers of the 34th at Cassino ranked among the bravest of any men who fought in World War II.

The Germans made an unsuccessful attack on Monte Castellone on February 12. On February 13, the Germans, under a white flag, sent an officer to the Americans asking if a truce could be declared. Much like the truce they granted earlier on the Rapido River, the Germans requested permission to pick up about 150 of their dead and wounded. These men lay on the slopes of Monte Castellone on the Monte Cassino Ridge. The truce was asked for between the hours of eight and eleven A.M. on February 14.

Both the 34th and 36th American Infantry Divisions were almost destroyed in the fighting around Cassino. For this reason, after the war ended, the 36th asked for a congressional investigation into the leadership capabilities and the battlefield decisions made by General Mark Clark.

Major General Francis Tucker commanded the Indian Division, which included the mountain-fighting, knife-wielding Gurkhas from Nepal. General Clark ordered the general to make a frontal assault on the monastery. General Tucker strongly disapproved of the plan and asked Lieutenant General Freyberg, head of the New Zealand troops, to intervene. Before Tucker's troops made the attack, he wanted General Freyberg to apply pressure on the Americans to bomb Monte Cassino.

It was the general opinion of the Allies that the Germans were using the monastery as an observation post from which to direct their incredibly accurate artillery fire. The decision to bomb the abbey was against the better judgment of most of the American staff officers, including General Clark. They were afraid of the repercussions from the Christian world if the monastery and its art treasures were destroyed.

In the early hours of February 15, 1944, most of the men were moved back from their gun positions. We were told the abbey would be bombed that morning. The previous day, leaflets were dropped on the abbey informing its occupants of the Allied decision to destroy the Benedictine monks' home.

The walls of the monastery were ten feet thick at the base, and the building was about 150 feet wide and 660 feet long. It looked beautiful atop the hill, but to us soldiers gazing at it from the valley floor, it reminded us of a fortress. Its long rows of narrow windows resembled gun ports. At the time and even after the war ended, the Germans disputed the fact that they occupied the monastery. With the abbey never out of our minds or our sight, we imagined that back in the shadows behind the window openings lurked guns pointing down at us.

The dawn of the 15th arrived crisp and clear. The sun, with a premonition of the events to come, crept cautiously over the Abruzzi Mountains behind the monastery. Unlike the beginning of most other great battles, no artillery barrage announced the approach of H-hour. Instead, all of the guns on both sides of the Gustav Line became silent. A deathlike stillness settled over the battlefield.

About nine-thirty A.M., the first wave of American B-17 bombers carrying 500-pound bombs came from the south. For too long, tears of blood had flowed down the slopes from the monastery. The bombers hoped to destroy the eyes of the abbey that most Allied soldiers believed were responsible for directing the artillery fire that kept the blood flowing.

It seems that the human race derives a twisted, inquisitive pleasure in witnessing the forces of nature destroy part of our planet or in watching men inflict torture and suffering on other humans. Down through the ages, cruel events took place in the Colosseum to the delight of thousands of spectators. Even in modern times, amphitheaters and arenas are filled to capacity with throngs cheering their favorite contestant, team, animal, or fowl on to victory. Cockfighting is a sport where roosters fight to the death. In bullfighting, the spectators take pleasure in watching a maddened bull be tortured until, finally, the heroic matador's sword is driven between the animal's shoulders in a death plunge. Even the execution method of hanging draws crowds to view the event. So it was with the preannounced destruction of the famous Benedictine monastery.

People came from as far away as Naples to watch a piece of history die. Many of them brought along picnic lunches. They stayed safely out of harm's way on Monte Trocchio, three miles to the south.

During the early phase of the American Civil War at the first battle of Bull Run, spectators acted much the same way. Carriages loaded with socialites and curious noncombatants drove down from Washington, D.C. They came to witness the slaughter of their fellow countrymen.

That morning in February 1944, soldiers from both armies sat in their foxholes, staring at the heavens. They waited for the curtain to be lifted on a performance that would make a few men happy but the rest of the world sad. The scene reminded me of a legend about ancient Rome where Nero supposedly played a lyre while Rome burned. I was no better than the other spectators at Cassino, for I didn't want to miss the show.

The monastery had been a source of controversy ever since the battle began. Most of the men in the trenches wanted the building that had been a cultural center in Europe for hundreds of years, destroyed. The morning of the bombing, with the sun reflecting on the ancient building of stone yellowed with age, I felt saddened to think that it had to go.

The drone of engines in the sky broke the stillness of the battlefield. As we watched, the first bombs were released from the planes. The dark specks in the sky descended in a sloping glide toward the abbey. Immediately after the black plume from the exploding bombs appeared, white clouds of smoke caused by flying debris enveloped the building. Wave after wave of planes emptied their loads of destruction. Still the walls of the monastery remained.

Later in the day, B-26 Marauder bombers with their 1,000-pound bombs appeared from bases in Foggia, Italy, and the island of Sardinia. Not all the bombs found their target. Some of them were dropped as far away as 17 miles to the south on mountain terrain similar to that in the Cassino area.

After the last dust settled around the monastery, though the roof was destroyed, the ten-foot-thick walls remained intact. No holes penetrated the base through which an infantryman could enter the building. There was no reason for the German troops not to occupy the rubble now and take advantage of the excellent defensive positions provided by the bombing. A total of 576 tons of explosives were dropped on Monte Cassino by 142 B-17 bombers and 117 medium bombers. The day's destruction only turned the building into a fortress.

The abbey was bombed at the request of the commander of the Gurkha troops from Nepal. Their attack, scheduled to coincide with the bombing, didn't take place until two nights later, on February 17. Because of this delay, when the attack finally came, Germans troops already occupied the abbey. The Allies lost their tactical advantage. The Indian Division suffered 530 casualties in their initial attack. That same day the New Zealanders, who were dug in on the left flank of Troop C of the 91st Recon, attacked the Cassino railroad station. Of the 200 men taking part in the attack, only seventy returned. Before the fighting ended at Cassino, the New Zealand 2nd Infantry Division was almost annihilated.

Communication between the fighting men and the generals making the assault plans continued to be one of the main problems confronting the men at Cassino. Most of the top brass never experienced the hardships and impossible odds that faced the infantrymen. The foot soldiers fought not only the enemy, but also the weather and terrain. Back at headquarters, the generals looking at a map calculated that only a few hundred yards separated their forward positions from the objective. They thought that by throwing in more men, they could gain a victory. They didn't understand the terrain. No invading army in the history of the Italian peninsula ever captured Rome coming up from the south. Cassino was a defender's dream of victory and an invader's nightmare of death.

Captain Maple continued to send me on patrol every night. On one of my last missions before we were pulled out of the front lines, an incident happened that made me so ashamed, I never talked about it for almost thirty-five years.

Before dusk of that unforgettable evening, I blackened my face and hands and checked all of my equipment before moving up to the captain's command post. His dugout, with a shelter half draped over it, was large enough to hold three or four men. After entering the oversized foxhole, I asked him, "Where do you want me to go tonight, Captain?"

He glanced up at me, and in the dim candlelight I could see that he had an embarrassed look on his face. He seemed hesitant to answer. Finally, he said, "Corporal, when you first started running patrols here at Cassino, I said that you would be in charge of them, even though some of the men assigned to the patrol would outrank you. Up until now, that has worked out just fine, but plans have changed. New orders have come down from II Corps headquarters that change the guidelines for night patrols on the Cassino front. From now on, an officer must accompany every patrol, and I have to let him take charge of the mission."

"That's okay with me," I said, "but what's the reason for the new directive?"

"They are concerned that some of the patrols aren't

venturing very far beyond their units' machine-gun nests. Headquarters suspects that some of them are remaining hidden for the night on this side of the river. The New Zealand troops ran up against heavily reinforced positions the other night when they attacked the railroad station. They suffered tremendous losses. General Clark claims this wouldn't have happened if the night patrols had learned of the German buildup. He suspects that some patrols aren't bringing back accurate reports of enemy activity in their area. For that reason I am compelled to send a lieutenant along on every one of your patrols."

"That's fine with me," I said. "At least it will take the responsibility off my shoulders."

When I first entered the command post, though I didn't acknowledge seeing him, I noticed my platoon officer squatted down in the corner of the dugout. After listening to the captain's explanation, the lieutenant spoke up and said, "You can rest assured that this patrol will complete its mission tonight, Captain. You'll get the correct information for your report. There will be no hiding out in front of any machine-gun nest on my patrol."

Shocked, I couldn't believe what I'd just heard. The lieutenant's words were like a slap in the face. As angry as I felt, their impact didn't jar my emotions to the point of becoming violent. The hostility would come later. Looking over at the captain, I said, "You know I've never done a thing like that on any of my patrols."

Totally embarrassed by the outspoken lieutenant, the captain said in an apologetic voice, "I know that, Corporal."

My platoon officer didn't have enough sense to keep his mouth shut or retract his first statement. I believe his only concern was to impress his superior officer, but at my expense. Again he spoke up and said, "I'm only telling you that I intend to see tonight's patrol carried out as ordered."

Throughout my life, I'd always been known as a quiet person, almost to the point of being an introvert. After hearing the lieutenant speak, I had a hard time suppressing both my mental and physical emotions. Rather than reply to his intimidating remarks and defend myself, I felt like clobbering him. I'd have made a terrible mistake in hitting him in front of the captain, but I vowed that my time would come.

During the rest of the briefing I remained silent, but the captain knew by my actions that the lieutenant had gone too far in trying to build himself up. He told me to proceed to our right flank and show the lieutenant where I'd crossed the river on previous occasions. Though fairly wide at that location, the water was shallow, which made for an easy crossing. The captain told us that once we reached the opposite bank of the river, we were to proceed along in front of Cassino, all the while listening for enemy troop activity. To me, these orders were routine. Little did I realize how far from normal this mission would be. Before the coming of dawn, the minds of two men would almost be destroyed.

Tonight's patrol turned out to be larger than usual. The lieutenant, because he'd been placed in charge, assigned two more men to the mission, making a total of four. We weren't a combat patrol, but the platoon leader figured there would be safety in numbers. He didn't take into consideration that the more men you have crawling around in front of the German lines, the greater your risk of being discovered. Even though exceptionally competent men were chosen to accompany us, I felt nervous.

Corporal Tom Thompson, recently promoted to squad leader in our section of the 2nd Platoon and one of my closest buddies, stood waiting outside the dugout when the lieutenant and I emerged. The fourth member of the patrol stood smiling beside Tom, little PFC Tom Miller, from Laurel, Mississippi.

The four of us moved in a northeasterly direction behind our lines. When we reached the last machine-gun nest on the right flank, we told the men to inform their relief that we'd be returning through their position sometime before daylight.

I led the men down the slope in front of the machine gun and headed for the river's edge. The lieutenant crept along ten or fifteen yards behind me. The two other members of the patrol followed at a greater distance but kept in visual contact.

I crawled through some shell-torn brush, then squatted down behind a fallen log only a stone's throw from the river. After surveying the area to my front for a couple of minutes, I motioned for the lieutenant to join me.

While waiting for him to move forward, I watched the water ripple over the rocks that protruded out of the shallow ford. The water sparkled like a glistening raft of diamonds floating downstream on a cloud of liquid moonlight. Suspended overhead in the night sky was what the airmen called a "bomber's moon." To the right of that majestic silver globe in the sky, a couple of small clouds, the only ones visible, drifted lazily above the monastery. A beautiful evening for a romantic, but a terrible night for a patrol, especially with so many men along. It only took a small mistake by one man to place everyone's life in jeopardy.

I'd previously instructed Corporal Thompson and little Tom Miller to bring up the rear and cover the lieutenant and me when we made the crossing. A smile crossed my face when I thought of those two comrades. They reminded me of Mutt and Jeff in the comic strips. Big Tom, well over six feet tall, towered above Shorty Miller's head, which didn't even reach up to Tom's shoulder.

Though I held only the rank of a noncommissioned officer, I knew I had far more experience on night patrols than the lieutenant. Even though he joined our outfit before we landed in Sicily, to my knowledge this was his first night mission. Except for his lack of experience, it didn't bother me that he'd been put in command. Just the same, with so many lives at stake, I couldn't let him make decisions that would imperil the safety of the patrol. Ever since we'd left the command post, his uncalled-for comments to Captain Maple were eating away at my pride.

Throughout my army career, I'd always adhered to the army's policy of observing strict discipline. I was taught that you either obeyed the orders given by your superior officers or else suffered the consequences. Since the battle of Hill 69, whenever I ventured out into No-Man's-Land, I let my conscience guide me, not the word of an officer. It took me four campaigns to learn that in the heat of battle, a man should be judged by his capabilities and performance under fire, not by his rank.

My new philosophy of making decisions in combat without first consulting my superior officers in the platoon didn't sit too well with them. This is the main reason that, lately, when assigned to patrol duty, I worked directly under the captain's supervision. No one reprimanded me for my change in attitude, for I did my job. Because of my actions, I became a very lonely person. Complying with the army's policy of going through a chain of command is fine when you are back behind the lines. When a few minutes' delay in taking control of a serious situation can mean the difference between life and death, a man must use his own judgment and take the initiative.

Because of my new attitude, recognition for any of the deeds I performed while on patrol had to come from the captain. He recommended me for the Silver Star on Hill 69, not my platoon officer. I knew that I would never advance in rank higher than a corporal, for I wasn't cut out to be a leader. No wonder the captain considered me a "maverick."

Ever since we left the command post, I'd been formulating a plan of how to deal with the lieutenant. Subconsciously, I believe I still held ill feelings against this officer for his actions toward me after the battle on Hill 69. I blamed our conflicting personalities as the cause of his refusing my request to award PFC George Porth the Silver Star he so rightly deserved.

As the lieutenant crouched next to me behind the log, I whispered, "Across the river and to our left, you'll notice a high bank. That is where I head for whenever I use this crossing. If the Germans open fire from the flat ground between the buildings in Cassino and the river, that bank will give us protection."

Before reaching the river, I had carefully rehearsed the words to my next statement. "Lieutenant, you were put in command of this mission. Up until tonight, I've led every patrol from Troop C that ventured out in front of our lines here at Cassino. Not once have I shirked my duty by asking another man to lead my patrol. Back in the captain's dugout, you seemed very anxious to take command of this mission and prove how brave you are. I was only instructed to show you the ford that I usually use, not lead the patrol." Pointing to the wide expanse of shallow water in front of us, I said, "Well, there it is. When you're ready, move out and I'll cover you until you get safely across."

Without giving him a chance to reply, I turned my back on him and crawled about twenty feet into the brush. By my own decision, I'd lifted the responsibility of the patrol from my shoulders. At long last, I breathed a sigh of relief.

For a brief moment I made a concentrated effort to relax, knowing that it is not mentally safe to venture into No-Man's-Land with a cluttered mind. I took a moment to glance up at the abbey that loomed above us, thinking how much it influenced all of our lives. I listened to the sound of the water tinkling like a thousand bells as it flowed over the rocks in the ford. It seemed to be playing a symphony, in this orchestra pit below the monastery. The shadows, falling up there on the stage that surrounded the jagged walls of the ancient building, danced on beams of moonlight, to the bell-like rhythm of the water. I waited.

One minute passed, then two minutes. After about five minutes elapsed, I began to wonder if something had gone wrong. Maybe the lieutenant spotted enemy activity; if so, then the delay was understandable. After waiting another five minutes, I crawled up beside him. He remained in the same position as when I left, staring across the water toward the enemy lines. He seemed to be in a trance.

"Lieutenant," I asked, "have you spotted something? What's the problem?" When he didn't reply, I said, "There's no use waiting for the moon to disappear. There's hardly a cloud in the sky. You better move out. We have a lot of ground to cover before we finish our patrol."

The lieutenant made no attempt to answer; he just sat like a statue next to that log. Realizing that he didn't intend to live up to his responsibilities, I decided to take charge and lead the patrol. I checked the actuator on the top of my 1928 Thompson submachine gun to make sure it was in firing position, then started to crawl alongside the log in the direction of the river.

Before I'd gone a couple of feet, in a voice cracking from emotional strain, the lieutenant whispered, "You know, Corporal, I've been watching and listening. I haven't seen or heard any activity coming from the German lines. I believe we can wait here a while longer, then go back and report that everything is all clear. I don't believe there are any enemy troops moving around in front of our sector."

In disgust, I looked back across my shoulder at my superior officer. All the anger that I'd built up inside of me since he tried to make a good impression on the captain came to the surface. I said, "Lieutenant, right now, no one is more afraid to cross that river bathed in moonlight than I am. Every time I leave the safety of our lines, I get this same feeling. If you can't overcome those feelings, then you don't belong out here leading this patrol."

I should have stopped talking and realized that the man was not responsible for his actions, but I didn't. Instead, I said and did things that have gnawed at my conscience even until now. I said, "Back at the command post, when the captain gave us our orders, you spoke the truth when you told him this patrol would complete its mission. You said that he'd get the correct information when you made your report. You're supposed to be leading this patrol tonight. So help me God, you better move out right now, or you'll never leave this spot."

I crawled back toward him. Just recently, I had attached the sling of my Thompson to the front of the barrel with a swivel. The sling, draped over my shoulder, was fastened to a swivel I screwed to the top of the buttstock. This allowed my gun to remain in an upright firing position at all times. The sling modification permitted my right hand to be free so I could toss a grenade if needed.

Swinging the stock of my Thompson around with the heel of my right hand, the cutts compensator on the front of the barrel pointed directly at the lieutenant, almost touching his belly. His mouth dropped open. As he stared down at the gun, I flipped off the safety. Later, I realized that I'd momentarily gone insane, for I took the slack up on the trigger and slowly began to apply pressure.

When he saw my trigger finger begin to move, he sucked in his stomach and hunched his shoulders but never said a word. Lifting his eyes from the gun, he looked at me in disbelief. After seeing the deranged look on my face, he must have realized he was staring at a maniac. He knew I intended to take his life.

I'll never forget the whites of those eyes that reflected in the moonlight. With my finger a breath away from applying the final pressure on the trigger, I don't know what stopped me from killing him. Thank the Good Lord, I didn't.

Slowly, he turned his body, and without uttering a word, he crept down to the river's edge. Unless you were there that night, it is impossible to imagine how hard it must have been for him to venture out from behind the safety of that log and walk across the shallow body of moonlit water.

Halfway across that mirrorlike river, he stopped, then turned his head and glanced back over his shoulder, probably hoping against hope that I'd have a change of heart. Unflinching in the decision I'd made, I knelt with my Thompson pointed at his back. I showed no mercy to the man who had already paid a high price for his mistake. No man who calls himself a Christian would have treated another man the way I did that night. The lieutenant should have been forgiven.

When he saw no mercy in my actions, he proceeded toward the opposite shore. Only a month previous, just a short distance downstream from where he walked, the river had flowed red with blood from the men of the 36th Infantry Division. I wondered, "Would it run red tonight?" If it did, the guilt would be on my shoulders. We had no guarantee that a German patrol wasn't lurking in the brush on the opposite shore just waiting for everyone to get across before wiping us out.

Even though I had crossed the river at this location on other patrols, tonight was different. The tension seemed explosive, not only because of my confrontation with the lieutenant, but also because there were more men involved. After the cruel and inhumane thing I had just done, if disaster befell us, it would be my fault for pushing a man beyond his breaking point.

My conscience was in conflict. One side of it kept telling me that I should have been compassionate and forgiving and obeyed the lieutenant. If I had, in a couple of hours, we'd be on our way back to the command post. The other side of my conscience said there was nothing else I could have done. We were given a mission to accomplish, and the river had to be crossed. More than the lives of four men depended on the information we would bring back. At the moment, I wasn't capable of coming to an understanding with either side of my conscience. I asked myself, "When will I ever start acting like a human being instead of a military monster?"

The lieutenant deserved a great deal of credit. With a little persuasion from my Thompson, he recognized his fears. Even though he might not have completely overcome them, he led us across the river. After he reached the safety of the overhanging riverbank, I motioned for my buddy Tom to move up and cover me. All of us made it across without any mishaps. Taking our time, we proceeded along the flats in front of Cassino. A couple of hours later, we reached Highway #6. Through the course of the patrol, the lieutenant didn't speak to anyone, but performed his job exceptionally well.

Without encountering a single flare or hearing any undue troop movements, the mission was uneventful. I don't believe the Germans expected a patrol to venture out on such a clear night. With a full moon painting shadows behind every bush, there was actually no need for them to use flares. We returned by a route closer to the river, just in case watchful eyes had detected our earlier movements along the edge of the town and were waiting to pounce on us. After re-crossing the ford, we entered our lines through the previously designated machine-gun nest, ending the patrol.

Tom and Shorty Miller dropped out of our little column and returned to their foxholes. The lieutenant and I proceeded on to the command post. When we reached it, I spoke to the lieutenant for the first time since I'd threatened to take his life. As humbly as I could, I said, "You did a fine job of leading the patrol tonight, Lieutenant. You might as well make the report."

Without looking at me or making a reply, he turned and lifted the canvas flap, then entered the captain's darkened foxhole.

Oh, how I wish I would have asked his forgiveness as we stood out there beneath the disappearing moonlight, for I never got another opportunity to ease my conscience. Turning my back on the command post, I returned to my foxhole, tired and dejected. I began to worry about the repercussions that were bound to come for what I did. There was no anger left in me, just sadness and a feeling of guilt and shame. Sleep didn't come for many hours. Over and over, I reviewed and relived the night's events, trying to justify my actions, but I couldn't.

That evening, after preparing for the upcoming mission, I walked to the command post for my orders. Not knowing what the lieutenant had told the troop commander, I dreaded the thought of facing my friend. As I lifted the canvas shelter half and stepped down into the bunker, I noticed the captain was alone. The lines across his forehead, caused by the heavy burden he carried, seemed to be deeper tonight. When he didn't look me full in the face, I surmised that I'd created the change that came over him. I knew that I'd added another problem to his responsibility of defending this sector of the Rapido River.

Attempting to break the tension, I asked, "What's the mission for tonight, Captain?"

Only then did he look up, but for only a second. Lowering his eyes, he seemed to ignore me. After a moment's thought, as if trying to find the right words to answer my question, he asked, "Corporal, what did you do to the lieutenant last night?"

I couldn't avoid the confrontation any longer; my insane actions had finally caught up with me. I felt like I'd been put between the firing squad and a prisoner about to be executed. If I told the captain that the lieutenant refused to carry out the mission given us, I'd disgrace him and he'd probably be court-martialed. On the other hand, if I admitted that I threatened to kill my superior officer, I'd be lucky if I escaped with my life. What should I do?

I made a spur-of-the-moment decision. Whatever happened to me, I couldn't inform on the lieutenant. According to army regulations, I should have obeyed his orders, whether I approved of them or not. Most important, I was morally wrong. To get out of my predicament, maybe I could act dumb.

I spoke up and said, "I didn't do a thing to him, Captain."

"You must have done something terrible," he said. Then for the second time, he asked, "Tell me, what did you do?"

The draft coming from beneath the canvas that covered the bunker caused the flame of the candle to dance a shadow across his face. I dropped my eyes, for I didn't have the courage to look into that face when I answered. "The lieutenant led the patrol across the river, and he did a good job. We completed our assigned mission and returned just before dawn. I left him outside your dugout. Didn't he come in and make his report?"

I knew the captain figured I was trying to evade the issue. He wanted to hear my side of the story. I couldn't rat on the lieutenant, no matter what tale he'd told. But for the Grace of God, I could have been the one who refused to cross the river. Lately, my nerves were getting shattered. My actions last night proved that I couldn't hold up much longer under the strain of combat.

The captain had finished his interrogation. Somehow, I sensed that he felt relieved by my response. If he surmised the truth, did he expect me to reveal it? I would never know.

"This morning," he said, "after making his report, the lieutenant asked to be relieved of his command and sent back behind the lines. He has left us."

With bowed head, I sat down on the dirt floor and remained silent. "What have I done?" I asked myself. Even though the lieutenant made a mistake, I'd committed a far more serious offense, violence to a man's soul.

The captain, knowing that he'd shaken me badly, waited for my reply. When none came, he dropped the subject. Questions raced through my mind. Did he know that I almost killed one of his fellow officers? Did the lieutenant think I would disgrace him by telling the men in the troop what he did? Maybe he figured I'd hold a grudge and kill him the first opportunity I got. I was unable to come up with the answers.

The lieutenant's name would never be mentioned again. All I could do was repent. The unanswered questions and the guilt of what I had done were added to the growing list of war memories that would forever haunt me.

I asked the captain, "What officer is going to accompany me tonight?"

I never questioned his reply when he looked at me and said, "From now on, there will be no officer assigned to your patrol."

I wondered if he was afraid of running out of officers or whether those that remained were aware of what I had done and refused to associate with me.

That evening's mission, and the remaining patrols I made along the Rapido River at Cassino, were routine. I continued to work alone or with only one other man. The incident with the lieutenant proved to be my downfall. From then on, I became more depressed and nervous. I knew that I had had every intention of killing an American officer in cold blood.

I kept telling myself, "Look what war has done to you. It has made you think you are a judge and jury over another man's actions." My conscience would ask, "Does war give me the right to convict and sentence a man to death, then let me carry out the verdict? How can I ever continue to live with myself for breaking the spirit of another human being?"

Just because the lieutenant faltered under extreme pressure in combat didn't mean he was a coward. I had been afraid many times. Didn't I run away from putting a young German soldier out of his misery, only because I feared that by firing my Thompson and making a noise, his comrade would kill me? I had no right to think of another soldier as a coward, for I was one.

That night along the river, I felt justified for my actions. Since then, I'd almost driven myself to the breaking point with guilt. My efficiency as a combat soldier began to deteriorate.

None of us men in the troop ever saw the lieutenant again. Many times, in the years following the war, I wished that I could have taken him by the hand and said, "Forgive me. I am sorry for what I did."

Everyone has experienced an episode in their lifetime they wish they could relive. Even though we may regret having said or done something to another person in a fit of anger, the hurt remains. Both parties have to live with that moment for the rest of their lives.

In order to ease your conscience, YOU have to be humble enough to say, "I am sorry." The other party has to be man enough to forgive someone who is truly remorseful. These acts of humility would ease the pain that two people hold in their hearts, sometimes for as long as they live.

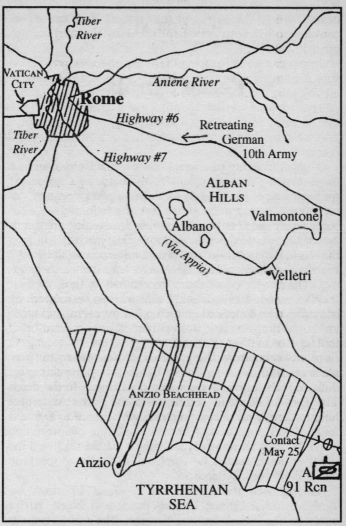

**Anzio Beachhead–Rome**

# CHAPTER XI

# Recon Patrols

A ghost from my past wraps a heavy black cloak around my shoulders whenever I think of the battle of Cassino. At the beginning of the struggle, the Allies hoped for an easy victory. Weeks turned into months of bitter fighting before the battle finally ended to become another horrible legend of war. Newspapers throughout the Allied world, when reporting on the war in Italy, spoke of "routine patrol action on the front." Fathers and mothers back home who read the war communiques had no idea what their sons endured on those patrols.

When moving forward into battle, we were surrounded by comrades who depended on each other for moral and physical support. A soldier psyched himself into a false belief that he wasn't afraid, for he couldn't show his true feelings in front of his buddies. Things were different when you were alone on a patrol in No-Man's-Land. It became extremely difficult to be brave. There were no witnesses to the deeds you were expected to perform and the fear that forever haunted you. You were on your own with no one to urge you forward with their acts of bravery. A feeling of impending doom hovered above you. Each time a soldier reentered the safety of his front lines, he wondered how much longer God would delay the inevitable.

Troops from the United States, Great Britain, New Zealand, India, France, Poland, Brazil and North Africa made up the Allied army at Cassino. The Gurkhas from Nepal, members of the 4th Indian Division, were excellent at fighting in close combat. With their deadly kukri, a heavy, curved slashing knife, they put the fear of God into their enemies. Oftentimes the French North African Goums brought back ears to prove they had killed Germans.

Ironically, when the spring offensive started, the French General Juin and his mountain troops were responsible for the breakthrough on the Cassino front. After thousands of men had been killed and wounded in frontal assaults, the tactic he proposed to the stubborn General Clark back in January proved to be the strategy that saved many lives. General Juin and his "Free French" forces outflanked Cassino and broke the Gustav Line.

Not until May 18 would the monastery fall to the Polish troops. The Germans evacuated Cassino voluntarily, and only after General Kesselring saw he would lose part of his 10th Army if they didn't retreat.

Soon after the war ended, a monument was erected in memory of the Polish soldiers who died at Cassino. The wording on the memorial expressed the feelings of all nations, including the German soldiers who survived the battle. Germany's brave men also gave their lives in one of the most senseless battles of the war. The inscription on the monument read: "We soldiers—for our freedom and yours—have given our soul to God—our bodies to the soil of Italy—and our hearts to Poland."

On March 10, 1944, the 91st Recon was relieved from combat duty along the Rapido River. We were sent back to reorganize and receive specialized training in mountain warfare. After being reunited with our vehicles, we traveled south, passing through the city of Naples. We were given a tour of the surrounding countryside, visiting the ruins of Pompeii, the ancient Roman Empire's city of sin.

Proceeding on to our training area, we established our camp near the town of Avellino. Looking west from our new bivouac area, we could see the active volcano, Mount Vesuvius. It erupted that March of 1944, destroying the village of San Sabastiano. We were continually being covered with volcanic ash, sometimes up to several inches deep. The smell of sulfur reminded me of my boyhood days when Mother forced me to take my daily spring tonic of sulfur and molasses. At night we'd sit and watch the red glow from the 3,891-foot-high volcano. The lava flowing out of the crater looked like spaghetti sauce bubbling out of an overheated pot.

All the equipment we lost since the start of the Italian campaign needed to be replaced. The box-shaped armored cars, issued to the 91st Recon when they were part of the 1st Cavalry Division at Fort Bliss, Texas, were replaced by the newer Model M8 scout cars.

The 2nd Platoon of Troop C received mountain training at the 5th Army Mountain Warfare School. This specialized training prepared us for the spring offensive of May 11, 1944. Most of the instructors at the school were Italian alpine troopers, but a few of them were from an advanced unit of the 10th Mountain Division. This division wouldn't arrive in Italy until the following winter or go into action until February 1945.

At the Mountain Warfare School, with a rope connecting us together, my squad learned how to climb cliffs that were almost perpendicular. The instructors taught us to drive a piton into a crack in a rock, then attach a carabiner, a steel ring that the rope passed through. Rappelling, the art of moving down the face of a cliff, interested me more than any part of the training. We didn't have fancy gear like the modern-day mountain climbers. A coil of half-inch manila rope, a hammer, a few pitons and carabiners were the extent of our equipment.

To rappel, we looped a long rope around a tree or rock on top of a cliff, and threw the two ends down over the sides of the precipice. With our back to the edge of the cliff, we straddled the double rope. Reaching down behind us, we brought the rope up across our buttocks, over our left shoulder, then down across our chest to our right hip. With your right hand still holding onto the rope at your hip, you bent down and grasped the rope in front of you with your left hand.

To control the speed of your descent, you moved the right hand forward or backward, letting it act as a brake. Leaning back at a sharp angle with your feet on the edge of the cliff, you leaped out into space as far as possible, while at the same time bringing your right hand forward. Applying the brake with your right hand while plummeting toward the valley floor brought you back to the face of the cliff. You continued these birdlike leaps until you reached the bottom of the cliff. Pulling on one end of the rope released it from around the tree above and allowed you to repeat the process of descending the mountain.

Oh, what a thrill to rappel down the face of a mountain. It not only gets your adrenaline flowing, but makes you feel like you've left all your earthly troubles behind. I believe that when God made heaven and earth and all things in it, he slighted us humans by only giving birds and angels the capability to fly.

I enjoyed watching the alpine troops work on the face of the cliffs. They seemed at home flying through the air. So graceful were their actions, you envisioned that they might have been born in one of the bird nests that clung to the rocky ledges. The feathers protruding from their alpine hats waved in the cool mountain breeze. When the birdlike figures sailed out beyond the face of the cliffs, an eagle in flight couldn't have been more graceful.

We weren't told the reason we were given mountain warfare training. When the spring offensive started and we saw the terrain we were expected to fight in, we soon realized the value of our time spent climbing up and down the face of those mountains. Eventually, we would go into action in the rugged coastal Aurunci Mountains north of the Garigliano River in the drive to connect the Cassino front with the Anzio beachhead.

While at our camp near Avellino, I received a five-day R-and-R pass to the town of Caserta. This was the only time while overseas that I got a pass with a note attached saying, "Just relax." The American army had taken over the king of Italy's beautiful palace at Caserta and used it as a rest area for the combat troops.

Our training area wasn't far from the town of Avellino. With no work scheduled for Sundays, my buddy Al Jerman and I went to church services in town. Walking back to camp one Sunday, we fished in one of the mountain streams and brought back a mess of fish for our buddies in the kitchen. If there'd been any Italian game wardens in the vicinity, I don't believe they would have approved of us using hand grenades instead of fishing lines.

One afternoon in late March, the entire squadron put on their best uniforms and fell out in formation. Decorations were awarded by Major General Geoffrey Keyes, commander of the American II Corps, the same general who had given me the combat jacket a few months earlier.

George Johnson and I each received the Silver Star for the part we played in getting machine guns and ammunition up to the men on Hill 69. Much to my regret, George Porth, equally responsible for the success of that operation, received nothing.

Throughout the war, I saw other deeds of heroism go unrewarded. Other times I've seen officers in Headquarters Troop receive medals they didn't deserve. Many men came home from the war without ever getting recognition for the deeds they performed above and beyond the call of duty. Any man who experienced the horrors of war on the front lines, whether he lived to tell about it or rested in peace under a white cross in some foreign cemetery, deserved a medal.

When I received the Silver Star, General Keyes' photographer took a picture of the general congratulating me. He sent it back to the States for publication in the local newspaper. When the general shook my hand, he asked, "Where have I seen you before?"

"Last October, when we were camped along the Volturno River," I said, "you gave me a combat jacket after you watched me make a vest out of a German army blanket. I want to thank you for the jacket, General. The vest you saw me making was blown up along with the ammunition the day I earned the medal you just gave me."

While at Avellino, 1st Sergeant Foote asked me if I wanted to become a sergeant. I told him that I had no desire to take on any more responsibility than a squad of eight men. I knew that I wasn't cut out to be a leader.

Just before leaving our training area, we were loaded into trucks and hauled to the courtyard of the king's palace at Caserta. There we received a shower. Each man took his turn enjoying the five gallons of warm water allotted him. The water sprinkled over our body out of the bottom of a can that had only recently contained dehydrated eggs. To put frosting on the cake, we were given freshly washed, woolen olive drab uniforms. We thought we were in "hog heaven."

After having received a few weeks' training and rest, we headed toward the front lines. We were sent north along the coast below where the Garigliano River empties into the Mediterranean Sea. There we were assigned beach patrol duty. Under cover of darkness, the Germans were sending raiding parties in small boats to infiltrate behind our lines. Our job was to intercept them when they hit the beach. This job kept us busy until the spring offensive.

On April 12, I met Albert Brown, a boy who grew up in the village with me in Pennsylvania. Albert had only recently arrived overseas with the 85th Infantry Division. When I mentioned that I always took the German prisoners' watches and pistols, he asked me if I could get him a watch. I told him the next one I confiscated would be his. The following day, his unit was scheduled to move up to the front to occupy defensive positions north of the Garigliano River.

Troop C of the 91st Recon continued performing patrol duty until May 10. The following day, all the mortar squads in our squadron were sent up to the front. At eleven P.M. on May 11, we participated in the largest artillery barrage the Italian campaign ever saw: 1,600 guns along the twenty-five-mile front opened up. As soon as the barrage ended, our 81-millimeter mortars were loaded on our vehicles and the drivers took them behind the lines. Once again, we were sent into action as dismounted cavalry.

When the attack began, none of the Allied troops from Cassino west to the Tyrrhenian Sea made any progress against the strongly defended German positions. The French Corps was made up of North African troops from Morocco, Algeria and Tunisia. They were the soldiers who finally broke through the Gustav Line in the Aurunci Mountains on the west side of the Liri Valley. The valiant French forces fought in terrain so rugged, all the Allied troops and

even the Germans thought it impossible to penetrate. The
American 88th Infantry Division, only recently arrived in
Italy, performed magnificently while supporting the French
in the attack. We men of the 91st Recon were attached to the
88th during this phase of the operation.

To show his gratitude to the American units who aided
his French forces, General Charles de Gaulle of France
awarded the 88th Infantry Division and the men of the
91st Recon attached to them the coveted Croix De Guerre
Avec Palme. We were proud to play a small part in the
eventual breakthrough on the Cassino front.

I don't believe any single objective fought for by Allied
soldiers on the western front in Europe in World War II
took as long to conquer as the Benedictine monastery of
Cassino. In comparison, after the Allies landed in France
in June 1944, it only took eleven months before the war in
Europe ended. The battle for Cassino and the monastery
lasted from January 20 until May 18, 1944.

With the spring offensive under way, we soon realized the
reason we were given mountain warfare training. On the
western sector of the Cassino front, the Germans were dug
in above sheer cliffs or steep, rocky terrain. Because of this,
General Frido Von Senger hadn't used as many troops to defend the area; he let the terrain work to his advantage. He
never thought the French and American forces would overcome the natural obstacles in front of them. The 88th Infantry Division, although fresh from the States, performed
gallantly and showed the German veterans the outstanding
courage of the American fighting man.

A few of the towns the 91st helped capture in the spring
offensive were Scauri, Formia, Gaeta and Itri. The 91st
claimed to be the first unit to enter Fondi and Sperlonga.
On the 19th of May, I had the honor of being the first
American to pass under the road sign at the entrance to the
town of Gaeta along coastal Highway #7. I will never forget
that sign, for under its shadow, I almost lost my life, all because of my stupidity.

The morning started out uneventfully, all except the

weather; it held a welcome of spring. Somehow, the sunshine reflecting off the blue Mediterranean to our left lifted everyone's spirits. It tried to make amends for the terrible winter just past. The air being sucked into my lungs had a crispness that forced me to breathe a little deeper. "Only good can come out of a day such as this," I thought. Even the breeze blowing in off the water seemed to encourage the tall grasses along the roadside to wave a welcome as we passed.

Our 2nd Platoon, under the command of Staff Sergeant Smith, reached a point about a half mile south of the outskirts of Gaeta. The white buildings in the town up ahead nestled on land that jutted out into the sea. They made a picturesque setting with their background of blue sky and water.

The sergeant called us together and said, "Gaeta hasn't fallen yet, so we better send a patrol into the town and find out how strongly it is defended."

I stepped forward and said, "I'll go, Sergeant."

"No, Corporal, I think I'll let Tom take his squad on this patrol," he replied. "He needs the experience."

My friend Tom Thompson, a scout car driver throughout the previous campaigns, had only recently been promoted to squad leader. He and three of his men moved down the road in the direction of Gaeta. As they left, I asked the sergeant, "Can I back Tom up just in case he runs into trouble?"

"Okay," he said. "Follow along behind his squad if you want to."

I motioned for three of my men who weren't jeep drivers to follow me. Taking the point position, I moved my arm from right to left. Pointing to the gutters on each side of the road, the men assumed a staggered formation in them. This tactic helped provide covering fire for each man when we passed buildings.

Tom and his men moved along about fifty yards ahead of us. When I saw his squad come to a halt at what looked to be a blown-out stone bridge, I raised my hand, the signal for my squad to stop. Tom's men went forward to investigate. They walked up to the edge of the demolished structure and peered down into the mass of rubble. Until recently,

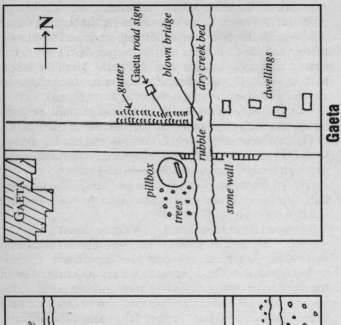

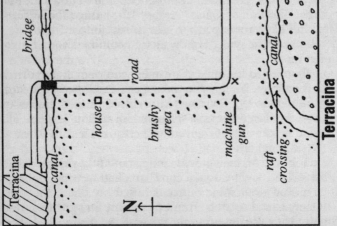

it had stood as another fine example of the beautiful masonry work of the skilled Italian craftsmen.

Without any warning, the stillness of the spring morning was broken by the chatter of a German machine gun firing from the far side of the creek bed. Dumbfounded, I watched Tom and his men fall to the ground. I knew Tom had been hit and could see that Pop Haggerty was in bad shape.

Ironically, on one of our patrols in Sicily, Pop was the fellow a German machine gunner had caught in the act of drinking a bottle of wine in a ditch. The bullets shattered the bottle and spilled wine all over Pop. This time, he hadn't been fortunate enough to escape injury, for the red fluid flowing down his arm and shirt front wasn't wine, but blood.

Even though the fairly steep approach to the bridge afforded Tom's men some protection, they were in serious trouble.

Manley, our 2nd Platoon first aid man, rushed forward from the tail end of my squad. Though wounded himself, Tom helped drag his men out of the line of fire. Later, Tom would receive the Silver Star for his gallantry. I instructed two of my men to assist the wounded.

A two-foot-high stone wall bordered the left side of the approach to the blown-out bridge. Using this to shield us from view, Paul Yenser and I crawled forward. Peering across the crater, we surveyed the area to our front. In the gutter on the right side of the road, fastened to the top of a pole about eight feet tall, I saw a metal road sign. In large letters, it announced the name of the town up ahead, Gaeta. Almost hidden among a few trees on the far side of the creek bed, we spotted the source of the firing. On the left side of the road leading into Gaeta stood a concrete pillbox.

No wonder Tom hadn't seen it, for the Krauts did a good job of camouflaging the pillbox. At first glance, Tom must have thought the Germans had destroyed the bridge, then moved north into the town.

Once again, I didn't have time to go back and ask Sergeant Smith for further instructions. We had to take the initiative and knock the pillbox out. Knowing Paul to be an excellent rifleman, I told him to take his M1 and keep peppering the slot in the pillbox. I figured that if he could get enough bullets ricocheting around inside of it, sooner or later the Krauts would have to vacate their position. At least Paul could keep them busy while the rest of us moved against it.

I told Paul that I intended to go farther up on this side of the creek bed, then cross the gully and try to outflank the machine-gun nest. I hoped the Germans were only trying to delay our advance and didn't have many riflemen protecting the flanks of the pillbox. Once I reached a point opposite it, on the other side of the creek, I might be able to toss a grenade across the road in front of the rear entrance. Hopefully, we could flush the machine gunner out.

Up until this point in the mission, I hadn't fired a round out of my newly issued .30-caliber, semiautomatic carbine. Although I'd shot a few practice rounds, I wasn't familiar with the operation of the weapon. How I wished I'd brought along my old Thompson submachine gun. Instead, I'd left it back in my jeep. A strange feeling came over me when I glanced down at the peashooter cradled in my arms, knowing that I might have to use it.

The 3rd Platoon, moving forward on our right flank, heard the machine-gun and rifle fire. A couple of their men ran over to assist us. As I turned to crawl away from Paul, I almost bumped into Corporal Arnold Eckert, former first gunner on my 3rd Platoon mortar squad in North Africa. He probably heard me tell Paul how I intended to handle the situation, for he asked, "Fred, do you want me to go along and back you up?"

"Thanks, Arnold," I said, "I sure could use your help. Let's go."

We moved across the road, behind where Tom and his men were ambushed. Manley was preparing to evacuate the wounded to a field hospital. Cautiously, Arnold and I worked our way alongside the creek.

Before venturing across the streambed, we visually searched the opposite shore, but found no sign of it being defended. Once across the creek, we stayed below the overhanging bank and headed back toward the blown-out bridge. Arnold needed no instructions, for we'd worked together in the African Campaign. I couldn't have wished for a more capable partner.

Upon reaching the old bridge abutment, I whispered, "Cover me, I'm gonna crawl down through the tall grass alongside the road."

Easing up over the bank, I parted the lush green stems of natural camouflage. With the .30-caliber carbine clutched tightly in my right hand, I proceeded to move down the gutter, which was only about a foot deep. Though warm, the weather didn't account for the excess moisture on the palms of my hands. After venturing three or four yards through the tall grass, I stopped. Glancing back over my shoulder, I noticed that Arnold hadn't crawled into the gutter yet.

Ever so slowly, I raised my head and peered as far down the ditch as possible. The coast seemed clear. If our luck held out a little longer and we didn't encounter any riflemen guarding the flank of the pillbox, we'd have it made.

All firing had ceased, even the bark of Paul's M1 rifle. The tension mounted. It seemed like I'd reached the calm in the eye of a hurricane. If I moved forward, the full fury of the storm could strike, but I couldn't remain here. After crawling a couple of feet, I halted again, then peered through the grass in front of me. Only a couple of yards to go and I should be in a position to lob a grenade at the rear of the pillbox.

Once again I advanced, stopping at the base of the road sign I'd noticed from the opposite side of the creek bed. Even though I couldn't see above my head to read the letters on the sign, I knew they spelled "Gaeta." The time for action had arrived. In preparation for throwing the grenade, I released my sweaty right hand from around the stock of the carbine, then transferred the gun to my left hand. My breathing quickened when I placed my hand around the pineapple-shaped grenade and made ready to pull the pin.

Gripping a grenade might give some fellows a sense of destructive power. To me, the handful of cast iron, marked with deep notches and filled with powder, seemed just another instrument of death used to accomplish a specific task. With a little luck, in a few more seconds the pillbox would be ours.

Suddenly I noticed a few blades of grass move not fifteen feet in front of me. Though the breeze drifting in from the sea carried a current of air down the ditch toward me and helped hush my movements, the grass swayed to both the right and left. Someone was parting that grass. Instantly I replaced the grenade in my belt and regripped my carbine. My breathing almost stopped when I recognized the top of a dark, German-shaped helmet. I knew that its flared-out edges rested atop the head of a Kraut soldier. Protected by that greenish black bucket of steel was a mind dedicated to the destruction of men like Arnold and me.

Without moving a muscle or twitching an eyelid, I watched. The helmet faced toward my right, which meant I'd not been discovered, but I couldn't wait any longer to react. If Arnold happened to make a noise, it would alert the German to the danger he faced. The gutter, which only recently carried water from the spring rains, would flow red with my blood.

Oh, how I longed for my old Thompson instead of the peashooter I carried, but there was no use thinking about that now. I had to do something, and fast. After pushing the safety button that traveled crossways through the receiver of my carbine, I took the slack up on the trigger.

In one quick maneuver I raised up, knelt on my right knee and swung the carbine in the direction of the enemy soldier. As the gun completed its arclike movement and lined up with his body, only then did I notice his Nordic features. Fair hair protruding beneath the dark helmet picture-framed the sides of his light-skinned face.

I'll never forget what happened during those next few seconds. But for the will of God, that road sign could have been my grave marker.

Because I'd raised up on my knee, I could see him clearly. The rifle, cradled across his left arm, pointed away from me, which meant he was right-handed. I didn't have time to thank the Good Lord for this break, but it probably saved my life. Before he could bring his rifle into play, he needed to swing his body to the right. Would he try to beat the odds?

Totally surprised when he heard me raise up, his mouth sprang open and he stared directly into the barrel of my carbine. I have learned that sometimes the look on a person's face will reveal their intentions, a split second before they physically attempt to execute them.

An incident from my past made me think I was looking into the face of the first man I'd ever killed. That horrible spring of 1943 seemed a lifetime ago. As with that soldier in North Africa, this man's superb military training took over. I just knew he was going to try and take me. Automatically his left hand that gripped the foregrip of the rifle started a maneuver that would mean either his life or mine. As my body leaned forward for the kill, what he didn't see was my finger squeeze hard on the trigger. I knew I had him beat. At this close range, I didn't need to focus my eyes on the part of his body where I expected the bullet to hit.

I can only imagine how he must have felt, when he turned his head and saw an enemy soldier with a gun pointed directly at his belly. No one can explain to another person the feeling that comes over a man when he stares death in the face. Most people shrug off the thought, thinking that when they come that close to cashing in their chips, the other person will die, not them.

Both of us were veterans and knew we faced reality. I was confident of success, but wait, something was wrong, dreadfully wrong. As hard as I squeezed the trigger, my weapon wouldn't respond. Looking into his terrified eyes, I gritted my teeth, crazily thinking that by doing so, more pressure would be applied on my trigger finger and the carbine would fire. Our blue eyes locked on each other, mine now as terrified as his.

In the fraction of a second it took for my brain to register that my gun refused to fire, I had visions of his rifle completing its arc. Would his eight-millimeter bullet tear my guts apart? At this close range he couldn't miss.

The same thought of impending doom must have been going through his subconscious mind, telling him that his reflexes weren't fast enough to beat me. Seeing my gun pointing at his midsection and about to spew death, midway through his swing he changed his mind. He figured that his only chance of survival was to drop his rifle and hope I'd let him surrender.

Before the gun left his hands to flatten the grass in front of him, I realized the terrible mistake I'd made. With lightning speed I pushed the safety button on my newfangled carbine in the opposite direction and continued my trigger squeeze. Only then did it register in my mind that he'd released his rifle, but the message came too late. I couldn't make my brain react fast enough to stop pulling the trigger. The bullet's mission couldn't be aborted.

When I saw the pleading look in those eyes asking for mercy, had the time finally come for me to show compassion to the enemy? Whatever the reason for my actions, I had no physical control over them. Some unknown force pushed my gun barrel up in the air, the same instant the bullet left the barrel. The 30-caliber metal projectile went harmlessly over his head to land far out in the blue Mediterranean.

For one brief moment we stared at each other, not fully understanding the reason we had spared each other's life. When he raised his hands above his head, I motioned for him to lie on the ground. Once again gripping my carbine in my left hand, I reached down and took a grenade from my belt. Pulling the pin, I lobbed it across the road behind the pillbox.

The minute Arnold heard my carbine fire, he moved forward to assist me. Seeing me hurl the grenade, he too hugged the bottom of the gutter. After the explosion, he asked, "What were you shooting at, Fred?"

When I nodded toward the German prisoner who had risen to his knees, Arnold's only response was, "You didn't kill him."

Unable to explain my behavior, I said, "They can interrogate him. Maybe they'll learn something."

When I confessed to Arnold that I had pushed the safety on my carbine in the wrong direction, he shook his head and said, "It's a wonder you didn't get yourself killed."

After relieving the German of his pistol and watch, I asked Arnold if he'd take charge of the prisoner. The pistol I confiscated was unfamiliar to me. Usually we confiscated a Luger or P-38 Walther pistol from the prisoners. This Browning, nine-millimeter, Model P-35 Belgian pistol held thirteen rounds in its magazine. Shoving it into my backpack, I decided that I'd better get on with my job. By now, the dust across the road had settled.

Having received no response from my grenade, I looked up the road toward Gaeta. After making sure the coast was clear, I dashed across the road to check out the pillbox. At the back entrance to the concrete structure I found the body of the machine gunner, killed either by Paul's ricocheting rifle bullets or my grenade.

What Arnold, Paul and I accomplished seemed to us like routine patrol action. We didn't talk about the incident. Tom and his men getting wounded overshadowed our part of the operation. For this I was thankful, for I would have taken a ribbing if Arnold had elaborated about the stupid mistake that almost took my life. It happened because I didn't familiarize myself with a weapon before taking it into combat. I knew more about the operation of German handguns and machine guns than I did about some of the weapons we were being issued. The two reliable German pistols that I carried were taken from prisoners in North Africa.

In a way, the incident at Gaeta had a profound affect on my mind. Sparing that German's life made me realize that my feelings of hate toward the individual enemy soldier were lessening. Ever since I had almost murdered my superior officer at Cassino, a psychological change had come over me.

After neutralizing the concrete pillbox at the edge of Gaeta, I gathered my squad together. The remainder of the 2nd Platoon moved forward and worked their way around the blown-out bridge. My squad joined them, and we rode into the coastal town.

Al Jerman, our radio operator, came very close to getting killed in the town when an artillery shell hit his jeep. He didn't receive a scratch, but wound up without a vehicle.

While rounding up prisoners in the town, I noticed that a few of them were from the Waffen-SS, Hitler's military watchdogs. We knew that after receiving humane treatment at the hands of their American captors, most of these men would discard the brutal and ruthless tactics indoctrinated into them by the Nazis. Once in a while we ran into a fanatic with the disposition of the men in the dreaded Gestapo, the secret state police arm of the SS. One such man appeared in Gaeta.

I motioned for the SS prisoners to place their hands above their heads and lean against a wall so we could search them for hidden weapons. One of the men raised his chin in an arrogant look of defiance. He threw his shoulders back and refused to obey my command. Instantly, a mental picture flashed before me. I saw my buddy Tom Thompson and his men lying wounded at the blown-out bridge. I began to lose patience with the SS trooper and wondered if he might not have given the order responsible for my comrades getting wounded.

Looking into the face of this fanatical Nazi, I saw an entirely different personality from that of the man whose life I had spared under the Gaeta road sign. The militaristic stance, the rigid jaw, and the hateful eyes of this young man were characteristic of a person who still believed he belonged to the superior race. His arrogant attitude dissolved all the compassion I'd shown earlier in the day to one of his comrades. It took only a fraction of a second for the short fuse attached to my better judgment to ignite my explosive nature.

Since making an almost fatal mistake earlier in the day, upon returning to my jeep, I had switched weapons. Once again, I carried my old reliable Thompson. Shooting from the hip, I fired three rounds so close to the side of the SS trooper's right boot that gravel sprayed over his legs. I didn't intend to kill or wound him if I could help it, only make him humble.

When he still refused to raise his hands, I asked myself, "Is this crazy Nazi willing to die for his beliefs?" With my patience exhausted, I fired another volley, this time much closer to his foot. One of the .45-caliber slugs grazed the side of his boot.

By now even his comrades were getting irritated with

him. They were probably afraid he would get me so riled up that I'd kill all of them. They shouted for him to comply with my request. He finally realized that he could die trying to uphold his beliefs. He didn't seem to understand that Hitler's cause was already lost.

Reluctantly, he raised his hands. With blood oozing from the side of his boot, he lowered his head in defeat. It's a good thing that all of Hitler's followers weren't as fanatical as this SS trooper, or the Allies' casualty list in Italy would have been much higher.

A similarity in beliefs existed between the soldiers on both sides of the conflict. Men from both armies believed in the cause they fought for. As the war progressed, many of the German soldiers heard about the defeat of their armies on the Russian front. In letters from their loved ones, they learned of the hardships endured in their homeland because of the Allied bombings. Many of them began to have doubts about the justification and validity of Hitler's policies. They started to realize that they were drawn into the conflict by a maniac.

On July 20, 1944, a group of German officers failed in their attempt to save their country from total destruction by assassinating Hitler. Rommel, my favorite German general, knew of the plot and didn't discourage it. Hitler later gave this brilliant officer a choice of committing suicide or being arrested to stand trial. To stand before a tribunal of Hitler's die-hard Nazis would mean destruction of Rommel's family. The general swallowed poison.

Mussolini, the former dictator of Italy, initiated many programs that were beneficial to the Italian people. He improved the canals built through the Pontine Marshes by the early Romans. The marshes covered about 175,000 acres south of Rome from Cisterna to just below the town of Terracina along the coast.

The 2nd Platoon was assigned the mission of going through the Aurunci Mountains and reconnoitering the area around Terracina, still under German control. We first had to penetrate the German lines before we could attempt to learn their plans for defending the port city. Terracina was the western terminus of the old "Hitler Line" of defense. Once the Allied armies breached the Gustav Line at Cassino, the German high command realized the "Hitler Line" would suffer the same fate. Wanting to disconnect their Fuehrer's name from defensive positions the Germans knew would inevitably fall, they renamed it the "Dora Line."

With over ten miles of enemy territory to penetrate, no one underestimated the tough job assigned to the 2nd Platoon. Carrying a rubber raft and two machine guns, Sergeant Joe Montoro led my squad and the few remaining able-bodied men from Tom Thompson's squad on the patrol.

Under cover of darkness, we slipped through the German lines. After leaving the foothills of the rugged mountains, we worked our way through the brushy countryside until we came to the system of canals on the lower end of the Pontine Marshes. The heavy undergrowth along the canal banks helped conceal our movements. Luckily, we managed to avoid German patrols. Undetected, we reached a point about a mile from Terracina. After shuttling everyone across the canal south of town, we tied the inflated raft to a bush along the bank. In case we were forced to retreat, the raft would be our lifeline.

Highway #7, the main road leading into Terracina from the south, was only a stone's throw away from the canal. On its way to the sea, this narrow channel flowed past the town. Once we left the edge of the canal where we tied the raft, we had to be extremely careful. If the Germans had any inkling that American troops were in the vicinity, someone using a pair of field glasses could spot us very easily.

Halfway between our present location and the town, the road crossed over the canal on a fairly large bridge. Sergeant Montoro figured that if we could crawl through the brush unnoticed and remain hidden next to that bridge, we could observe the Germans building their defenses. We noticed a lot of activity around the town, but none between there and the bridge.

The afternoon sun wouldn't be swallowed by the sea to the

west for at least two hours. This made everyone extremely careful when crawling the half mile to the bridge. Though we were making a bold move, the sergeant knew that any information we obtained concerning the German defenses would be invaluable to the 85th Infantry Division. Within the next few days, they were scheduled to attack the town.

We left one man to guard the raft, our only means of escape. The remainder of our small body of men moved forward. The Germans had left the bridge unguarded, never suspecting a patrol would venture ten miles behind their lines, especially in broad daylight. Keeping well back from the road, we finally reached our objective. From the security of the thick brush growing along the water's edge, we noted the location of the gun emplacements. With our hands cupped over the front of our field glasses to keep the sun from reflecting its telltale glare, we watched the Germans build their fortifications.

My buddy Paul Yenser, raised only a few miles from my home in Pennsylvania, had received intensive training in the art of using explosives. While the rest of us watched the Germans at work, Paul's inquisitive nature led him down to the water where he investigated the underside of the bridge. Scurrying back on his hands and knees, he became so excited that he stuttered when he told me what he'd discovered.

In a voice that betrayed a touch of his Swedish ancestry, he explained, "This bridge is wired with explosives. The Krauts can blow it anytime they see our troops advancing up Highway #7 from the south. All they have to do is push a lever, and that darned bridge will blow sky-high."

When the Americans reached the outskirts of Terracina, the infantry might be able to ford the canal and climb its steep banks without using the bridge. If the bridge could be saved, our engineers wouldn't have to construct a "Bailey bridge" to carry tanks and other equipment across in support of the foot soldiers.

Paul said, "I can break the wires leading to the explosives so the Krauts won't suspect they've been tampered with. I have cutters and the other tools I'll need in my pack."

After listening to Paul's proposal, the sergeant gave his consent to disable the explosives. Taking a couple of us with him, Paul crawled under the bridge on the side farthest from town. Like a kid with a new toy, he went to work removing a few of the charges hidden from view behind the beams. He told us to conceal the explosives in deep water, upstream from the structure.

If the Germans discovered us now, we'd be sittin' ducks, and probably dead ones at that. When Paul figured he'd severed enough wires to make blowing the bridge an impossibility, we crawled back to our former positions along the bank of the canal.

Sergeant Montoro informed us that he'd obtained enough information. He said, "Fred, we better not press our luck any further. Let's get out of here."

Joe wanted to get away from the bridge, for if we were spotted near it, the Germans might get suspicious and discover we'd tampered with their demolition charges. Cautiously, we worked our way back toward our rubber raft.

As on all patrols where a number of men are involved, the chances of discovery are greatly increased, especially when traveling during daylight hours. Up until now, we'd been very fortunate.

Though there was still light enough to see the town, the evening sun had disappeared behind the waters of the Tyrrhenian Sea. Joe decided that before making our final move to the canal, we'd stop for a rest. Only a hundred yards separated us from our raft. Being overconfident, after having successfully escaped from beneath the very nose of the enemy, proved to be our downfall.

Just as we were about to move out and close the final gap, a machine gun in Terracina opened up at us. Someone had become careless and exposed our position to the enemy. The Krauts probably thought they'd spotted a small recon patrol advancing toward the town from the south. Because most patrols operating in enemy territory traveled at night, they would never think we were heading away from Terracina. Luckily, we were a good distance from the bridge before being discovered.

No one needed to be told the urgency of reaching the opposite bank of the canal. Sergeant Montoro yelled out orders: "Salter, take one man with you and set up your machine gun over there in the bend of the road. Keep those Krauts off our backs until we get everyone ferried across. I'll holler when they are all over."

Before the spring offensive, I had received a couple of new replacements in my squad. Henry Mahaney, the lad who had asked so many questions about survival back at Cassino, was one of these new men. So far he'd proven to be very reliable. Without looking in my little black notebook, I knew his name came up next to serve on a combat mission. I motioned for him to follow me with his machine-gun receiver. "Henry, you and I are going to be rear guards. Stay with me," I said.

George Rogers, carrying the tripod, set it down on the edge of the ditch, which was about three feet deep. At this point in the road it made a bend, then headed straight for the bridge. One of the other men dropped two boxes of .30-caliber ammo into the bottom of the same depression. I hoped that with 500 rounds of ammo, we'd be able to keep the Krauts busy, at least until Joe and the men reached safety. As long as the Krauts didn't open up on us with mortars or artillery, we'd be okay.

Glancing to the west, I noticed the final rays of the sun disappear over the distant horizon. Twilight is a beautiful time of day on the shores of the Mediterranean, but right now I couldn't wait for it to disappear into the darkness. I prayed for the caretaker of the night to draw the curtains a little faster.

Joe and the men headed for the canal, throwing all caution to the cool evening breeze. Because of the great distance we were from the German machine gun, its bullets weren't very accurate.

Henry and I lay in the ditch while a steady stream of bullets buzzed above our heads. It sounded like a symphony orchestra, playing Rimski-Korsakov's "The Flight of the Bumblebee."

After scraping loose gravel from the side of the road, we were able to lower the tripod of the Browning machine gun. Piling the gravel on either side of the gun, we made a breastwork for more protection. We positioned the air-cooled barrel an inch or two above the roadbed. Taking one of the canvas belts laced with 250 rounds of ammo, we loaded the gun and swiveled it directly toward the bridge. I figured there wasn't any advantage in revealing our position by firing at the Germans moving down the opposite side of the canal. Let them think they were going to get out of this fracas without paying their dues.

Unlike the smokeless and flashless powder of the German ammunition, the puffs of light blue smoke and tiny flashes from our gun would betray our location. We'd give the Krauts heck once they hit the bridge. Looking down the gravel road, we could see both approaches, and the entire deck surface of the structure.

While watching about a dozen German soldiers running from the town toward the bridge, we heard the sound of vehicle engines. In the gathering twilight, we could see a couple of motorcycles with sidecars leave Terracina, then race down the road and head for the bridge. Following them came an open-top Kubelwagen, sounding like the gasoline engine on my mother's old-fashioned washing machine.

The foot soldiers had almost reached the bridge when the lead motorcycle passed them. With a sidecar slowing him down, the driver didn't rev up his engine until after he completed his 90-degree turn and climbed the slight grade to the bridge.

Up until this time, the Krauts had things their way, for their machine gun on the edge of town still harassed Joe and the rest of the men. Henry and I had yet to fire a shot, but now it was our turn to play games. The moment the cycle's front wheel hit the decking, our machine gun came alive. I walked the first few rounds down the roadway in front of the bridge and kept those that followed ricocheting across the decking in front of the speeding cycle. Because of the distance and poor visibility, I couldn't see his face, but I'll bet the cyclist's expression changed. With the tables turned, he probably realized that to drive an unarmed vehicle across that bridge in the face of machine-gun fire would be suicidal.

The ricocheting bullets finally found their target. Though our belt of ammunition contained a few tracers and armor-piercing rounds, I don't believe a tracer bullet hit the gas tank. I think a bullet probably punctured a tire on the side-car. The cycle careened sideways, then catapulted on the decking. The man in the sidecar looked like an acrobat leaving a trapeze. He flew through the air and over the low railing, landing in the canal with a splash. The belly flopper he took reminded me of the ones we kids used to take down in the old swimming hole.

The driver, competing with the night birds for flying space, flapped his winglike arms and raced the tumbling cycle to the end of the bridge. Both he and the machine cleared the bridge decking and made it to the gravel road. Before coming to a complete stop, the machine exploded. Miraculously, the driver got up and staggered into the brush.

The burning motorcycle halted the remaining vehicles and the men advancing on foot, but not for long. Within a couple of minutes, a few of the more daring and reckless soldiers braved our steady fire and made it across the bridge. They fanned out on either side of the road, but were reluctant to advance rapidly.

Even though it didn't take long for Joe Montoro to shuttle our men across the canal, to Henry and me it seemed like an eternity. We emptied one box of ammo but were trying to conserve what we had left in the second container. I thought how lucky we were that the Krauts weren't prepared to use their mortars or artillery. Up until now, we'd encountered only small-arms fire.

High cumulus clouds, like floating icebergs drifting over a jagged arctic wasteland, began to fill the sky from the mountains to the sea. These clouds worked in our favor, hastening our friend, the darkness.

A burp gun opened up halfway between where we lay and the bridge. They were getting close. A moment later, a dreaded MG42 light machine gun, capable of firing 1,200 rounds a minute, filled the air with its steady staccatolike music of death. Henry said, "Fred, let's get out of here."

"Not until we've used up all the ammo," I said. "We've got to hold them off a little longer."

With the road in front of us barely visible, I squeezed off the remaining rounds as enemy bullets kicked dust from off the parched roadbed.

"Take the receiver, Henry," I hollered. "I'll keep them busy until you reach the canal, then you give me covering fire. I'll bring the tripod."

I was proud of Henry. No one could have asked for a better partner, or done a better job. As soon as he reached the canal and began firing, I grabbed the tripod and raced back. If necessary, we could make a stand at the water's edge. If things became too hot, we could always dump the machine gun in the drink and take to the water.

Just as I reached the canal, Joe grabbed my arm and said, "Get in the raft, those Krauts are too close for comfort."

The men had formed a skirmish line on the far side of the canal to give us covering fire if the Germans silhouetted themselves against the night sky before we got safely across. The raft no sooner touched the opposite shore when welcome hands dragged it into the brush and deflated it.

Before the Krauts reached the edge of the canal, we were long gone. We entered the thickets, protected beneath a cloak of darkness that embraced our ghostlike figures. The Germans probably wouldn't consider our small force a big threat to their security. For that reason, we didn't expect them to venture across the water and follow us, especially in the darkness.

Moving southward for a couple of hours, with only our compass as a guide, we didn't cover much ground. Before long, though, the clouds disappeared and, aided by the moon and stars, we soon made up for lost time. So as not to slow our progress after we crossed the last canal, we discarded the rubber raft.

Trying to return safely with the valuable information we'd

obtained turned into a game of cat and mouse. All night long the Germans reached in every nook and cranny, trying to search us out with their felinelike claws. We knew the soldiers at Terracina had alerted their forces to the south to be on the lookout for an enemy patrol. Twice we vanished into the safety of the thickets to escape the probing lights of a vehicle on road patrol. Fortunately, our luck held.

Without another shot being fired, we reentered the American lines, a tired and brush-torn body of men. Though haggard and worn, everyone felt a sense of accomplishment, knowing that very few Recon patrols wind up with such a happy ending. Once again, we thanked our guardian angels for letting us share the light of another day.

# CHAPTER XII

# Weary Are the Warriors

Until the spring offensive of 1944 pushed the German war machine farther up the boot of Italy, the 91st Recon's major role was in support of the infantry. After the 2nd Platoon returned from our Terracina patrol, we rejoined the troop, where our vehicles awaited us. Once again C Troop became mounted reconnaissance, performing the job we were originally trained for.

While driving along the winding, narrow road leading to the front, we passed infantrymen from the 337th Regiment of the 85th Division. When I heard my name being yelled above the noise of the jeep engine, I saw my boyhood buddy, Albert Brown, marching in the staggered column of men.

In late April, Albert had told me that he needed a wristwatch. When the jeep pulled up beside him, I took a watch off my arm and handed it to him. Reluctantly, he accepted it, but said, "Fred, I don't want to take your watch, you'll need it on patrols."

"Albert, I have more than one," I replied. "Only a few days ago, I took this one from a machine gunner at Gaeta."

With no further chance to talk, I waved good-bye. Our column of vehicles continued on down the road. I wouldn't see Albert again until after the war.

In the early morning hours of May 25, the 91st Recon made contact with the Anzio beachhead. A Troop had the honor of officially making the connection. Since February, the gallant men occupying the narrow strip of land along the coast had been surrounded by Germans and a hostile sea. Every square foot of the beachhead could be shelled by the enemy artillery. The men of the 91st were proud to say that their unit from the Cassino front joined hands with the brave men of Anzio.

The *Pictorial History of the Second World War* shows a picture of General Mark Clark bravely leading a column of soldiers to the junction where the Cassino and Anzio forces met. The heading reads, "Clark leads beachhead forces to junction." This photo was taken quite a while after the men from the 91st had made the historic union. Recon scouts didn't have press agents and photographers accompany them on patrols.

While the men from C Troop celebrated with the enlisted men from the beachhead, our troop commander, Captain Maple, talked to their colonel. Even though the unit we made contact with wasn't a recon outfit, the men treated us like long-lost brothers.

After a few minutes of joyful reunion, I heard our captain tell the colonel, "I'm sorry we can't spend more time with you, but we have to continue north. The Krauts aren't far ahead of us."

The captain shook hands with the colonel and gave him a waving salute, then he climbed into the lead jeep and moved on down the road. As usual, when we were on mounted patrol, my vehicle carrying the mortar brought up the rear of the column. I walked over to my jeep, then raised my hand in a friendly gesture to the men I'd been talking to. "Good luck," I said.

I had just placed my left foot on top of the sandbag in the floor of the jeep and was preparing to swing into the vehicle, when the colonel approached me and said, "Hold on a minute, Corporal."

Stepping back out onto the gravel roadbed, I turned around and asked, "What do you want, Colonel?"

"I imagine you are aware of the 5th Army directive concerning contraband," he said. "It states that no soldier is permitted to use or have in his possession any German equipment."

When I said, "Yes, sir," I thought to myself, I'll bet this

son of a gun has spotted the butt end of my German P-38 Walther pistol. It stuck out of the U.S. Army holster on my right hip. Still, I wasn't quite sure of the reason for his remark, not until I noticed his eyes focus on the large German 10 × 50 Dienstglas field glasses hanging around my neck. With his mouth half open and a greedy look in his eyes, I could almost see the saliva drooling down over the side of his lower lip. He reminded me of the hungry wolf about to devour Little Red Riding Hood.

I watched him hunch his shoulders, moving them from side to side. I swear that he only made this gesture so that the polished eagles on top of his jacket would sparkle in the early morning sunlight. Neither his manner nor his movements intimidated me. In a voice rumbling with authority, supposedly to impress me and his men, he asked, "Those field glasses you have around your neck are German, aren't they?"

"Yes, sir," I replied.

"I'm afraid I'll have to confiscate them, Corporal. They are contraband."

A group of the colonel's men, after listening to their leader's outrageous demand, moved closer so they could hear my reply. Many of the men looked at each other in disgust, for they realized the officer intended to pull his rank on a lowly noncommissioned officer. The legal technicality in the army regulation might get him a pair of beautiful German field glasses, but it wouldn't endear him in the hearts of his men. By the looks on their faces, if they could help me out of my predicament, the colonel would lose his case.

For a long moment I remained silent. The sneaky tactics of this officer were obvious. He had waited until Captain Maple and the rest of the troop left before making his demand. I tried to remain as calm as possible and choose my words carefully so as not to be accused of insubordination.

I said, "I'm sorry, Colonel, I can't let you have these glasses. I took them from one of General Rommel's officers when he surrendered in North Africa. I'm afraid you'll have to get a pair the same way I got mine."

If looks could kill, I'd have been "deader than a boiled mackerel." The colonel must have realized that with his men listening, I'd not only contested his authority, but challenged his ability as a soldier to obtain booty in combat.

Losing his self control, he shouted, "Hand those glasses over, and that's an order!"

On the surface, I tried to appear undaunted by his command, but my guts were churning faster than the inside of Mother's butter churn. Reaching in my left shirt pocket, I brought out my battered, steel-covered New Testament. Opening the cover, I removed a slip of paper and handed it to him, saying, "Read this."

The document, written by our squadron commander, also a colonel, authorized me to carry the German binoculars. The paper stated that the glasses were not only more powerful than those issued by the U.S. Army, but contained a built-in millimeter scale. The nature of my job exempted me from the order issued by the military high command.

Later, I realized that I should have read the document out loud and made the colonel's men aware of its contents.

When he finished reading, he turned and literally threw the paper at me. Too angry to reply, he spun around and walked away, never waiting for the smart salute I intended to bestow on his deflated ego. If the American eagles on his shoulders were real birds, they would have flown the coop. They'd have been too ashamed to rest atop the shoulders of such a man.

The men witnessing the event could only surmise what the paper said, but they knew their arrogant commander ate crow for breakfast that morning. Smiles appeared on many of their faces, and one of the men winked at me and nodded. When I climbed into my jeep and said to George, "Let's go," a corporal stepped forward. Defying the wrath of his superior officer, he raised his hand and joined his thumb and forefinger in a circle of approval.

Very few American officers were of the colonel's caliber. Once in a great while, a man is given authority beyond his capabilities. He knows only how to dictate, not lead by setting a good example to his men. The soldiers in his command are the ones who suffer. The dirty trick the colonel tried to pull on a man from the ranks would never win him a popularity contest. How different Captain Maple and even General Keyes, our II Corps Commander, were from this officer. He needed to be sent out on night patrol and assigned the point position. There he'd have to depend on lowly privates and noncommissioned officers for survival. Maybe then he'd realize that the birds atop his shoulders couldn't help him fly away from death any faster than one or two stripes on an enlisted man's arm.

The colonel reminded me of the roving principal in our rural school district back in Pennsylvania during the 1920s. When I was a young boy in grade school, the principal often visited our two-room schoolhouse. One morning, he stood before me with a ruler in his hand, threatening to crack my knuckles if I didn't turn over the plug cut of apple chewing tobacco I held behind my back. Like most young boys of that era, I'd been experimenting with a vice that was acceptable to most of our male elders. Even a few of the more hardy women in the backcountry saw nothing wrong in having a chew. When I defied the principal's request to turn over the compressed plug of tobacco, I paid the price.

Later in the day, while rubbing my raw knuckles, I saw my confiscated "stunt your growth, chaw," bulging the principal's cheek. He was one of the few men I knew who didn't spit; instead, he swallowed the juices. In that little two-room schoolhouse, I learned more than my three Rs. I found out at an early age, many people in high offices use their authority for their own benefit.

After waiting a couple of weeks for my knuckles to heal, I gladly got them scarred again when I brought another plug cut of tobacco to school. The fun started when the principal found the outhouse door locked from the inside. He didn't know that I'd loaded the plug cut with cascara, the next best thing I could find to store-bought Ex-Lax.

When our squadron left the Anzio beachhead, we traveled northeast, heading for the Alban Hills. There we went into action between the 1st Special Service Force and General Juin's mountain troops from North Africa.

Advance units from Truscott's VI Corps were nearing Valmontone on Highway #6. Once they reached this road junction, they'd be in position to cut off the retreating army heading north from Cassino. General Mark Clark issued a surprise order to General Truscott, commander of the beachhead forces. He instructed him to halt his drive toward Valmontone and invalidate his former plan of cutting Highway #6. Instead, he instructed him to swing northwest toward Rome.

General Keyes, our II Corps commander, formed a task force made up of recon, infantry, tanks and tank destroyer units. Under the leadership of Colonel Howze from the 1st Armored Division, it spearheaded the drive to Rome. The 91st took part in the historic drive to capture the Eternal City.

The breakthrough came on June 4, 1944. With his small army of publicity men and photographers, General Mark Clark fulfilled his dream of becoming the first Allied commander to enter the Eternal City. Because of his determination to go down in history as the first conqueror of Rome from the south, most of General Kesselring's 10th Army retreating from Cassino escaped the trap that the British hoped could be sprung. General Alexander and his British 8th Army were justified in being angry at the glory-seeking Clark.

The 91st Recon never had the opportunity to see many of the historic sites or enjoy the hospitality of the grateful inhabitants of Rome. We continued in hot pursuit of the enemy. As we drove through the city, the structure that impressed me the most was the Colosseum.

Never again would I enter the Eternal City or have the opportunity to visit the mysterious Vatican. The retreating Germans spared Rome for a couple of reasons. Many of their generals, including Kesselring, held strong religious convictions. Hitler and his advisers also saw the political gains to be made in the eyes of the Christian world by sparing the city. They knew that by destroying the

Benedictine monastery at Cassino, the Allies gave the Third Reich valuable propaganda material.

Because the 91st Recon led the drive north of Rome, II Corps command named the force we led "Task Force Ellis" after our colonel. The Germans failed to blow the bridges when they retreated from Rome, enabling the Allies to move across the Tiber River in style. We enjoyed the scenery much like tourists. Instead of being loaded down with travel brochures, we were armed to the teeth, waiting for the scenery in front of us to explode.

The next six weeks turned out to be a repetition of roadblocks, ambushes and sniper fire, one delaying action after another. General Kesselring planned to slow us down, so the German war machine could make an orderly withdrawal to their next line of defense. He did it successfully without incurring too many losses. The 91st Recon continued to remain in front of the action. We knew we'd have no rest until the Germans quit retreating. This was the type of warfare we were trained for.

One evening, after we stopped for the night and secured our positions, First Sergeant Foote called me back to the command post. He said, "I'm sure you are aware that every month since January 1944, two men from each troop have been sent back to the States on rotation. This policy came about because we have been overseas since the latter part of 1942. Sometime before the end of August, you are scheduled to leave us. Be prepared."

At a loss for words, I said, "Thank you, Sergeant," then walked away.

I'd been assigned guard duty that night. After leaving the first sergeant, I checked our perimeter to make sure things were secure. After completing my rounds, in a daze I walked back to my foxhole to think. I couldn't believe my good fortune. I'd never expected to return home until after the war ended and couldn't figure out why they chose me. Were they trying to get rid of a maverick? Ever since I'd threatened to kill my lieutenant at Cassino, I'd retreated into a shell. I kept the burden of guilt locked inside me. After gazing into life's crystal ball for so long and seeing nothing but death, I began to wonder if a future existed for me.

As the days passed, I realized that nothing I'd experienced in the entire war was harder on my nerves than waiting to be relieved from combat duty. If only the sergeant had waited until the day of my departure to tell me the good news. Instead, the glimmer of hope riding down on the rays of the summer sun seemed threatened by dark clouds moving toward me from the German lines.

To notify a soldier ahead of time that he is going home in a few weeks makes it harder for him to put his life on the line every day. He may not realize that he is acting any differently in combat, but, subconsciously, his mind is carrying a heavy burden. A haunting fear, that he will depart this earth before he leaves for home, hangs over his head.

Thirty years after the Vietnam War ended, I listened to a speech by the general of the Communist forces of North Vietnam. An interviewer asked the speaker what he thought defeated the American forces in Southeast Asia.

The general replied, "The American fighting men in Vietnam fought magnificently during their first six months of combat. Knowing they only had a year to serve overseas, during their last six months of duty, they became overly cautious. They worried more about getting killed than they did about fighting the enemy. Looking into their imaginary crystal ball, the face of death stared back at them. Behind that ghostlike figure, they saw all the dreams they'd experienced while out on patrol or lying in a muddy foxhole. They knew that if they could survive another six months, all those dreams would become a reality. Above anything else in the world, even patriotism to the divided nation they left behind, they wanted to get out of the war alive."

The Communist general glanced over at a few of his disabled veterans attending the ceremony and said, "In contrast, the Communist soldier fought until he was either wounded or killed, or the war ended. He had nothing to look forward to but fighting. Like the newly arrived American soldier, he gave his all, oftentimes with a fatalistic attitude."

Military men have often debated the humaneness of the policy of requiring a man to serve only one year in combat, and the effect it has on a man's fighting ability. A person who has never faced the enemy, knowing that on a specific date he will be sent home, can never fully comprehend this controversial situation.

In my opinion, the Communist general came up with the wrong reason why the United States lost the war in Vietnam. Though his reason was valid, I feel that political issues in the United States were the cause. The American people thought the politicians had drawn them into an unjust war. With so much controversy at home, the military's ability to win the war was hindered by Congress and our leaders.

As the Allies advanced north of Rome, C Troop liberated the private wine cellar of General Kesselring. Before we departed from the underground buildings where the cache of wine was stored, our vehicles were loaded with enough bottles of antidepressant fluid to float our rising spirits all the way back to the States.

One evening, after losing contact with the retreating Germans, we camped in a small grove of trees. Jack Jones, my musical buddy from Crane, Missouri, brought out an old guitar. As we sang and played, the night shadows danced beside the memories of buddies who once joined us around our campfire. Though their voices were stilled, they lived on in our hearts.

The following day, Jack and the lieutenant riding with him were killed. The officer was scheduled to leave for Rome the next day, then return to the States on rotation. Their deaths pounded a couple more nails into my imaginary coffin. I began to wonder if I'd survive until the time came for me to be pulled out of the line.

Another friend, Ralph Allen, from Coatesville, Pennsylvania, lost his life shortly after Jack Jones was killed. Ralph lived only a few miles from the village where I'd been raised.

John Manley, our 2nd Platoon medical corpsman, like all medics who served in combat units, considered himself a

noncombatant. Constantly being exposed to enemy fire
while attending the wounded made a medic's job far more
dangerous than those of the men he treated. Talk to any soldier who served in combat and he'll tell you the combat
medics were true heroes of the war. We were all saddened
when Manley lost his life on Monti Catini. He patched me
up twice. At one time or another, with no regard for his own
safety, he treated nearly every man in the 2nd Platoon.

Al Malaker from Aurora, Illinois, was wounded the
same day Manley died. When Leroy Folkenflik, a Jewish
boy from Elizabeth, New Jersey, lost his leg, my buddy Al
Jerman dragged him back to safety. Al later received the
Silver Star for his actions.

During one point in our advance north of Rome, we were
delayed by heavy rifle fire erupting from a stone farmhouse.
Sergeant Montoro's section of the 2nd Platoon had the job
of driving the Krauts from their fortified position. A few
Italians in the northern part of Italy were sympathetic to the
Germans, more so than those in the southern provinces. The
civilian men in this farmhouse were supporting the Germans. When the skirmish ended, the Italian survivors raised
a white flag and threw down their weapons. With their hands
above their heads, they walked out the door.

Joe Montoro, speaking fluent Italian, asked one of the
civilians if there were any Germans in the stone barn and
the other outbuildings. The Italian arrogantly refused to
answer Joe's question, telling him, "Find out for yourself."

Moving through the house, I knelt beside a rear window that gave me a good view of the barn and the area
around the other buildings. Resting my Thompson submachine gun on the windowsill, I searched for a target.

A flickering light in the room distracted me. Glancing
about, the first thing my eyes focused on was an ancient
flintlock pistol sitting on top of a box. It lay within arm's
length of where I knelt. The handcarved pistol grip and the
wood surrounding the barrel of the old weapon reminded me of the pistols I'd seen buccaneers carry in pirate
movies. While I stared at the antique weapon, it almost

disappeared from view. The sun, bouncing off a bright chunk of yellow metal lying on the table next to the gun, temporarily blinded me. Sunburst rays of light rebounded off the jagged sides of the metal object. It seemed as if an invisible hand turned a kaleidoscope, projecting its patterns on the white walls of the room.

Reaching out, I picked up the piece of metal. Never before had I seen such a treasure. "This must be gold," I thought.

With no remorse, all through the war I'd confiscated weapons and watches from German prisoners. Never had I taken anything from a civilian. Like most GIs, I gave food to the Italian people to lessen their misery. They were to be pitied.

The civilians in this farmhouse who took up arms against us were different from the majority of the peasants in the area. They had plenty of food and seemed prosperous, which meant they had probably cooperated with the Germans. Most of the other peasants were near starvation. The more I thought about the bitter struggle we endured to capture the farmhouse, the angrier I became.

I shoved the shining piece of metal and the pistol into my backpack. Trying to justify the wrong I committed, I imagined myself a judge, speaking to the inhabitants of the farmhouse. I said, "For collaborating with the Krauts, you are going to pay dearly. Your penalty will be a chunk of gold and this pistol."

After the episode at the farmhouse, we moved farther up the road and dug in for the night. When the kitchen crew brought us chow that evening, I gave the pistol to one of the cooks for safekeeping. I never mentioned the one-and-a-half-pound piece of gold that I'd stolen in retaliation for what the Italian civilians did to us. The treasure lay safely hidden in the bottom of my backpack.

During the rest of my trek up the boot of Italy, I carried that chunk of shining metal on my back. It weighed as much as a hand grenade, yet wasn't of any value in saving my life. Unless the war deteriorated to the point where both sides ran out of ammunition and threw rocks at each other, the piece of gold was useless.

There is more than one moral to this story. Besides learning never to steal or take an eye for an eye to get even with another person, I found truth in the old cliché that says, "All that glitters is not gold." The crime I committed not only weighed heavy on my conscience, but also weighted down my backpack as well. Not until years later, when I started prospecting in Alaska, did I learn the true value of the heavy piece of metal. It was nothing but a beautiful piece of iron pyrite: worthless "fool's gold." I've kept that polished piece of metal as a reminder that we should never judge someone by their outward appearance. As with real gold, the true beauty in a person lies beneath the surface.

The 91st Recon moved relentlessly northward against the stubborn resistance of the retreating Germans. Like the probing tentacles of an octopus, patrols investigated every side road as well as the main thoroughfares leading to the enemy's next line of defense.

One afternoon our mess sergeant, Edwin Volcik, from West, Texas, took his kitchen truck loaded with chow and headed out to deliver food to each of our three platoons. Being conscientious, he wanted to make sure that none of us went hungry. One of the cooks drove the two-and-a-half-ton truck, while he stood up and manned the machine gun mounted on top of the vehicle.

Somehow, the two "hash slingers" became disoriented and took the wrong turn in the gravel road. They drove into an area we hadn't reconnoitered. Barreling along at a good clip, they ran smack dab into a roadblock. The Germans were just as surprised as the mess sergeant and his helper. Before the Krauts had time to man their machine gun or reach for their rifles, the sergeant's machine gun was dishing out hot, unappetizing morsels of metal. The Germans were unable to digest his .30-caliber recipe.

When Sergeant Volcik finally released his finger from the trigger, we had one less roadblock to worry about. For performing a duty far beyond that expected of a mess sergeant, he received the Silver Star.

On one of my last patrols before leaving Italy, I confiscated a piece of German equipment that helped preserve many of my war souvenirs. Almost certain that a German ambush awaited us at a road junction up ahead, we outflanked it and approached from the rear. Looking down upon the intersection from atop a small knoll, we spotted our unsuspecting quarry, dug in between the two roads. With a clear field of fire to his front, the German machine gunner waited for us in ambush. Sitting beneath the shade of a small tree about thirty feet behind the gun, two of his comrades tried to escape the heat of the midday sun.

We watched the two men open a large portable metal container and remove food. After spreading their noonday meal on a blanket under the tree, they called to the soldier manning the machine gun. Confident that we Americans were far down the road, the gunner didn't ask one of his comrades to relieve him; instead, he joined them.

At this opportune moment, we moved in on them from the rear. In a matter of minutes the confrontation ended. The road junction, along with the prepared food, fell into our hands.

We probably were getting tired of eating our small cans of stew, beans or hash. It could be that we hadn't eaten regularly. Whatever the reason, we couldn't resist consuming the elaborate feast laid out before us. Everything was superb, especially the canned rice pudding. I have never tasted any better.

Leaving a couple of men to secure the roadblock, the rest of us patted our satisfied paunches and prepared to head back to our lines. The rest of the troop could now move forward. Propped up against a tree, next to all the Germans' gear, I spotted a beautiful Hohner accordion. Though far more complicated than the small concertina my mother taught me how to play, the German instrument intrigued me. Knowing that its owner had no further use for it, I slung the miniature piano over my shoulder.

Upon returning to the troop, I made my report to Captain Maple. A strange look came over his face when he glanced at the instrument on my back. As I turned to walk away, he squinted his eyebrows and asked, "Corporal, what in thunder are you going to do with that accordion?"

I had been afraid to approach him on the subject of the musical squeezebox. Now that he had broken the ice, I felt relieved. "Can I ask a favor of you, Captain? I haven't sent a package back home to my folks since we left North Africa. Will you give me permission to send this accordion to my mother? It sure beats the little concertina she plays."

At first I thought he'd refuse, but after a moment he nodded his head and said, "Okay, Corporal. Have one of the cooks scrounge up a wooden box. After you have it packed, leave the lid open so I can inspect it. It is so large I can't guarantee we can get it approved by the army post office, but we'll try."

The captain's reply was far more than I had expected or even deserved. Up until today, I'd always been aboveboard in my dealings with him. Now I felt guilty. I had played on his good nature and deceived him by not revealing the real reason I wanted to ship the accordion to my mother. Oh, I hadn't lied about her playing the concertina, but the rest of the story was a bunch of bull. If the squeezebox ever reached home, it would be in no condition for her to play. Ever since the day I learned the army intended to send me home, I had tried to figure out a way to save my German gear. If it could speak, every item I carried could tell a story of how it came to be in my possession. Through four campaigns, that equipment had been partly responsible for my survival.

Without getting written permission, no soldier was authorized to carry German equipment into combat, let alone send it back to the States. After getting the captain's approval, my stomach began to rumble like that of a belly dancer performing her sensuous movements. If my plan worked, I'd be able to give my heirs the war souvenirs.

At this point in the war, the government didn't X-ray packages sent to the States by military personnel stationed overseas. Every letter or package was visually inspected by an officer from each unit. The captain might have gone along with my devious plan if I'd confided in him, but I didn't want to implicate him in something illegal.

That evening, after we dug our foxholes, I took the accordion apart and removed the reeds and internal parts. I left the outer case intact. Stuffing toilet paper around it, I packed the small 7.65 mm Saur pistol. It had remained hidden beneath my left armpit since before we left North Africa. Next to the pistol I placed the German night compass and the Browning pistol that held thirteen rounds of nine-millimeter ammo. I had taken this weapon from the machine gunner at Gaeta. The $10 \times 50$ Dienstglas field glasses were too large to put in the accordion without taking them apart. Wrapping the prisms in toilet paper, I packed them along with my stag-handled German dagger. After carrying the knife for over a year and a half, it seemed strange not to have it strapped to my leg beneath my trousers.

I felt like a pirate loading a treasure chest full of booty prior to burying it on some deserted island. Many a buccaneer never lived to enjoy the fruits of the adventurous life he led. I hoped the outcome of this night's effort would be different.

Finally, everything was packed except the P-38 Walther pistol I took from the officer who surrendered to me at the end of the African Campaign. With no room left in the accordion, I decided to keep the gun with me. Not knowing how long it would be before I returned to the States, I didn't want to go on patrol without a pistol. I would take a chance on getting it home some other way.

It seemed a shame to ruin such a beautiful accordion, but it was my only hope of keeping the souvenirs. Intentionally, I broke the strap that held the accordion in a closed position. I then took a piece of wire and wound it around the outside of the instrument to band it together. After carefully lowering it into the wooden box, I thought, "Never again will it vibrate to the sound of beautiful music when those keys are caressed."

Knowing I'd broken almost every rule in the army's book of postal regulations, I prayed I wouldn't get caught and jeopardize my chances of being sent home. Though none of the items in the box were U.S. Government issue, they were still considered contraband. I closed the lid, but didn't fasten it. When I took the box to my superior officer, I said, "I've got the accordion all ready to ship, Captain."

He looked down at the instrument and said, "It sure is a beauty."

While he stood admiring it, the blood pounding against the walls of my chest sounded like a lazy woodpecker beating against a hollow tree. I loosened my combat jacket so he wouldn't notice the war drum beat of my heart.

The captain had joined our outfit as a cavalry replacement officer after the North Africa Campaign. Many a night since then he'd listened to Jack Jones and me, along with our other buddies, play and sing ballads around a campfire. With all of my guitar-playing comrades watching from astride cavalry mounts up in the sky and me about to leave the troop, the captain decided to ask me one last favor.

Smiling, he swept his hand back across his coal black hair and said, "I'll okay your request to ship the accordion, Corporal, but first you have to play me a tune."

The time had come for me to face the music. Even though I'd prepared myself for the guilt-driven task of confronting the captain, I almost broke down and confessed the deceitful thing I'd done. Instead of crossing my fingers to cancel out the white lie I was about to tell, I was so shook up I crossed my legs to keep from messing my pants.

Putting on my best poker face, I looked up and said, "I'd sure like to oblige you, Captain, but the darn strap holding the accordion together got broken." Pointing down to the three strands of wire wrapped tightly around the instrument, I said, "See how I had to hold it in place. I'd have to take all that wire off to play it."

He looked down in the box and said, "That's okay, Corporal, don't bother. Go ahead and close the lid."

When the ordeal was over, I felt relieved, but also a little guilty. After the captain had treated me so well, I deceived him. Even though he might have stuck his neck out to help, I hated to ask him to knowingly perform an illegal act. The gutted accordion and its contents eventually arrived home. When I returned to the States and opened the box, things were just as I had packed them.

Since the start of the spring offensive on May 11, 1944, the 91st Recon never stopped reconnoitering in front of the American II Corps. For well over two months, we kept pressure on the enemy as they retreated up the boot of Italy.

On our trek northward, we came upon the village where the Germans had lined up 300 Italian civilians and shot them. The murderers claimed they did it in retaliation for a criminal act committed against them by the Italian partisans. The Nazis performed many such barbaric acts during the war. Picking their victims at random, they shot them in front of their neighbors. The Germans used this cruel method to keep the civilian population under control.

Food seemed to be more plentiful in northern Italy. Many of the peasants harvested what they could from their gardens before the German soldiers confiscated the produce. We didn't see as many starving children with bloated stomachs protruding from their bodies. Even so, the youngsters were so thin and frail you wondered how they had the strength to beg for our discarded scraps of food.

During my tour of duty in Italy, in exchange for garlic, I gave the peasants candy and crackers. After chopping up a clove of garlic, I stirred the pieces into each can of type-C rations that I ate. This onionlike plant probably kept me from getting sick. Many of us hadn't slept under a roof since we were with the French Foreign Legion back in North Africa. I'd never been bitten by bedbugs since then either, probably because they couldn't stand the smell of garlic.

An interesting event took place before we reached the Arno River south of Florence. One of the many roadblocks we encountered along the way delayed C Troop's advance. We were preparing to knock it out when a high-ranking officer, accompanied by one of his executive officers from squadron headquarters, approached us. The senior officer wanted to know the reason for the delay. We informed him that a German tank, positioned at the road junction up ahead, was temporarily delaying us.

Because the Krauts didn't have flank guards out, we figured it would be a simple matter to knock the tank out with a bazooka. By feinting an attack on the left of their position, we hoped to draw fire away from their right. The terrain, filled with gullies, afforded excellent cover. It would be no problem to crawl close enough to fire a bazooka round into the tank's vulnerable bogie wheels.

Since leaving Rome, all the troops of the 91st Recon had encountered similar obstacles and overcome them. To the men in the line troops, these delays were all in a day's work. If the situation proved too difficult for us to handle, we called on the 1st Armored Division for tank support or on the foot soldiers of their 6th Infantry.

After loading our bazooka, we sent a couple of men across the road to open fire on the left side of the tank. Rifle bullets are no match for the armor on a tank. When our fellows started bouncing bullets off the heavy steel shell, it was like a mouse scratching the back of an elephant. Getting annoyed, the tank crew swung the turret around in the direction of the small-arms fire. After the large-caliber gun sent a couple of shells toward our concealed comrades, we knew the Krauts had taken our bait.

Hidden behind a bank, the men of the 2nd Platoon prepared to fire the bazooka. Not being in any grave danger, the officers from squadron headquarters remained with us. The senior officer said that he'd fired a bazooka back in the States and asked if we'd mind letting him fire at the tank. Figuring it to be "no big deal," we handed him the stovepipe-looking weapon. Resting it on top of his right shoulder, he raised it above the top of the bank and fired. The projectile found its mark and disabled the tank. Realizing they could either surrender or make the tank their coffin, the Krauts raised a white flag.

After sending the prisoners back for interrogation, we prepared to move forward. Having no further conversation with the two officers, we watched them climb into their jeep and return to headquarters.

A week or so later, after we reached the Arno River and were relieved from front-line duty, awards were presented to men of the squadron. We were shocked to learn that the subordinate of the high-ranking officer who helped us clear the roadblock had recommended his superior for the Distinguished Service Cross. Except for the Congressional Medal of Honor, this was the highest decoration a soldier could receive.

Since first entering combat in North Africa, no member of C Troop had received a medal higher than the Silver Star, one step lower than the Distinguished Service Cross.

With every soldier having a specific job, each man became part of a team. As in all combat units, victory is achieved through the joint efforts of men who depend on one another. Very few men ever thought of or expected to get a medal for doing their duty.

To receive a medal, there had to be a witness to the act of heroism performed above and beyond the call of duty. The witness put the man up for the decoration. Upon learning that the junior officer recommended his superior for the DSC, we shook our heads in disgust.

An officer who very seldom visits the front lines might perform a task that he thinks is much more hazardous than his usual job. In his eyes, he believes he is a hero. A combat soldier does the same job and considers it all in a day's work performed in the line of duty. He expects no recognition, and usually gets none.

Quite a few staff officers assigned to headquarters units in the infantry received medals under similar circumstances. I've often heard infantrymen say, "Many times after a group of officers visit the front, you can expect them to pat each other on the back with one hand and hang a medal on their colleague's chest with the other."

Back in the States, people were impressed with the large, false bouquet of "lettuce" many of these officers plastered across their chests. Most high-ranking officers deserve a lot of credit for organizing and executing the tactical maneuvers that helped to win the war. Not all of them earned the medals they flaunted, awarded, supposedly, for gallantry and heroism in action.

When I think of the men in C Troop who risked their lives over and over with no thought of receiving recognition, then medals take on an insignificant meaning. Names such as John Manley, George Porth, Paul Yenser, George Rogers and Arnold Eckert would be added to the list of thousands of men who fought and received little credit for their heroic deeds. The only awards many of their families received from the War Department were the Purple Heart and a folded flag. The flag was similar to the one that should have covered their son's shattered body before it was lowered into the alien ground of a distant land.

In preparation for my return to the States, George Rogers, who had been wounded twice, took command of my squad before we reached the Arno River south of Florence. Soon after becoming squad leader, he started leading night patrols. Though he had gained a lot of experience on patrols, fate turned against him. A couple of nights after he became squad leader, while returning through our lines, he was killed. George and I had both joined the 91st Recon at A. P. Hill, Virginia, in 1942. He'd been my faithful companion on many a patrol. The unforgettable night we lay in the gutter at Cassino, with a German patrol standing next to us, would forever be a reminder that a man doesn't have to die to live a thousand deaths. After sharing so many harrowing experiences, it was hard to say, "Farewell, Old Friend."

Paul Yenser took over my squad after George's death. That same day, I went back to bring up tanks from the 1st Armored Division, for we'd run into a heavily fortified roadblock. Returning that evening, I sat in a foxhole and talked with my good friend Paul. We were both saddened after having lost our comrade George.

Staring out into No-Man's-Land, Paul said, "Fred,

you're heading back to the States in a couple of days. When you get home, will you do me a favor?"

"Sure thing, Paul, anything you ask," I said.

Though the night was exceptionally dark, I saw him lower his head. After swallowing real hard, he asked, "Will you drive up to Reading and see my mom and dad for me? Tell Mom that I love her, Fred. I don't believe I'll ever see her again."

He spoke with such choked emotion, I'm certain that if my eyes could have penetrated the darkness, I would have seen tears moisten his cheeks. "Don't talk like that," I said. "I'll be glad to visit your mom and dad, for Reading is only a few miles from home. I'll tell your mom how much you love her, but when the war's over, you'll be able to give her a big hug and a kiss and tell her yourself. Don't be so depressed, Paul. You're going to make it home. I know you will."

"Fred," he said, "I have a gut feeling that I'll never leave Italy. Just look how many men are left in our squad. Of those who came from the States with us, only George Johnson, Porth and I remain. The rest are gone. With the job we have, the odds are against me ever getting home. You and I both know it. Fred, you are the lucky one."

Nothing I could say seemed to cheer Paul up, for he had a premonition of impending doom.

Later that night, the Germans shelled our positions. Before morning, Paul was just another silent memory. We began our army careers together, leaving Pennsylvania for the cavalry post at Fort Riley, Kansas. Through four campaigns, we played and fought. Because men in combat depend on each other for survival, we became as brothers.

Looking down at his lifeless body, unashamed, I cried openly, letting the tears wash gullies through the dust caked on my face. I clutched a limp hand, already beginning to turn cold. When I stroked his head, I stopped where the hair lay matted with dried blood against his forehead. His blond hair reminded me of a tangled mass of parched grass atop a windswept knoll sprinkled with splotches of Indian paintbrush.

Lifting his shoulders off the ground, I held his limp

body to my breast, and buried my face in his bloodstained blond hair. He'd always been proud to say he inherited his thick mop of hair from his Swedish ancestors. I cried out, "Why God, why?"

Silently I prayed, whispering words I should have told him before today. I hoped my thoughts would penetrate his deaf ears, even though his spirit had drifted away to join those of our fallen comrades.

The conversation between Paul and me, only a few short hours ago, came back to haunt me. All I could think about was the need to fulfill his last request. How hard it would be to face his poor mother.

That morning, about eight or ten battle-weary German soldiers entered our lines and surrendered. Sergeant Smith, our platoon leader, said, "I need a volunteer to take these prisoners to the rear."

Leaping off the ground, I said, "I want to take them back, Sergeant."

After pulling the actuator back on my Thompson submachine gun, I switched the safety off, then started walking toward the prisoners. My distorted mind kept telling me that all I need do is put pressure on the trigger. Thirty rounds of vengeance would help ease the pain of my comrade's death.

Sergeant Smith knew that Paul and I were like brothers. He saw the look on my tearstained face that reflected the pain in my heart. It alerted him to the fact that he'd better not send me back with the men responsible for Paul's death. He held up his hand and motioned for me to stay put, then told Sergeant Charles Sturn from McMechen, West Virginia, to take charge of the prisoners. He said, "I'm sorry, Corporal, but I can't let you take them."

At the time, I resented the sergeant's decision. When I came to my senses, I realized how wrong I'd been. What if the situation were reversed, and I was one of those enemy soldiers. The Germans, undoubtedly, had the same feelings of compassion for their comrades killed in combat. If a man reacted to his emotions and let them control his decisions instead of doing what is morally right, the war could turn a

man into a murderer. How thankful I am that Sergeant
Smith stopped me.

In North Africa, one of my friends in another troop
emptied a box of machine-gun ammo into a column of
prisoners. He wanted to avenge the death of his brother
killed next to him earlier in the fighting. Unless you have
walked in that soldier's shoes, you will never understand
his feelings. When he came face to face with those men responsible for his sorrow, the urge for revenge overpowered
his will to think like a civilized human being.

After almost three months of continuous combat, when
the 91st reached the Arno River, II Corps relieved our
squadron from combat duty. We moved to a secluded
bivouac area in the rear. When the award ceremonies were
over, the troops assembled for speeches and entertainment.
On a hillside shaped in the form of an amphitheater, we sat
and listened to our colonel commend us for a job well done.

Among some of the German equipment that the
squadron captured north of Rome, one of the men had
found a public address system, complete with microphone.
The maintenance crew put it to good use at the gathering.
Knowing I was scheduled to leave the outfit, the men in C
Troop thrust an old guitar into my hands, and made me
get up in front of the squadron. They asked me to lead
them in singing some of the songs that had comforted us
around the campfires in Africa, Sicily and Italy. The men
requested that Al Jerman and I sing "The Rough and
Ready Recon," the marching song we wrote for our outfit.

I hated to leave these men. Many of them I would never
see again, for the North Apennines campaign was about to
begin. There were still mountains to be crossed before the
war finally came to an end. The day I left the squadron, I
presented my 1928 Model Thompson submachine gun to
one of the men in my squad. How I wish I could have
taken it with me, for it held so many memories.

With moistened eyes, I bid farewell to my comrades and
left for Port Piombino, south of the Leaning Tower of
Pisa. There I boarded a Liberty ship bound for Naples.

Carrying my Walther P-38 pistol concealed in my back-pack, I hoped to somehow get it back to the States.

On board the Liberty ship, I met a sailor who lived about ten miles from my home in Pennsylvania. Although I'd never met him before, after he heard the story of how I acquired my P-38 pistol in North Africa, he offered to conceal the gun in his personal gear and smuggle it into the United States. His ship was scheduled to return to its home port within a couple of weeks. My spirits lifted, for I never expected to be so fortunate.

When we arrived in Naples, military personnel inspected every piece of our gear. We were told that if any of us had German military equipment in our possession, we wouldn't be allowed to leave for the States. The following day, we boarded a troopship loaded with mostly wounded soldiers.

Before the evening sun tinted the hulks of the sunken ships in the harbor, we departed Naples. We sailed out past the beautiful Isle of Capri and into the Mediterranean. The rising and falling swells seemed to be bluer than ever, but my spirits were anything but blue. Those rolling waters were carrying me home.

When the ship left the port of Algiers, and later Oran, I whispered good-bye to North Africa. I knew I'd never set foot on the Dark Continent again.

Before we sailed through the Straits of Gibraltar and into the Atlantic Ocean, off to our left on the shores of Spanish Morocco I could see the white houses of Tangier. Gazing at the distant buildings brought back memories of the time C Troop raced to the border of Spanish Morocco. Fearing the Germans were going to cross the straits from Spain and attack his forces in French Morocco, General Patton had sent his cavalry scouts, the 91st Recon, out to meet them.

On our ocean voyage in 1942, we were continually harassed by the German submarine wolf packs. Unlike those trying times, once we sailed out into the Atlantic Ocean, our convoy experienced no difficulties.

On board ship, I slept on the deck 'neath the sky that had served as my comforter for hundreds of nights. Looking up into the heavens, I talked to the same stars that had guided me on so many patrols. With plenty of time to think, I wanted to sort out the events of my life that had taken place over the past couple of years. The happy-go-lucky, carefree young boy who enlisted in the horse cavalry had long since vanished. In his place stood a young man, old for his years, a person who very rarely smiled. The pain in his heart could be seen in moistened eyes whenever he reflected on those bygone days.

I felt guilt-ridden because of the decisions I'd made that affected the lives of so many. While trying to cope with my past, I tried to figure out why I'd been spared. Though staying alive became a science with me, what saved me from the many mistakes I made? Who guided the bullets and shrapnel away, letting them strike down buddies touching my elbows? If I didn't quit thinking about these things, I'd go insane trying to come up with the answers.

Like a new world being born from out of the depths of the North Atlantic, the shores of my homeland rose above the horizon. As I stood leaning against the railing, I unbuttoned my shirt collar and pulled out the chain from around my neck. There, next to my dog tags, was the Miraculous Medal I'd picked up on the battlefield near Troina, Sicily. Reaching into my left shirt pocket, I removed the battered, steel-encased New Testament that covered my heart. Opening it, I stared at the faded poppy pressed between its pages. I'd picked that once beautiful flower on the plains of North Africa as the shrieking sound of a Stuka dive bomber released its bomb above me.

Could the tiny medal I held in my hand and this small book of sacred scriptures be responsible for the miracle that brought me safely home?

# CHAPTER XIII

# The Bugler Sounds Retreat

The tears of joy falling over the railing of our troopship into the waters of Chesapeake Bay swelled the incoming tide. On shore, the crowds cheered when the sailors secured the lines and lowered the gangplank to the dock in Newport News, Virginia.

I watched the uplifted faces in the waiting crowd. Bulging eyes searched the deck of our ship, hoping against hope to catch a glimpse of their wounded son or husband. The war had changed the physical appearance as well as the mental attitude of their loved ones. The scene reminded me of a group of parents looking into a crowded nursery, searching for a newborn child they'd never held in their arms.

When we stepped from the gangplank, Red Cross workers gave us doughnuts and lemonade. Twilight settled over the land. For the first time since 1942, I watched a city untouched by the violence of war light its halo. It brought back memories of the America I once knew.

The buses and ambulances awaiting our arrival hauled us to Fort Patrick Henry. The following day a group of us left for Camp Meade, Maryland. Before we left the camp, we were given a brief medical exam. Afterward, each of us received a twenty-one-day furlough. I traveled to Pennsylvania on a train with Alton Knappenburger, a 3rd Division infantryman who had recently received the Congressional Medal of Honor in Italy. News of Alton's arrival in the States preceded him. He told me that later in the day he was scheduled to lead a large parade given in his honor.

"I just hope I don't need any more money before I get home, because I'm almost flat busted," he said.

As the P&W train rolled along past villages that I remembered as a boy, I said, "You're a national hero now, Alton, and you might be delayed before you get home. You better take this twenty-dollar bill I have, just in case you need some extra cash."

"Won't you have use for it before you reach home?" he asked.

"Heck no," I said. "My family has no idea that I'm even in the States. They think I'm still over in northern Italy. I didn't want to write and build up their hopes for fear I'd be killed and never make it back. Once I get off this train and walk through the woods into the village of Gulph Mills, I'll be home. There's no brass band waiting to welcome me."

Alton was raised in the Quaker religion, also called the Society of Friends. Its members didn't believe in violence; instead, they lived a quiet and law-abiding life. Their church let each man decide for himself whether he should enter the armed forces in time of war. Alton chose to follow his conscience and serve his country in combat. In Italy, he received the highest medal the United States could bestow on a soldier.

When the train pulled into the station at Gulph Mills, I waved farewell to Alton. Leaving the bullet-shaped car, I stepped onto the wooden platform. There wasn't a soul in sight. It made for a lonely welcome, but that's the way I wanted it.

"I better not just walk home and surprise Mother," I thought. "The shock might be too much for her. There's a phone down in the village. I better call her from there."

Picking up my duffel bag, I walked to the historic Bird In Hand country store. When the telephone operator connected me with Mother, I asked, "Can I speak to your son Fred?"

"I'm sorry, but that's impossible," she said. "He's in the army, somewhere in northern Italy. We haven't seen him since 1942."

Realizing that Mother didn't recognize my voice, I

asked if she was seated in a chair. Thinking something dreadful had happened, she began to cry, saying, "Yes, I'm sitting down. Has something happened to my son?"

Not wanting to cause her any more anxiety, I said, "Mother, this is your wandering boy, Fred."

"You can't be him," she said. "Please don't tease me."

She wouldn't believe me, not until I started to sing, "The Little Shirt Me Mother Made for Me," the song my father sang in Wales as a young boy. After I told her, "I'll see you later this afternoon, Mother," I hung up the receiver.

As I walked through the village, everyone came out to greet me. Unlike the brass band awaiting Alton's homecoming, I heard the rhythmic beat of steel pounding against steel. The old familiar ringing sound floated out from beneath the branches of the apple tree next to old Dan McDermott's blacksmith shop. In the summer heat, he always worked outside at his portable forge.

Before Dan's daughter Alice called to tell him I'd returned home from the war, I stood in the middle of the road and listened. It seemed like Dan was playing "The Anvil Chorus" just for me. Down through the years, the sinewy arms beating the hammer on that age-old anvil had cradled nearly every child in the village. No youngster could recall the time when Dan's hair turned to silver.

After I finished talking to my old friend and his family, I proceeded down the road. The news of my arrival spread like wildfire. I noticed that a few of the faces showing joy at my return, were also moistened with tears of sorrow. Many of these families had lost loved ones in the war. Seeing me come home reminded them they would never be able to enjoy a reunion such as mine.

Because Gulph Mills lay nestled between steep, wooded hills, the shadows had lengthened by the time I reached the far side of the village. Before opening the wooden gate leading to our front yard, I leaned against the giant oak tree that grew beside the road. I stood for a moment, watching my gray-haired mother rock back and forth in her chair on the porch. Unaware that I'd arrived in the vil-

lage, she busily knitted a scarf for some unknown soldier
boy in Europe.

I walked up behind her chair and spoke. Tears filled
both our eyes. Reaching down, I hugged her close and
kissed her moistened cheek. When Dad and my sister
Ethel and brother George returned home from work, they
welcomed me with open arms. The trouble I caused when I
left home and joined the horse cavalry would never be forgotten, but no one ever mentioned it. My folks were just
thankful that I'd returned safe.

Even though it seemed wonderful to be home, I
couldn't get rid of the tensions that plagued my troubled
mind. Foremost was the promise I'd made to my buddy
Paul Yenser before he died. How could I ever deliver that
final message of love to his heartbroken mother? Until I
fulfilled my promise to Paul, I couldn't begin to think
about enjoying my reunion with family and friends.

The next morning, I walked through the village to visit
the blacksmith's oldest son, Pat. Wounded during the invasion of North Africa, he had only recently been discharged from the army. Pat offered to take me to see Paul
Yenser's parents the following morning.

Pat's brother George was also home from the service on a
furlough. Bright and early the next day, the three of us drove
the few miles to the town of Reading where Paul's folks lived.

Trying to console Paul's mother turned out to be one of
the most difficult things I've done in my life. Although she
had previously received official notice of her son's death from
the War Department, she refused to believe he'd been killed.

Before I could begin to unravel the heartrending conversation Paul and I had the night before he died, my tears
moistened that poor woman's shoulder. When I explained
how he sat on the edge of his foxhole and spoke of his premonition of death, the look in her eyes made me wish
God had taken my life instead of Paul's. I told her how
much he loved her, but no words seemed to ease the pain
in her broken heart.

For his family's sake, Paul's dad tried to be strong, but I

could tell his world had collapsed. Before the McDermott brothers and I left, Mrs. Yenser finally came to the realization that the war had taken her eldest son. I spoke of the good times we'd spent together since entering the army and of the places we visited in our travels. Her eyes sparkled when I told her of all the fun we used to have reminiscing about childhood days and our families. The moisture in her eyes might have made the sparkle more pronounced, but I think they shone because she wanted to have those fond memories to caress in the lonely years ahead.

I promised to keep in touch with Paul's parents, his younger brother John and his two sisters. The heartaches and suffering I saw them go through made me realize what thousands of families all over the world were experiencing. Scenes like this were taking place, not only in the Allied countries, but in Germany as well. The pain might be over for the young men who made the supreme sacrifice for their country, but the loved ones left behind continued to suffer the rest of their lives. Many of the survivors died from a broken heart. Somehow, I had to keep this from happening to Paul's mother. I vowed to keep in touch and comfort her.

After returning from the mission of mercy with the grieving family, I headed for New England. I visited my childhood friends on their mountain farm in New Hampshire. Upon my return to Pennsylvania, everyone in the village turned out to honor me at a dinner party. They held the event in the old hall where our country-western band used to hold its Saturday-night barn dances.

The guitar I took overseas was destroyed the same day my buddy Henderson lost his life in North Africa. The one I made out of an ammunition box, in Italy, suffered the same fate near Cassino. The loss of these two instruments prompted my folks to buy a new guitar and present it to me at the ceremony.

Jake Moser, my best friend and former trapline partner, was home on furlough from the Marine Corps. Jake was the leader of our hillbilly band. Though some of the other band members were off to war, Ann Pribula, Bill Mitchell, Jake and I got together and had a big shinding in the village. Ann and I reminisced about the times she and I used to sing duets with the band. Though we were only teenage kids, and the youngest members in the group, we played in nearly all of the parks in the area. The summer of 1941, at Chalfont Park, Ann and I refused a talent scout's offer to go to radio station WSM and the Grand Ole Opry in Nashville, Tennessee. Instead of accepting the once-in-a-lifetime offer, I joined the cavalry. Over the next few years, I sang around lonely campfires with my buddies, instead of on a stage.

The accordion I had sent home from Italy, loaded with German weapons, arrived intact. After showing the souvenirs to my family, I stored them with my muzzle-loading rifles in the attic of our old stone house. The stories of how I obtained each of the pieces of equipment remained locked in my memory. I wanted to forget about the war.

With my brother George now fourteen years of age, I prayed the fighting would end before he would have to enter the service. I hated to see him march down a road similar to the one I'd trod.

Even though Mother aired out my bedroom in the attic, none of the family could understand why I felt uncomfortable cooped up in a room where the ceiling sloped almost to the floor. Each night, I carried my blanket outside, and unrolled it on the back porch. After having slept so long in the open, I had claustrophobia.

Mother volunteered to send a package to my buddies in the 2nd Platoon of C Troop. She baked an assortment of cookies and candy. When I said that I wanted to enclose an unsliced loaf of bread in the package, she asked, "Don't the fellows get bread in Italy? By the time the package arrives, the bread will be stale."

Shaking her head, she watched me hollow out the freshly baked loaf and discard the center. Her eyes widened when I inserted a bottle of whiskey in the cavity. During the war, my mother and sister sent packages to the men overseas, but never again one that contained a bottle of moonshine.

The pleasant reunion I spent with family and friends soon came to an end. After bidding farewell to everyone in the village, I boarded a train for Camp Butner, North Carolina. Many of the other soldiers on the train were also returning from furloughs. As in most passenger trains of the era, soot from the coal-fired locomotive filtered in beneath the loose-fitting windows. Before reaching camp, our light khaki uniforms were the color of a burnt omelet saturated with black pepper.

When the conductor announced our arrival at Butner, we stepped off the train and found ourselves within walking distance of camp. As the autumn sun headed toward the Blue Ridge Mountains to the west, we marched along the road leading to the post.

The permanent cadre of Camp Butner was assembled on the parade ground. As we approached the area, without any warning, the cannon used for retreat boomed its gutless message across the southern landscape. Before the sound of the explosion had a chance to echo off the freshly painted white buildings, I dove headfirst into the ditch beside the road. The part of my brain controlling my body movements took me back to those never-to-be-forgotten days in Italy. I wasn't alone in the ditch. Lying scattered up and down the depression were many of the men who had recently returned from combat. A few of the soldiers standing upright on the roadbed didn't understand the reason we responded as we did. They laughed and one of them jokingly yelled, "You guys better sober up before we enter camp."

To us men in the ditch, our reactions were no laughing matter. I soon came to realize that the remainder of my life would be a repetition of what happened that day at Camp Butner. If I heard a boom that reminded me of an artillery piece firing in the distance or heard a whistle that sounded like an incoming shell, I either ducked my head or fell to the ground. A noise like the chatter of a machine gun brought on the same reaction. Try as I might, I could never control my reflexes and keep them from reacting to those sounds.

No one knows how sheepish and self-conscious a man

feels, when he gets up off the ground with people staring at him. I never held it against anyone who laughed at me, for I knew that unless they'd been in combat, they wouldn't understand.

The day after my arrival at Camp Butner, I had a complete examination. Physically, I was in good shape, even though I still carried a scar on my chest from the shrapnel wound I had received at Cassino. A doctor saw the scar on my left eardrum and wanted to know what had caused it. I told him about the artillery shell that landed next to my head as I lay in a ditch. Even though the shrapnel passed harmlessly over my head, I received a concussion from the violent explosion.

Part of every physical exam given returning veterans included a visit to a psychiatrist. When that doctor finished examining me, he leaned back in his chair and propped his glasses up on top of his head. With a questioning look, he folded his hands on his lap and sat staring at me.

I began to feel uncomfortable under his gaze. Finally he asked, "Tell me, soldier, what kind of a job did you have overseas?"

Having a backwoods impression of doctors, I thought the only reliable ones were those who carried the tools of their trade in a satchel and charged two dollars for a house call. Only insane people went to a psychiatrist like this fellow. I took offense with his inquiring nature and answered his question with more questions. "Why do you ask me about my job? What difference does it make what I did overseas? Do you think I'm crazy?"

Ignoring my defensive attitude, he replied, "Young man, I've examined a lot of returning servicemen, but very few with nerves that react like yours. Your every move is that of a stalking cat, wound up and ready to pounce on its prey. I've never seen anyone so tense. Why can't you relax?"

Acknowledging his assessment of the problem I knew existed, I said, "Doc, I've just left a recon outfit that fought through North Africa, Sicily and Italy. When out on patrol, we had to make believe an enemy soldier lurked behind every tree and boulder. A man continually had to anticipate his next move. If a German happened to be lying in wait up ahead, and you didn't have a plan of action, a fellow didn't live very long. Every movement you made, while crawling through the darkness, had to prepare you for the inevitable. A scout's mind has to be continually working. If you relax for just a second, you can wind up dead. The slightest sound, or even a shadow out of place, can warn you of your would-be executioner's presence."

Instead of looking at the doctor sitting in the chair in front of me, I was talking to the replica of a skeleton hanging from the ceiling in his office. When the psychiatrist remained silent, I kept jabbering. I tried to justify my actions, not for the sake of the man listening to me, but to keep my own sanity. "When German artillery is firing, having your mind tuned to the sound of a projectile that could scribble your name in blood on the ground beside you, keeps your nerves forever tense. Once a man learns how to tell if a shell is going to land nearby, he has a better chance of survival. If you wait for a shell to explode before making a move to fall to the ground, you'll never escape from the mushrooming, cancerlike, flying shrapnel."

Knowing that he'd hit upon the subject and cause of my tension, the doctor tried to calm me. He backed off from asking any further questions and treated me kindly.

By the time I approached the last doctor performing the exams, I felt like an interrogated prisoner. When this physician asked if I'd ever had malaria, for some unknown reason I lied. "No," I said, even though I'd contracted the disease in Sicily.

As if to pay retribution for the stupid lie, the day after completing my physical, I came down with a high fever. I couldn't even get out of bed to report for sick call. The following morning, the medics lifted me onto a stretcher and carried me to the base hospital. My temperature got so high, I became delirious. A couple of days later no one recognized me. My face was a mass of sores and broken skin. Because of the high fever, I lost nearly all of my hair. I wondered whether I'd contracted malaria again because of lying to the doctor or because I'd been shipped to a hot and humid part of the country.

The large amount of quinine the nurses gave me, although not a cure for the disease, did reduce the fever. Twice the doctors released me from the hospital, and each time I had to be readmitted. The last time I entered the malaria ward, I was nothing but skin and bones. In a uniform, I would have looked like "Sad Sack," the comic-strip character.

Fearing I might cash in my chips, I asked a nurse for a notebook and pencil. Some inner force kept driving me to record my war experiences. I'd kept a small diary in my New Testament all the time I was overseas, but I wanted a more detailed account. The notes I made were condensed, but were enough to jog my memory loose if I survived and ever decided to write about the war. My nerves were so bad, I feared my mind would snap before I finished the brief journal.

After jotting down the main events from most of my patrols, I added other incidents that I had experienced over the past few years. Placing the notes in a box the nurse gave me, I had her send them to Mother. In an enclosed envelope, I told Mom to put the package away in the trunk with my personal belongings. Forty-five years would pass before the contents of that box were opened and read. Without those notes, many of my experiences would have been almost impossible to recollect. Even though I could never forget most of the things that happened, memories have a way of fading with the passing years.

During my eleven weeks of intermittent hospital care, I received treatment for malaria and my shattered nerves. The doctors informed me that I suffered from combat fatigue and was unfit to return to the front lines. Along with a group of other patients recently discharged from the hospital, I boarded a train headed for the U.S. Disciplinary Barracks at Fort Harrison, Indiana.

Though I was not qualified to handle a weapon in combat, the army figured that I was well enough to man a machine-gun tower and guard American soldiers convicted of major crimes. Many of the prisoners were a hardened group of men, having been sent to Fort Harrison from the overcrowded U.S. penitentiary at Leavenworth, Kansas.

Two rows of chain-link and barbed-wire fencing surrounded the compound. The machine-gun towers reminded me of a pack of wolves silently watching a flock of sheep. Like tongues hanging from open mouths, the machine-gun barrels seemed ready to spew instant death on anyone who tried to escape from the enclosure. The prisoners were housed in wooden barracks located inside of the double row of fencing. During the short time I manned the tower, I encountered no trouble. I never came in close contact with the prisoners.

A couple of weeks after arriving at the complex, I was assigned to a two-man detail scheduled to travel by train to the federal penitentiary at Chillicothe, Ohio. We were ordered to pick up a prisoner and escort him back to Fort Harrison. Upon arriving at the prison, when the huge gates slammed shut behind us, a strange feeling came over me. I looked at the confined cells of the inmates and witnessed the strict disciplinary action enforced on the prisoners. Feeling like a trapped mountain lion fresh out of the wild, I automatically began making plans of how to escape if I was ever sent to prison.

During the return trip to Fort Harrison, our prisoner remained handcuffed to either me or the sergeant in command. After our mission was completed, the sergeant of the guard relieved me from further duty on the machine-gun tower.

My new assignment inside the compound took me to the basement of a building set apart from the other structures. Little did I realize that I was now part of a team of men who administered severe and inhumane punishment on the less-than-model prisoners. These guards used a different method of control.

Most citizens of our country were unaware that the belowground, individual cell units called "black boxes" even existed. Each cell measured approximately six feet square. There were no fixtures or furniture of any kind in the cell. The smooth ceiling and walls provided no place for a prisoner to tie a piece of clothing from which to hang himself. Many of the occupants would gladly have taken this means of escape in preference to an extended stay in the black boxes. The six-inch-square, half-inch-thick piece of reinforced glass, located near the top of the solid door, might just as well have been painted black. Most of the time, the entire basement remained in darkness.

Prisoners in the main compound who disobeyed the guards or tried to incite their fellow inmates in any way were thrown into the black boxes. Sometimes the men were sentenced for up to thirty days.

The first day I worked at my new job, I felt like walking out the prison gate and going "over the hill." One of the men in the boxes had become sick during the night. When I opened his cell door, the stench that filled my nostrils was horrible. It smelled like the prisoner's bile duct had broken, then fermented before passing through his lower intestines. I leaned against the outside wall of the cubicle and vomited. The greasy potatoes and gravy I'd eaten for breakfast splattered on the concrete hallway. With nothing left in my stomach to eject, I staggered to the restroom. After locating a mop and bucket, I filled it with hot water and poured in a whole bottle of ammonia.

When I returned to the cell and examined the prisoner, I realized he was too weak to swill out his cell floor. The poor fellow couldn't even stand up. As soon as the sergeant of the guard left the building, I mopped out the cell myself. Outside in the hallway, my partially digested breakfast was slowly winding its way down the sloping floor.

Though the guards weren't supposed to become friendly with the prisoners or show them any compassion, a man has to do right by his conscience. When I was told the man wasn't sick enough to be sent to the base hospital, I decided to break the strict guard rules and help him. Later in the day, I went to the prison mess hall and smuggled out a pint of broth and some strong tea. When I returned to my job, I gave the two containers to the sick prisoner.

On the first morning of my new assignment, the sergeant told me to hand out the prisoners' rations. I looked around the guardroom, expecting to find a cart loaded with a stack of trays filled with food. Instead, all I found was a large box of bread.

When I opened each of the cell doors, I couldn't look the unfortunate occupant in the eye. Handing him his breakfast, dinner and supper baked into a single loaf of day-old bread, I wished I had more to give. The incident reminded me of Marie Antoinette during the French Revolution. When she asked why her subjects were angry, the reply was, "Because they have no bread." The arrogant queen said, "Then let them eat cake."

Though I realized the prisoners had to be punished for their crimes, I couldn't understand how our government could justify starving an American just to subdue him. There had to be a more humane method. During these war years, the government treated foreign prisoners of war like royalty.

Most of the prisoners tried to control their bowels. They knew they'd have to lie in their excrement until a guard got around to attending to them. They were allowed out of their cell only once every morning and evening to get a drink of water and go to the toilet. Sleeping on the cold hard floor, with only a single blanket for warmth, almost always assured the men of catching a cold before their punishment ended.

Confined inside a dark dungeon, and having no one to converse with for days and sometimes weeks at a time, could drive a man insane. Some prisoners learned a lesson from their stay in the black boxes. For others, the inhumane treatment broke their spirit. Many of the hard-line prisoners became more embittered and seemed willing to suffer the punishment. They probably figured their fellow inmates would show more respect for a martyr who continually fought the system.

While on guard duty, I had time to do a lot of thinking. During my childhood, I read quite a few books. Most of them were about the early frontier and the American West. I'd never read stories to prepare me for my present job of dealing with the criminal element in our society. Over the past few years, each page I turned in my book of life taught me more about the inner workings of my fellow man. I could never have learned these lessons out of a textbook or from a psychology professor.

In the spring of 1945, just prior to Germany's surrender, a race riot broke out inside the compound at Fort Harrison. Many of the frame barracks went up in flames. Because I hated my assigned job, instead of my nerves improving, they were worse than those of the unfortunate prisoners in the black boxes. The periods of depression I felt during the day fueled the nightmares I experienced. Although the war was thousands of miles away, I often woke up in a cold sweat, reliving one of my night patrols. As hard as I tried, I couldn't escape the exploding shells and the whine of machine-gun bullets.

One morning when I reported for sick call, the doctor relieved me from duty and sent me to Wakeman General Hospital at Camp Atterbury, Indiana. After being examined, I was transferred to that post. The doctor said I'd be able to receive more advanced treatment for my mental condition.

While I was receiving therapy as an outpatient at the hospital, Germany surrendered. During this final phase of the war, the military initiated a system of discharging returning servicemen. Personnel received a point for each month spent in the service, plus an additional point for each month served overseas. Five additional points were given for every campaign a man participated in and also for each decoration he received. Although I had enough points to be discharged, I continued to remain an outpatient at the base hospital.

Camp Atterbury, like many other military posts across the country, was the site of a German prisoner of war camp. Many of the prisoners interned there worked on farms in the area. With men being discharged from the camp under the point system, a shortage developed in the guard unit overseeing the German prisoners. The officers at Atterbury took every unassigned enlisted man on the post and made them perform guard duty. With my service record listing one of my qualifications as a machine gunner, I became one of the first men ordered to report to the guard-house.

Quite a few of the German prisoners at Atterbury had served in Rommel's Afrika Korps. Those not assigned to farm labor around the camp worked in bakeries, laundries and other service shops on the post. The prisoners performed a valuable service and made it possible for many of the local farm laborers to join the military.

Like most people of German descent, the prisoners were excellent workers. They got along well with their civilian and military supervisors. Fate did an injustice to the German people when it chose the former leader of their country. A great majority of its citizens began to realize that Hitler's policy of world domination could only bring disaster to their homeland.

With the upcoming Fourth of July being a national holiday, everyone on the post with a job not essential to keeping the compound secure was given the day off. Because of their seniority, the older guards were relieved from duty. Since I was one of the new replacements, the sergeant of the guard ordered me to work on the holiday.

The German prisoners also had the day off because there was no one to supervise them in the fields. I became disgusted for having to work on the first Fourth of July I'd spent in the States since 1942. The thought of babysitting German prisoners on the day our nation celebrated its independence griped me. These men were responsible for my being in the army. When Hitler set out to dominate the world, he also threatened the independence of the United States.

Whenever a group of men are banded together, you always find a troublemaker among them. A few of Hitler's fanatical followers, the hard-core SS troopers, seemed to be the only men in the prison compound with a chip on their shoulders.

Surrounding the prison area, and spaced about twenty feet apart, two rows of chain-link fence topped with barbed wire. The rectangular-shaped compound had six machine-gun towers around its outside perimeter, three on each of the longest sides. A short set of stairs led up to each tower. Directly behind the middle tower on the long side of the compound stood the guardhouse.

After I reported to this building, the sergeant of the guard took me into his office and said, "Because your records show that you are a qualified machine gunner, I won't need to brief you on its operation."

Having a new guard in his command and wanting to keep a watchful eye on him, the sergeant assigned me to the tower nearest the guardhouse. A person standing on the catwalk of this tower could throw a rock and hit the guard building.

I followed the sergeant up the few steps leading to the tower. Once inside, he pointed to the Browning machine gun and said, "You'll probably never have reason to use it, but there she is."

A green metal box beside the gun held 250 rounds of ammunition laced into a web belt. The belt wasn't threaded into the receiver of the gun. Mounted on a track, the machine gun could be slid out through the window to cover the prison yard and the buildings that housed the prisoners.

Squinting his dark, bushy eyebrows, the sergeant said, "Under no circumstances are the prisoners allowed to touch the inner fence. If they venture near it, go out on the catwalk and order them away."

Later that day, I had good reason to remember his next words. "If necessary," he said, "get rough with them. Whatever you do, make them stay back from the fence."

Pointing to a telephone on the wall, he said, "If you have any trouble, pick up the receiver and the relief guards will be at your side in a matter of seconds."

I mentioned to the sergeant that I'd worked in a tower at Fort Benjamin Harrison and understood his instructions. Before leaving for the guardhouse, he said, "Most of the prisoners are relieved from work detail today. The prison yard will be quite crowded, but the men should be in good spirits."

After the sergeant left, I looked out across the compound. I sucked in a deep breath and thought, What a beautiful day to celebrate the Fourth of July! The warm

Indiana sunshine reminds me of the summers I spent in Sicily and Italy. Though no one could hear me, I said, "Before next Fourth of July, I'll be out of this darn army and can spend the holiday as I see fit. I won't have to put up with playing nursemaid to a bunch of Krauts."

Figuring that I better get on with my job, I walked out onto the catwalk and surveyed the prisoners lounging in the yard. Off to my left, almost directly under the corner machine-gun tower, I noticed a group of prisoners watching me. Because the guard in the tower directly above them was sitting down, the men were out of his line of sight. I presumed the prisoners were sizing up the new guard in the middle tower. Because most of the Krauts had been in the German army for a long time, they probably figured the young light-haired kid must be a new recruit. I watched the group of men huddle together and start talking, then a couple of them began to laugh.

Out of the corner of my eye, I saw the entire group casually stroll over to the inner chain-link fence. All of them placed their hands upon it. I realized they were testing me, trying to see how far they could go with the new guard. The sergeant of the guard said they would be in a playful mood.

Walking around the catwalk to the side nearest them, I rested my foot on the center railing. Without saying a word, I casually raised my right hand and motioned them away from the fence. I didn't want them to think they'd upset me. Without hesitating, they obeyed my command. After they walked away from the fence, I turned around and reentered the tower.

Most of the other prisoners loafing around the compound witnessed the testing of the new guard. I imagine these men led a boring life when not working in the fields. There wasn't much for them to do to pass the time away. They made their own entertainment, which was what they were in the process of doing at the moment. The Fourth of July meant nothing to them except to bring them one day closer to returning to their homeland and loved ones.

Not long after I asserted my authority over the prisoners,

the same group of men stared up at my tower again. Their comrades seemed to be egging them on to some sort of mischief. When they approached the fence for the second time, they jokingly made like they intended to climb it. Needless to say, I became quite provoked. I noticed that a number of the young ringleaders were wearing light brown jackets and caps. Their uniforms were similar to those of the men in the Hermann Goering Division, many of whom we captured in North Africa. I surmised that most of the men had served in the Mediterranean Theater of Operations.

I began to wonder if they were just having fun or were using our Independence Day to show me they also had a right to express a desire for freedom. If such was the case, the supposedly raw recruit guarding them had no intention of putting up with their shenanigans. I knew these warlike Prussians were masters at manipulating and intimidating their victims.

I looked down at the ringleader of the troublemakers. A picture from my past flashed across the view screen of my mind. I remembered the incident that took place over a year ago, on May 19, 1944. Could it be possible that the man below me was the arrogant SS trooper I'd almost killed at Gaeta, Italy? Was my mind playing tricks on me? In this soldier's facial expression, I could see the same man who refused to obey my command and raise his hands so I could search for hidden weapons. I closed my eyes for a brief moment, remembering how in my frustration, I shot next to his feet with my submachine gun. I kept firing until he obeyed my command. The SS trooper knew that if he didn't bend to my wishes, I intended to kill him.

Regaining my composure as best I could, I walked out onto the catwalk. The prisoners knew they had finally "got my goat," for, in an angry voice, I shouted at them to get away from the fence. With a look of triumph on their faces, they removed their hands from the wire and walked away. I could tell that the prisoners sitting in the shade of the buildings were enjoying the holiday performance staged for their benefit. They all laughed and pointed in my direction.

When one of them yelled, "You'd make a good Boy Scout," the remark added fuel to my emotional fire.

I'd never been trained to handle a situation where I was forced to play games with my sworn enemy, especially when they made me the brunt of their jokes. Always before, the stakes in the game were much higher and pitted my wits and life against theirs.

They are making a fool of me, I thought, and I can't even fight back. If the SS trooper out in that yard is the same one who gave me all the trouble in Gaeta, he has finally beaten me. There is nothing I can do to stop him. With a defeatist attitude. I entered the machine-gun tower.

After declaring a brief truce, the group of tormentors pushed their advantage to the hilt and began to heckle me again. They walked over and gripped the chain-link fence. A couple of them reached up high enough to lift their feet off the ground, making like they intended to climb the heavy-gauge wire.

If any of the guards in the other five towers were watching the performance, they never intervened on my behalf. They were either accustomed to the prisoners' supposedly harmless antics or were waiting to see how the new guard would handle the situation.

When the ringleader of the tormenting prisoners glanced up at my tower, and I saw the smirk of victory on his face, I lost my self-control. All the bitterness bottled up inside me against those responsible for the heartaches I'd suffered over the past three years came to the surface. Depressed and nervous since returning to the States, I stood inside the machine-gun tower and shook like a pair of rolled dice in the cupped hand of a crapshooter. If I'd had a fever, I might have thought it was the start of a malaria attack.

I no longer thought of myself as a guard on a machine-gun tower in the peaceful Indiana countryside. Once again I was back in Italy, trying to outsmart the enemy. Something strange had happened, the enemy were all around me, but they carried no guns. That didn't seem to matter, for the daggers thrown from their eyes had penetrated my heart. I wanted revenge.

In the time it takes lightning to flash across a summer sky and you hear the crash of thunder, I built an ironclad case against the men in that prison compound. Though no one could hear me, I spoke to the window-covered walls of the tower and said, "If you Krauts think you're going to make a fool out of me, you're dead wrong. I don't have to take any of your crap. Some of you are probably responsible for the death of more than one of my buddies."

After looking back on the events that led up to my breakdown, I realize that my emotions had reached such a high pitch that I went temporarily insane.

Walking over to the phone connected directly to the guardhouse, I lifted the receiver. Immediately a voice answered, "Guardhouse."

"You better get every ambulance on the post over here," I said, "for you're going to need them."

Without waiting for a reply, I slammed the receiver down. I must have thought I was preparing for battle, for I walked over to the .30-caliber machine gun. Knowing it had helped me out of tight spots before, I probably figured that it could solve my latest problem.

By now, all the prisoners in the compound had turned their attention to the men teasing the new guard. They were all jubilant and having the time of their lives. On the stage before them, the curtain was about to go up on the third act of a play presented by none other than the elite performers of Hitler's Third Reich. While the Americans observed their independence from King George III of England, the German prisoners were celebrating their sovereignty over a new guard.

My emergency call must have been broadcast over a loudspeaker and heard throughout the guardhouse. Within a matter of seconds every relief guard sprang into action. Unbeknown to me, four or five of them raced the short distance from the guardhouse to the base of my tower. Each man tried to be the first to climb the ladder leading to the catwalk. While this was in progress, I pulled

the ammo belt through the receiver of the machine gun
and rolled the weapon out to the edge of the window. In
one quick movement, I swiveled the gun to my left and
lined it up on the prisoners at the base of the fence.

In shocked disbelief, they stared up at the open window.
With hands clutching the fence, and their feet a foot or so off
the ground, for just a split second they froze in place. Only
then did they realize they'd gone too far with their practical
joke. They shouldn't have listened to their comrade from the
SS. If the crazy young kid in the tower followed through with
his threat to end their performance, they'd never get a chance
to hear the applause from their comrades. They could see that
I was about to draw the curtain on the third and final act.

To the prisoners, the open window centered in the small
room atop the four-legged tower must have looked like the
mouth of a ferocious dragon. The hollow, black metal
tongue pointing in their direction seemed ready to spew
devouring flames of death.

In one swift movement, I pulled back the bolt with my
right hand. Though I hadn't fired a machine gun since the
firefight at the Terracina bridge in Italy, my forefinger
moved rapidly toward the trigger. Because I'd gone past
the point of no return in trying to control my emotions, I
was about to commit murder

My finger touched the sun-warmed, metal trigger. Before I could apply pressure, a miracle intervened. Both my
arms were almost torn from their sockets. Insane with
rage, I never heard the relief guards scramble up the ladder and enter the tower.

My body hit the wooden floor with a crash. I didn't re-
gain my senses until I felt myself falling through the air
into the waiting arms of the guards at the base of the
tower. They broke my descent, but I still landed with a
bone-crushing jolt on the sunbaked ground. One of the
guards twisted my right arm behind my back in a ham-
merlock. Another man put a choke hold on me. Even if I
wanted to talk, I couldn't. After hauling me into the
guardhouse, the men literally threw me on the floor.

Because of the bitterness I now felt toward the entire human race, I refused to speak to the officer of the guard. How could he, or anyone else for that matter, understand how I felt? I no longer cared what they did to me.

About an hour after the incident happened, an officer entered my room. He informed me that I was to be given a preliminary court-martial the following morning.

I never slept all night. The pounding in my head sounded like a loudspeaker blaring a warning of things to come. Over and over, it kept repeating, "Your maverick ways have caught up with you. Before this is over, you'll be lucky if you don't wind up in the dreaded black boxes."

A guard brought breakfast on a tray, but I pushed it aside. I lost my will to fight the very system that I had dedicated and almost given my life to uphold. At nine-thirty that morning, a guard led me into a temporary courtroom and seated me in front of a long table. Behind it sat a group of army officers, surveying me with contempt. Their faces held the same expression you'd expect to find on a judge about to sentence a man accused of trying to machine-gun a group of nuns. Because of my refusal to speak out in my own defense, everyone I came in contact with had already convicted me of trying to murder the German prisoners. No one understood.

The chests of the officers on the tribunal were plastered with good conduct ribbons and marksmanship medals. I saw nothing that indicated any of the men had served in combat. How could any of them understand why my mind snapped? With these men judging me, my cause seemed hopeless.

As I pondered my dilemma, a door swung open behind the officers seated at the table. A colonel entered the room. When an orderly yelled, "Attention," everyone stood up and pulled back their shoulders, trying to impress their superior. The senior officer walked to the armchair reserved for him at the center of the table. "At ease. Be seated," he said.

From beneath his left arm he removed a folder that contained a sheaf of papers and placed it on the table. After glancing at me in the straight-back chair across from him, he silently began to study the contents of the folder.

Twice in the course of his reading, he lifted his head and
looked at me. The last time, with eyebrows raised, he
gazed out over the top of his glasses and stared long and
hard in my direction. He seemed to be trying to read the
inner thoughts and judge the character of the man opposite him. When he lowered his head, he leafed through the
documents once more. During all of these proceedings,
everyone in the room remained silent.

I could tell by their faces that the officers flanking the
colonel were anxious to have the preliminary hearing over.
They looked like an impressive bunch of military elite.
Glancing under the table, I could see their spit-and-polish
shoes shining like bald heads in the front row of a burlesque
show. None of them had ever been soaked in the oozing
mud of a foxhole. Their immaculately pressed uniforms,
with creases singed by a hot iron at the post laundry, had
never felt the heat of an enemy's bullet. Even the marksmanship medals they earned on the firing range, where the
bullets only travel in one direction, were highly polished.

The superior attitude of these officers showed in the
stretch marks below their uplifted chins. They reminded
me of the pictures I'd seen of Hitler and Mussolini ad-
dressing their subjects. In comparison, when the colonel
lowered the sheaf of papers and stood up, he seemed not
interested in impressing anyone. Instead, his face held a
sad expression, as if he hated to perform the task assigned
to him. Would his decision spell my doom?

Before uttering a word, the colonel studied the face of
each officer to his right and left. A moment later he said,
"We are holding this preliminary hearing to decide whether
to court-martial Corporal Salter for attempting to assassi-
nate German prisoners of war. Ordinarily, with the evidence
submitted by the guards who subdued the defendant, there
would be no question about the outcome of this hearing.

"After reading the defendant's medical and military
records, I have an entirely different perspective of the case.
While walking around the catwalk of his machine-gun
tower, Corporal Salter probably recognized a few of the

insignias on the prisoners' uniforms. Many of those men fought against him in the Mediterranean Theater of Operations. From evidence submitted by a couple of the guards in the other machine-gun towers, the prisoners were heckling the defendant. Jokingly, they tried to climb the inner fence of the compound. These acts by the prisoners do not justify Corporal Salter's actions."

When I heard this last statement, all of my hopes vanished. The colonel paused for a moment and poured himself a glass of water from a pitcher on the table. During this brief lull in the proceedings, I noticed a couple of the junior officers glance at each other and smile, then nod their heads up and down. They were confident of my conviction.

Continuing with the summary of my case, the colonel said, "This man's service record shows that he is a decorated Recon Scout. Looking at his medical history, I find that on his return from Italy, the psychologists classified him as suffering from combat fatigue. Under the circumstances, I find that instead of this soldier being recommended for a court-martial, the officers who allowed him to stand guard over German prisoners should be the ones in front of this tribunal. Didn't any of you men read this man's records before assigning him to guard duty?"

Every officer in the room shifted uneasily in his chair. For the first time since the hearing started, the smug, over-confident expressions disappeared from their faces. Most of them lowered their heads, realizing they'd been thoroughly reprimanded.

In a voice that echoed the strength of his character, the colonel almost shouted. "I am not condoning this soldier's behavior, but how can a man who has fought through five campaigns and watched comrades die at the hands of these prisoners, be expected to act any different than he did yesterday?"

Before passing the sheaf of papers to the officer on his right, he waved them in the air and said, "Before any of you leave this room, I want you to read this man's records." Pointing a finger at me that was so rigid, it looked like it stood at attention, he said, "Even though this soldier did wrong, ask yourself if you can honestly blame him for his actions. I don't want to hear of a situation like this occurring on this post again."

Looking directly into my eyes, he lowered his voice and apologized for the behavior of his fellow officers. "Corporal, I am sorry you had to undergo the ordeal this command put you through. Your records show that under the point system you are eligible to be released from the army. Don't worry, none of these proceedings will appear on your military record; you will receive an honorable discharge. Return to your barracks and wait for further orders. As soon as I can arrange the necessary papers, you will be released from the service."

After giving him a much deserved salute, I spoke for the first time since being incarcerated. "Thank you for your kindness, Colonel. You have restored my faith in the military. I never expected anyone to understand the reason I went berserk. I'm sorry that I've caused so much trouble."

As he turned and walked away, I gripped the arm of my chair and slumped into it. Exhausted from the pressures and tension of the past two days, I lowered my head into sweaty hands and tried to unwind. Unashamed, I lost control of my emotions and let the teardrops ooze between my fingers. They fell to the floor, like tiny strands of severed rope falling from around the neck of a condemned man.

What a way to end a military career, I thought. I've sure made a mess out of my life.

The colonel left the room, but the panel of officers remained, for their superior officer had ordered them to read my army records. After relaxing for a few minutes to gain my composure, I wiped the moisture from my eyes and walked to the door. None of the officers spoke or looked in my direction. I could understand their feelings, for I'd been the cause of their reprimand.

Returning to my quarters, I proceeded to get my gear together. I wanted to be ready when the order came through for my release. Time passed swiftly. I spent it meditating and reassessing the past few years of my life. The colonel, who had exonerated me from the crime I almost committed, made me realize the time had come to forgive the shortcomings and flaws in the character of my fellow man. I had been pardoned for mine.

I couldn't continue to hold hatred in my heart toward the German soldier or be bitter against my superiors in the military. They were only doing the job assigned to them as best they could. Thanks to a compassionate and forgiving colonel, I'd reached a turning point in my life.

Within a couple of days, orders came through for me to report to the Army Separation Center at Indiantown Gap, Pennsylvania. I lost no time in carrying out those orders and boarded the first train heading east. After arriving at the camp, I underwent a complete physical examination. As in the exam I took at Camp Butner, the doctors made note of the shrapnel scar on my chest. They examined my left ear and saw the results of the concussion I received from an artillery shell.

"You'll probably have that ringing noise you're complaining about for the rest of your life," the doctor said.

My past history of malaria didn't seem to concern them, for the disease had remained dormant for several months. I handled my medical exam fairly well up until the psychiatrist told me that I would have to enter the base hospital and undergo further tests for "combat fatigue." I knew that once I entered the hospital, my discharge could be delayed indefinitely.

"All I want to do is get out of the army," I yelled. "I have enough points to be discharged. You can't keep me here, I'm not a psycho case."

If the colonel at Camp Atterbury had written the details of my preliminary court-martial on my service record, I could never have talked the doctor into releasing me. Fed up with my explosive attitude, he threw up his hands in disgust. I signed a paper stating that I was physically fit even though, psychologically, I needed help. The document released the government from any further responsibility for my mental condition.

At the end of my exam, the doctor informed me that I would receive a disability pension.

When I read my discharge papers, I saw two Military Occupation Specialty (M.O.S.) numbers listed. Number 1607 covered the time I served as a heavy mortar crewman. Before leaving Italy, number 761 had been placed on my service record. I looked upon this military occupation number with pride, for it designated me a "Scout."

I chuckled when I saw the paper attached to my discharge. It read, "Your military experience makes you eligible to become a guide in a national park." This was the only type of civilian job that my years in the army qualified me for.

Before joining the recon, I received commando training and attended an armorer school, which provided me with specialized instruction in the operation and use of small arms. In Italy, I had gone to a mountain warfare training school that taught rappelling and mountain climbing. These three schools were the extent of my specialized education.

Looking back over my military career, I didn't have much to show for all those years. I originally joined the cavalry so I would be better qualified to get a job on a horse ranch in Montana. A young boy and his fantasies are soon separated. Those dreams were shattered when the army retired our horses before we sailed for North Africa. If all of my personal experiences were tallied up, I probably received more of an education than most young men my age. I also felt that I paid the debt my immigrant parents owed to the country that adopted them.

Even though I did things in the army that I wasn't proud of, the lessons I learned would prove invaluable in the years ahead. Nothing I experienced during my entire life had a greater impact on me than those years spent in the army. I had taken orders from my superior officers and obeyed them (well, most of the time) whether they were right or wrong. Those days were gone forever. From now on, I vowed to be my own man. Never again would I be brainwashed or forced to do anything against my will.

My boyhood dreams of settling in Montana were still

tucked away in the muddled corner of my mind. Before I could fulfill those mental images, I had to sort out my life. I needed time to think, time to forget about the guilt I carried in my heart. Somehow, I had to heal my mind.

Early the following morning, I walked out of the army post clutching a piece of paper that granted me freedom. Earning the right to possess that document taught me how to love, especially how to love life. I knew I wasn't ready to settle down. I'd never be content to return to the kind of life I led before the war. Somewhere out in this great land, I had to find peace of mind, even if it meant starting out on a new adventure.

I lifted my face to the cool morning breeze and savored the breath of freedom it brought. I was free at last. For the first time since the war began, I intended to control my own destiny. The future beckoned me—just waiting to be lived. It was then I decided to head west—and search for peace in the source of the wind.

## THE END

This isn't the end of my adventures, just a new beginning in the life of "The Maverick Tumbleweed."

## EPILOGUE

# Out of War, Came Love

The supporting role I played in the battlefield scenes of World War II had a profound effect on my life, more so than any other event I've ever participated in. Those war years changed the innocent personality of my youth, transforming me into a clone of a hardened combat veteran. I became bitter and thrived on the emotions of hate that I felt toward my supposed enemies.

While becoming an expert at taking another man's life, I soon discovered the meaning of fear. I learned that the things I'd been taught to do to another human being could also be done to me. Staring death in the face, I witnessed firsthand the many horrible ways a man can die.

The more involved I became in the fighting, the more I realized that God continually spared my life, when all around me, comrades fell. Every night when I laid my head on the helmet I used for a pillow, I thanked the Lord for guiding me through another day. I would ask Him, "Why do you treat me so mercifully?"

Unable to come up with an answer, I found that my outlook on the war changed. The conflict took on a new meaning. I still believed we fought for a just cause, and if necessary, I would give my life to uphold it, but I needed something to give me renewed strength and courage. I reached out for love, and found it existed all around me.

In a wheat field in North Africa, I discovered love in a simple flower that brushed against my face when I fell to the ground. Amidst the exploding shells, that innocent poppy, with its red petals protruding outward like blood flowing from an open wound, shared its beauty with me.

I saw love in the eyes of a child, when it reached out for help with skin stretched over bones that resembled a hand from out of the grave. It grasped a scrap of dried bread that only partially eased the pangs of hunger in a bloated belly. The pain and sorrow I felt for those starving children would never be forgotten.

On the outskirts of the town of Gaeta, Italy, a look of impending doom appeared on the face of a surprised enemy soldier, when he turned his head and saw me lower my gun. He dropped his rifle, realizing I intended to spare his life. No words were spoken, but when his eyes returned to their normal size, and the gasp of air expelled from his lungs caused his shoulders and hands to relax, I knew he would forever be grateful. That incident benefited me as much as it did the life I spared. Now I knew that in my search for love, all was not lost. I had the power to stop killing.

Love seemed to be everywhere. To find it, all I needed to do was open my eyes and look beyond the cause I fought for. Because of my newfound feelings, I learned to value and depend more on the companionship of my comrades. In the heat of battle, except for the man at your side who would risk his life to save yours, you were alone. A bond of love that lasted a lifetime was formed between us all.

To ease my conscience for some of the things I continued to do in the line of duty, I showed more compassion to the unfortunate civilians caught up in the conflict. Hoping to justify my deeds on the battlefield, by finding love, I tried to escape from beneath the shadow of death that I feared would devour me. My efforts were to no avail, for a voice calling from the hidden depths of my soul kept whispering, "Look around you, there is no escape. Sooner or later death is inevitable."

Putting my life on the line day after day made me realize how precious life really is. I learned to love life more than anything else in the world. I wanted to rediscover all the joys and simple pleasures that, up until now, I had taken for granted.

Though it took a long time, eventually I learned to forgive my enemies, the soldiers of the opposing forces. Like them, I, too, had fallen into the trap set by rulers of countries who remain safely behind the front lines while urging their youth onward to commit mortal sin.

Not until my combat days were almost over did I become aware of the fact that hating a person only breeds a hate that could eventually destroy me. Because God gave me a second chance at life, I learned how unimportant materialistic things are in achieving happiness. I first had to experience a "Hell on Earth" before being able to appreciate and accept the gifts of life available to all of us.

When the conflict finally ended, I had spent almost half a lifetime searching for a solution to heal the festered wounds of my mind. The war that almost destroyed me taught me one of the most important lessons of life: The true meaning of Love.

I found Love, but would spend years of wandering before ever erasing my feelings of guilt and achieving a lasting peace.

Only after attaining the gifts of Love and Peace could I tell the world, "At last, I have found the greatest treasure a man can ever hope to possess; I have found Happiness."

# Glossary

**Ack-ack**   Antiaircraft fire.

**Ammo**   Ammunition.

**Bazooka**   American antitank rocket-projector.

**Burp gun**   A German MP40 Schmeisser automatic hand-held machine gun.

**Corps**   A group of divisions, assembled under the command of a lieutenant general.

**Division**   A military unit comprised of 12,000 to 18,000 men, commanded by a major general.

**88**   A highly accurate 88-millimeter gun that could be used for antiaircraft or artillery fire or be mounted on a Tiger tank. It was the most feared German artillery weapon of World War II.

**Foxhole**   A pit dug by a combatant for protection against enemy fire.

**H-hour**   The time set for a military attack: also called zero-hour.

**Jerry**   The nickname given to the German soldier by the British and picked up by the Americans.

341

**Kraut**   A nickname given to the German soldier by the American GI, mostly because the Germans in the U.S. were noted for eating sauerkraut.

**LST**   A landing ship, tank; used in World War II.

**MG42**   A German machine gun. One of the finest weapons of the war, combining reliability, accuracy and an extremely high rate of fire.

**Mortar**   A muzzleloading cannon used to fire shells at low velocity and high trajectories. The barrel, bipod and base plate could each be carried by a soldier

**Nebelwerfer**   A German, electrically operated, six-barrel rocket launcher.

**OSS**   The Office of Strategic Services (U.S.A.). The wartime foreign intelligence service and forerunner of the CIA.

**Pillbox**   A small, round, concrete emplacement for a machine gun or antitank gun.

**Pineapple**   A small fragmentation bomb, designed to be thrown by hand.

**Platoon**   A subdivision of a troop, commanded by a lieutenant. It consisted of two sections, with two squads of eight men in each section.

**Potato masher**   A German hand grenade with a wooden handle attached for throwing (resembling an old-fashioned potato masher).

**Recon**   Abbreviation for Reconnaissance, the eyes and ears of a military unit advancing against enemy forces. Its main purpose was to obtain information about the enemy.

**75s** A 75-millimeter gun mounted on American Sherman tanks.

**SS** Schutzstaffel; Nazi protection detachment.

**Sherman** The name of the largest American tank used in World War II. First used in the latter days of the African campaign, it weighed 28 tons and was equipped with a 75-millimeter gun.

**Shrapnel** Shell fragments from a high-explosive mortar or artillery shell.

**Squad** The smallest unit in the military. In the cavalry, it usually consisted of eight men commanded by a corporal.

**Squadron** A reconnaissance squadron usually consisted of five or more troops of cavalry, with a total of around 1,000 men, commanded by a colonel.

**Thompson** A .45-caliber automatic handheld submachine gun. The same gun used in the United States by the gangsters during Prohibition.

**Tommy** The nickname given to a British soldier.

**Troop** A cavalry unit corresponding to a company of infantry, and commanded by a captain. It had three combat platoons and a head-quarters service platoon.

**Wadi** Usually a dry bed of a watercourse or ravine in North Africa.

**Waffen-SS** The military arm of the SS. Supposedly the Nazi Army.

**Walkie-talkie** A handheld portable radio, used by front-line soldiers.

# Index

From the bloody shores of Africa and Italy to the murderous Omaha Beach at Normandy and on across the Rhine—the Rangers led the way.

# Rangers in World War II

by Robert W. Black

They were ordinary men on extraordinary missions, experiencing the full measure of fear, exhaustion, and heroism of combat in World War II as the spearhead of the U.S. Army.

Published by Ballantine Books.
Available at bookstores everywhere.

The classic account of tank warfare in
World War II by a German general who was there

# Panzer Battles

## by Major General F. W. Von Mellenthin

Published by Ballantine Books.
Available at a bookstore near you.

Read eyewitness accounts by the soldiers, sailors, airmen, nurses, and civilians who survived the day that will live in infamy.

# Remembering Pearl Harbor

**by Robert S. La Forte and Ronald E. Marcello**

Published by Ballantine Books.
Available at a bookstore near you.